Daniel O'Connell and the Repeal Year

LAWRENCE J.
McCAFFREY

Daniel O'Connell
and the Repeal Year

UNIVERSITY OF KENTUCKY PRESS

To Joan, Kevin, Sheila,
and Patricia McCaffrey

Preface

DANIEL O'CONNELL remains a neglected man of Victorian history, although he was the most discussed figure of his time. Members of the British Establishment despised this Irish demagogue. Their newspapers and periodicals described him as a mendacious, avaricious vulgarian agitating nationalism to collect contributions from ignorant and impoverished Irish peasants. The British public was told that O'Connell was the leader of a vast conspiracy dedicated to subverting the British Constitution by imposing Popery on the British Isles. He was the principal target of no-Popery sentiment—the basic ingredient in British nativism. The aristocracy all over the Western World viewed him as a menace to privilege, and liberals and democrats considered him their champion. He was the symbol of hope for those attacking the Metternich system. In 1829 he had confronted the British aristocracy on the Catholic emancipation issue, and he had left the field victorious.

O'Connell deserves the attention of historians because he was the most controversial man of his time and because he presents an interesting case study in public opinion and image and in political legend and symbol. But O'Connell was more than an image, a symbol, or a legend. He was an active politician—a shaper of institutions,

political parties, public opinion, issues, and events. No
man had more of an impact on Victorian Britain and
Ireland. He mobilized the Irish masses and created
modern Irish nationalism. From the period of O'Connell's
entry into politics until the creation of the Irish Free
State the Irish Question was the most important emotional
issue dividing British political parties and British public
opinion. He gave lessons to British politicians in the
techniques of organization and agitation. His successors
in the leadership of Irish nationalism continued the
instruction. They demonstrated the effectiveness of a
disciplined parliamentary party always ready to exploit
a balance of British parties to extort reform legislation.

Any thorough evaluation of the personalities shaping
Victorian Britain would have to rate O'Connell equal to
Peel, Gladstone, Disraeli, or Parnell. But his greatness
was European as well as British and Irish. In a period
when liberals, democrats, and nationalists challenged the
Metternich system he created a nationalist movement
that won substantial victories over the forces of status
quo, privilege, and aristocracy. His triumphs encouraged
and inspired leftists and nationalists in France, the Ger-
manies, the Italian States, and the Hapsburg Empire. And
because Irish nationalism was to inspire and influence
liberation movements in Asia and Africa, O'Connell's
importance extends beyond the frontiers of Western civilization.

Since it is obvious that O'Connell was a major factor
in molding modern Irish, British, Continental and even
global history, why has he not attracted sufficient consideration from historians, particularly the scholars of
Britain and Ireland? British historians are perhaps still
touchy about the Irish Question and its relation to no-
Popery and probably find it difficult to cope with Irish
personalities, particularly complex ones like O'Connell.
The leading British Victorian politicians were Protestants

from the aristocracy or upper middle class who shared a common educational experience. Their styles and assumptions were for the most part similar. O'Connell was a Catholic with a Continental education, a clan chieftain, a peasant hero, a demagogue, an artist in vituperation, and the pragmatist supreme. Any analysis of his character, virtues, achievements, and influence demands a different set of standards than one can apply to persons like Peel and Gladstone.

However, a politician's reputation is primarily the responsibility of his own countrymen, and in contemporary Ireland O'Connell does not seem to rank in the pantheon of heroes with Parnell, the Fenians, the men of 1916, or the leaders of the 1919-1922 period. His reputation has become a victim of a conflict of ideology within Irish nationalism. The Young Irelanders created an image of O'Connell entertained by many present-day Irishmen. They held the position that O'Connell's post-1829 control over the forces of Irish nationalism injured the prospects for self government. They argued that his pacifism, acceptance of British constitutional methods of agitation, willingness to compromise Repeal of the Union for reform legislation, alliance with and confidence in the Whigs, jealousy of talented young nationalists, complete trust in the decisions of his mediocre but ambitious son John, and loyalty to old comrades weakened the national cause and demoralized the Irish masses in time of crisis.

As long as constitutional methods of agitation held a promise of independence O'Connell retained the affection and respect of those committed to Irish nationalism. But in 1914 constitutional nationalism and the third Home Rule bill fell victim to Liberal compromise and timidity, British no-Popery, and Ulster Protestant nativism allied with Tory ambitions for power. Then physical force republicanism took charge of Irish nationalism and in 1921 won an independent parliament for twenty-six Irish counties. With the victory of physical force, the Young Ireland image of O'Connell as a symbol of ineffective constitutional agitation captured the imagination of the revolutionary and post-revolutionary generations. The efforts of Sean O'Faolain, Denis Gwynn, Michael Tierney, and others to rehabilitate the reputation of the father of Irish nationalism has failed to erase the partisan portrait presented by Charles Gavan Duffy, John Mitchel, Michael Doheny, and their twentieth-century disciples. Historians are still faced with the task of presenting a balanced interpretation of O'Connell—one which will indicate his significance for modern Irish and British history. But to do justice to O'Connell, they will also have to place him within a European as well as an Irish and British context.

This book, then, is both an effort to focus attention on a man shortchanged by historians and an attempt to demonstrate the impact of O'Connell and Irish issues on British history. It deals with one of the most controversial episodes in O'Connell's career, the Repeal agitation of 1843. In October 1843 O'Connell canceled the Clontarf Monster Meeting to avoid a clash with British troops. This decision antagonized the Young Irelanders in the Loyal National Repeal Association and inspired much of the criticism they directed at O'Connell. They argued that his failure to meet the challenge of the British Government destroyed the Repeal movement at the summit of its influence and demoralized the Irish masses. Duffy, Mitchel, and Doheny accused the Repeal leader of misleading and betraying the Irish people in 1843.[1] They emphasized O'Connell's 1843 speeches, particularly the Mallow Defiance, to prove that he gave the Irish masses the impression that he would resist any British Government effort to crush Repeal. The Young Irelanders insisted that if

[1] Sir Charles Gavan Duffy, *Young Ireland* (London, 1896); John Mitchel, *Jail Journal* (Dublin, 1913); Michael Doheny, *The Felon's Track* (Dublin, 1914).

O'Connell was not prepared to lead a rebellion to preserve the Repeal movement he should not have asked the Irish people to endorse and support the agitation. They also argued that even the slaughter of Repealers at Clontarf would have been better than surrender to a Government ultimatum. Duffy went so far as to suggest that the enthusiasm, the high morale, and the discipline of Repealers would have been more than a match for the armed and trained British army.

I am convinced that O'Connell did not consciously mislead the Irish masses in 1843. His tactics of that year followed the pattern of his previous agitations and were inspired by the strategy that had achieved Catholic emancipation. In 1843 he was a captive of that great victory of the 1820's, and he misjudged the British political atmosphere of the 1840's and the character of and alternatives left open to his adversary, Sir Robert Peel.

This study also takes issue with the Young Ireland thesis that O'Connell suffered a total defeat in 1843. Since he was willing to accept extensive Irish reform legislation which would make Ireland an integral part of the United Kingdom rather than a conquered and occupied colony as an alternative to Repeal, his success in forcing Peel and his Conservative cabinet colleagues to reconsider traditional Tory responses to the Irish Question was a considerable victory. If the famine had not interrupted the normal course of events, and if the Conservative party had not been divided into progressive and reactionary factions, Peel's comprehensive program of Irish reform might have had permanent beneficial influences on the course of Anglo-Irish relations. Instead, his attempt to destroy Irish nationalism by conciliating its various components widened the gulf in his own party and brought about the collapse of his Government and a generation of impotency for British Conservatism. But Peel's downfall in 1845 was not a total or permanent defeat for his sane approach to

Irish policy. Gladstone was a Peelite, and even a Tory like Balfour came to realize that there must be a better reply than coercion to Ireland's demands for freedom and reform.

II

I do not wish to leave the reader with the impression that no one has presented balanced or favorable portraits of O'Connell. In my opinion the two best studies of O'Connell's career are William Edward Hartpole Lecky's essay in *The Leaders of Public Opinion in Ireland* (London, 1871, 1883, 1903) and Sean O'Faolain's *King of the Beggars* (London, 1938). Lecky, although an opponent of the goals of Irish nationalism and a critic of O'Connell's introduction of the priest into Irish politics, was able to appreciate the genius of O'Connell, his work in improving the lot of the Catholic masses, and his basic sincerity. Lecky understood better than most Anglo-Irishmen and Englishmen both the Irish mind and character and the nature of early nineteenth-century Irish politics. He realized that O'Connell had to wear many masks because he played many roles—lay Catholic leader, champion of nationalism, Benthamite radical, clan chieftain, practical politician, and British parliamentarian. But Lecky left us with a question deserving answers from historians: "But when to the great services he rendered to his country we oppose the sectarian and class warfare that resulted from his policy, the fearful element of discord he evoked, and which he alone could in some degree control, it may be questioned whether his life was a blessing or a curse to Ireland."[2]

O'Faolain's brilliant biography portrays O'Connell as

[2] William Edward Hartpole Lecky, *The Leaders of Public Opinion in Ireland* (London, 1871), 320.

the father of the modern Irish nation—the liberator of his people. He emphasizes the degradation of the leaderless Irish peasant masses at the beginning of the nineteenth century and describes how O'Connell gave these millions of demoralized wretches dignity, hope, and confidence in the strength of their united numbers. O'Faolain does not ignore the obvious weaknesses of O'Connell—his vulgarity, his avarice, his quickness to compromise long range goals for immediate benefits, and his sometimes unscrupulous tactics in dealing with those who challenged his leadership, but he makes it clear that O'Connell's strengths and weaknesses were forged in the contest for Catholic emancipation and in the cockpits of early nineteenth-century British and Irish politics. O'Connell's personality was a product of a struggle for survival—a struggle that was both personal and national.

Denis Gwynn's *Daniel O'Connell* (Cork, 1947) and *Daniel O'Connell,* a book of essays edited by Michael Tierney (Dublin, 1949), are both useful for anyone interested in a favorable and scholarly view of O'Connell's achievements. James A. Reynolds' *The Catholic Emancipation Crisis in Ireland, 1823-1829* (New Haven, 1954) is a well documented, well written, and comprehensive study of the greatest victory in O'Connell's career. But Father Reynolds' fastidious hostility to the vulgarity of O'Connell and the people he led conditions him to view the Irish leader and his cause from the assumptions and prejudices of the nineteenth-century British Establishment.[3]

[3] Kevin B. Nowlan's *The Politics of Repeal* (Toronto, 1965) was published after the completion of my manuscript. Nowlan's book is a well written discussion of British-Irish relations during the 1841-1850 period and presents an excellent analysis of the issues dividing Young Ireland and O'Connell. The early chapters of his book treat the beginnings of the Loyal National Repeal Association, the Repeal agitation of 1843, and Peel's Irish policy in 1844-1845, but are not concerned with a detailed analysis of the ingredients that contributed to the Repeal enthusiasm of 1843 or with O'Connell's shifts in tactics during that crucial year. Nowlan seems reluctant to discuss and generalize about the motivations behind Peel's Irish policy in the 1843-1845 period.

Most of the sympathetic biographies of O'Connell, including the O'Faolain and Gwynn studies, pass quickly over the 1840's and treat his efforts in this decade as the anticlimax of a great career. After he was released from prison in 1844 O'Connell was obviously only a shadow of his earlier self, but in 1843 he exhibited the intelligence and skill of former years. O'Connell did not lose his bid for Repeal in 1843 because he had lost either his genius or his nerve. It was the political climate of opinion in Britain and the balance of forces in the House of Commons rather than the Liberator that had altered in the 1840's. This failure to understand the changing political situation is an indication that despite the excellent O'Faolain and Lecky portraits and the good Gwynn and Tierney books, O'Connell needs and deserves the same sort of detailed investigation that Norman Gash is now giving to Peel.

III

In preparing this book I had the advice and cooperation of many people. My good friends Gil Cahill, Emmet Larkin, Dick Loftus, and Alf MacLochlainn offered valuable suggestions and insights into the Irish Question. As Assistant Keeper of Manuscripts in the National Library of Ireland, Alf made available much of the original source material used in this study. I also discussed my research with R. Dudley Edwards, and my friend and teacher Bill Aydelotte read portions of my work. Sean O'Faolain was kind enough to invite me to his home in Killiney to talk about O'Connell. Tom O'Neill of the National Library of Ireland made valuable suggestions concerning the use of the Peel Papers and British newspaper sources. The staffs of the National Library, Dublin, University College Library, Dublin, State Paper Office, Dublin, Public Record

Office, London, British Museum, and the State University of Iowa and University of Illinois libraries went out of their way to provide me with the necessary research materials. I had two valuable research assistants, Mrs. Mina Carney in London and Eileen Riordan at the State University of Iowa, and I learned a great deal from reading the seminar papers of Mary Ann Harper and James D. Cochrane, graduate students at the State University of Iowa. Danute Gudaites Ernst and Mrs. Alwynne Paulson typed the manuscript which was submitted to the publisher. Without grants from the Penrose Fund of the American Philosophical Society and the Graduate Research Board of the University of Illinois I could not have made my research expeditions to Dublin and London. The Graduate Research Board of the University of Illinois also provided me with a typing grant. For six years my wife, Joan McCaffrey, patiently listened to me discuss Peel and O'Connell while she fed babies, changed diapers, washed and ironed clothes, and prepared meals. She also read my manuscript and suggested changes. Three small McCaffrey children, Kevin, Sheila, and Patricia, tolerantly sacrificed their father to a typewriter. To all of these friends, relations, institutions, and research foundations I express my gratitude.

Marquette University   LAWRENCE J. MCCAFFREY
January, 1965

Contents

1

Background of the Repeal Agitation of 1843

INVOLVED IN A LIFE and death struggle with the French Revolutionary armies, William Pitt the younger in the late 1790's decided that an autonomous Ireland was a weak link in Britain's chain of defenses. Using the power of the British Government and the wealth of its treasury he managed to achieve a legislative Union between Britain and Ireland. Pitt's efforts were aided by the fears of many members of the Irish Protestant aristocracy and gentry that Ireland was in danger of conquest by either of two dangerous enemies—French inspired radical democracy or the revitalized forces of Popery. The inadequately French-supported Irish rebellion of 1798, which allied the radical middle class United Irishmen, the Catholic peasantry of the South, and the Protestant peasantry of the North in an effort to establish a democratic Republic seemed to confirm the fears of the Establishment. So in 1800 a majority of the Protestant Irish Parliament —some members frightened by Jacobinism and Romanism and others bribed with British money—voted the extinction of their legislature. They exchanged Irish sovereignty for a permanent Protestant ascendancy supported by the British Government and its armed forces.

By the terms of the Union twenty-eight Protestant peers and four Protestant bishops represented Ireland in the British House of Lords and one hundred Protestant M.P.'s represented Ireland in the House of Commons. The reform bill of 1832 increased the number of Irish representatives in the House of Commons to 105. The Irish Church was joined with the English Church in the United Church of England and Ireland, and by 1817 the treasuries of the two countries were one. But the separate existence of an Irish executive branch in Dublin Castle indicated that Ireland was not completely assimilated like Scotland into the British system. On August 2, 1800, the Irish Parliament held its last session in College Green. In January 1801 the Irish representatives took their place at Westminster in the Parliament of the United Kingdom of Great Britain and Ireland.

The Union was accomplished, but Irish patriotism persisted, and men like Henry Grattan continued to hope and argue for Repeal and the restoration of the Irish Parliament. Pitt, to win Catholic support for the Union, led the bishops to believe that the Union would be followed by Catholic emancipation. He was sincere in his conciliation efforts, but he retreated when confronted by the Protestant conscience of George III. Disappointed by a continuation of second class citizenship, Catholic leaders became champions of Repeal. The greatest of them, Daniel O'Connell, used Catholic grievances as instruments to construct modern Irish nationalism.

In British terms O'Connell was a member of the Catholic gentry, but to Irish peasants he was a Kerry clan chieftain. Reared by his uncle Maurice, a man made moderately wealthy by smuggling, O'Connell was sent to

France and Belgium for his secondary education. His continental training was interrupted by the French Revolution, and shortly after Louis XVI was guillotined he and his brother left a school at Douay for Calais and then England, where he studied for the bar at Lincoln's Inn. The combination of his conservative clerical teachers and the violence of the French Revolution made him a permanent enemy of physical force as a method of political action. But his continental experiences did not leave him with a mental block against liberalism. He read the philosophes of the Enlightenment and developed into an enemy of the Old Regime, and while in England he became a disciple of Jeremy Bentham.

When O'Connell became active in Irish politics Catholic emancipation was the key issue. The leadership of the emancipation movement was in the hands of the Catholic nobility and gentry. Also prominent was the equally moderate Catholic middle class. In Parliament the Protestant patriot Henry Grattan led the forces agitating the Catholic cause. Emancipation held the allegiance of many Whigs and a few Tory M.P.'s and on occasion could even command a parliamentary majority. But the Tory Government resisted Irish Catholic and parliamentary opinion and enlisted anti-Catholic British Protestant public opinion in defense of Protestant ascendancy. However, emancipation did seem to have one chance for success. Tory leaders indicated a willingness to repeal the penal laws restricting Catholic political rights in exchange for a veto over the appointment of Catholic bishops in Britain and Ireland by the Vatican. The veto was a compromise satisfactory to most of the Catholic emancipation leaders in Ireland, many of the Catholic bishops, Grattan, and even the Vatican.

O'Connell, although sometimes willing to compromise the issue, threw in his lot with the minority anti-veto section of the Catholic community. He argued that

Government intervention into the affairs of the Catholic Church would be detrimental to the interests of religion. His attack on the veto was consistent with his Benthamite opposition to the union of Church and State. But more important, O'Connell's anti-veto position was an extension of his nationalism. Catholic emancipation was of secondary importance. Repeal and reform took precedence. O'Connell on January 13, 1800, told Dublin Catholics that he would rather retain the Irish Parliament with the continuation of Catholic disabilities "than lay his country at the feet of foreigners." He never ceased to advocate an alliance of Irish Catholic, Protestant, and Nonconformist opinion to restore the "King, Lords, and Commons of Ireland."[1]

O'Connell realized that the Catholic Question could be exploited to arouse the demoralized and impoverished Irish masses and to mobilize them into a disciplined national opinion demanding the restoration of the Irish Parliament. The Church and her hierarchy and clergy were potential instruments of national agitation. Most of the bishops and priests came from the peasant class. The clergy was the only educated class in rural Ireland close to the people and therefore their natural leaders. If the British Government controlled the nomination of bishops, members of the hierarchy would be potential agents of British interests, and it would be difficult if not impossible to organize an effective national movement in the face of their neutrality or hostility. Therefore O'Connell believed that it would be better to postpone Catholic emancipation if it meant the sacrifice of the most important institution in Ireland to British control. He mobilized clerical opinion against the veto. His efforts delayed emancipation, but they pushed the hierarchy and clergy in the direction of nationalism.

In 1813 the House of Commons approved the principle

[1] Michael Tierney (ed.), *Daniel O'Connell* (Dublin, 1949), 160.

of Catholic emancipation coupled with the veto, and Rome supported the compromise. O'Connell rallied Irish Catholic opinion against the Vatican-endorsed British offer and forced the Irish bishops to reject the measure and to defy the wishes of Rome. The 1813 conflict over the veto destroyed the unity of the Catholic emancipation movement. Anti-vetoists left the Catholic Committee and organized the Catholic Association. Neither group could promote a successful agitation, and O'Connell tried to restore unity. He was even prepared to permit a limited Government veto over episcopal appointments to heal the divisions in Irish Catholic opinion, but compromise failed and the emancipation cause continued to drift.

In 1823 O'Connell, Thomas Wyse, and Richard Lalor Sheil met at the home of O'Connell's son-in-law in the Wicklow mountains and formed a new Catholic Association. In the beginning so few people attended meetings that it was difficult to obtain a quorum. But in 1824 O'Connell devised tactics which made the Catholic Association the model for all nineteenth-century British and Irish agitations. He decided that the Association needed a fighting fund, and to obtain money he made every Catholic parish in the country a unit of agitation and every priest a recruiting agent for the Association. Tenant farmers, agricultural laborers, and the urban proletariat were all invited to become associate members of the Catholic Association. All they would have to contribute was one shilling a year, and they could pay it out at a farthing a week or a penny a month. They could make their contribution outside the church or chapel door on Sunday mornings. Priests encouraged contributions with fiery sermons endorsing the methods and the goals of the Association.

O'Connell's tactics not only swelled the treasury of the Catholic Association; they also captured the support, enthusiasm, and confidence of the Catholic masses. He had created an organized, passionate, and disciplined Irish Catholic opinion. The poverty racked farmers and workers sacrificed their liquor and tobacco to pay dues to the Association, and this great sacrifice committed them to the cause. Modern Irish nationalism emerged as a badge of dignity and a promise of hope for a people who in the century before O'Connell had lost these human qualities. O'Connell became "the uncrowned King of Ireland," the Liberator, the man who held the Irish masses in the palm of his hand.

From the beginning it was clear that the Catholic Association was more than just an organization agitating Catholic grievances. It was a national movement demanding reform and ultimately repeal of the Union. Catholic emancipation had provided the issue and pioneered the method of creating a national will. By the end of 1825 the Catholic Association had a war chest of £15,000 safely invested in Government securities. In 1828 the Association came out for an extensive franchise reform and shorter parliaments. O'Connell had married Irish nationalism to Benthamite radicalism.

The British Government was worried. O'Connell used constitutional methods, relied on the pressure of organized public opinion to achieve justice and freedom for Ireland, and strongly denounced physical force. He insisted that no cause or principle justified violence. But never before had the British encountered unified Irish Catholic opinion so deeply and emotionally committed to a cause. And while O'Connell preached nonviolence, he frightened British politicians with the threat of civil war. He warned that if the Government would not come to terms with constitutional Irish nationalism, the masses might turn in frustration to leaders who recommended physical force nationalism.

Government efforts to smash the Catholic agitation failed. In 1825 and again in 1828 laws were passed declaring the Association illegal, but O'Connell used his legal dexterity to reorganize his movement within the context of the law and then expanded its activities. The Association became a committee of grievances and an agitation against the payment of tithes and in support of mass education, land reform, expanded suffrage, and parliamentary reform. Irish newspapers, gave more attention to discussions in the Corn Exchange, the meeting place of the Association, than to debates in the British Parliament.

The general election of 1826 provided the first public test of strength for the Catholic Association. O'Connell and his colleagues decided to support pro-emancipation candidates against powerful representatives of the Protestant gentry in a number of constituencies. Landlords threatened tenants with eviction if they voted for O'Connell-endorsed candidates, but the priests led the people to the polls and to a series of spectacular victories. Irish nationalism displayed its potential, and intelligent British and Irish politicians realized that concessions to Irish grievances were inevitable.

Six months after the election Lord Liverpool was forced by ill health to retire as Prime Minister. George Canning, his successor, was friendly to the Catholic cause, so the Association toned down the agitation to give the new British leader time to introduce an emancipation proposal into the House of Commons. But in a few months Canning was dead, Wellington was Prime Minister, and Sir Robert Peel was Government leader in the House of Commons. The Duke appointed C. E. Vesey Fitzgerald President of the Board of Trade, forcing a by-election in County Clare.

Fitzgerald was a popular Irish landlord and a supporter of Catholic emancipation, but the Catholic Association decided on bold strategy: a Catholic would challenge a Cabinet Minister, and O'Connell, against his inclinations, was put forward as the candidate. The Government, engaged in a direct confrontation with the enemy, threw its energy and resources into the contest, but O'Connell, with the help of the priests, controlled the loyalty and the votes of the forty shilling freeholders. O'Connell's victory began the retreat of Protestant ascendancy; it also threatened the political influence of the landlord and demonstrated to Ireland, Britain, and all Europe the power of organized public opinion under the direction of a political genius.

In conscience Wellington and Peel opposed Catholic emancipation, but to deny O'Connell the fruits of victory was to risk civil disturbance in Ireland. Britain could not rule Ireland through coercion and military occupation. To deny Ireland the benefits of the British Constitution was to doubt the value of British political institutions. Irish Catholics had demonstrated their determination to win civil rights, and a majority of British parliamentary opinion probably supported the Irish Catholic claims. So to preserve the peace in Ireland and political stability in both islands Wellington and Peel decided to ignore British no-Popery opinion and their own prejudices and to concede Catholic emancipation. But they were not gracious losers. In exchange for emancipation O'Connell was forced to surrender the suffrage of the forty shilling Irish freeholders, to contest Clare in another election, and to take an insulting oath of allegiance before taking his seat in Parliament.

After O'Connell took his seat in the House of Commons he continued to agitate the Repeal question, but Tory and Whig administrations made full use of coercive legislation to frustrate the growth of an effective Repeal organization in Ireland. In fact, the Whig Government that took office in 1830 demonstrated more diligence in curtailing Irish agitation than the preceding Wellington-Peel administration. Although Whig leaders tried to woo O'Connell's support with Government office, Lord Anglesey, the Lord Lieutenant, and Lord Stanley, the Chief-Secretary, quickly outlawed every political organization launched by the Irish leader.[2]

O'Connell worked very hard for the cause of parliamentary reform and deserved much credit for the success of the 1832 bill. He entertained the hope that a reformed British Parliament would consider Irish grievances and then concede reform, and perhaps Repeal. But the contents of the reform bill were a major disappointment to the Irish leader. By taking away the vote of the urban proletariat the bill completed the disfranchisement of the Irish masses begun when the emancipation act eliminated the forty shilling freehold suffrage. Irish nationalists also protested that the additional five seats in the House of Commons awarded to Ireland as a result of parliamentary reform were inadequate to express the weight of Irish opinion. However, O'Connell refused to cut his ties with the Whig party although he was disappointed with the results of 1832, and Lord Grey and other Whig leaders did little to disguise their contempt for their Irish ally.

Against his better judgement but under the pressure of Irish nationalist opinion O'Connell introduced a Repeal motion in the parliamentary session of 1834. The humiliating result of this effort—only one British M.P. supported the motion—convinced O'Connell that the House of Commons would never seriously consider Repeal until it was buttressed by an organized, disciplined, and enthusiastic agitation in Ireland.

For five years the Whigs had the benefits of O'Connell's support in Parliament without the inconveniences and political risks of an alliance with the Repeal leader. But in 1835 they needed Irish votes to form a Government,

2 Anglesey personally urged O'Connell to accept a government office, but he refused (Denis Gwynn, *Daniel O'Connell* [Cork, 1947], 200).

and O'Connell was in a position to trade these votes for Irish reform legislation. The Lichfield House Compact, an alliance between Whigs, Radicals, and Irish nationalists, promised O'Connell reforms in the government of Ireland and a satisfactory solution to the tithe question in return for his guarantee to help keep the Whigs in office and to aid them in their effort to govern Ireland. This meant that O'Connell agreed to abandon the Repeal agitation. Of course the Tories denounced the Whig, Radical, Irish treaty as a dishonorable and unholy alliance, and many Irish nationalists shared this view. Lords Russell and Melbourne replied that there was nothing in the contents of the Lichfield House Compact contrary to Whig principles, and O'Connell insisted that his arrangement with the Whigs did not violate his political convictions.

While O'Connell had always been an advocate of Repeal he had no inherent objection to the British connection. He asked for an Irish parliament because he was convinced that only Irishmen could solve the political, religious, and economic problems which prevented their country from keeping step with the rest of western Europe. He believed that the Union reduced Ireland to a junior partner role and that her needs were subordinated to British interests. But he was prepared to have British politicians prove him wrong. O'Connell often told Irish audiences that if Ireland was treated as an equal partner in the Union, if her problems received a sympathetic hearing in Parliament, and if a successful effort was made to promote Irish prosperity, he would be happy to accept the Union as a final solution to Anglo-Irish differences. O'Connell was not a fanatic nationalist. He was not impressed with the myths of cultural nationalism which emphasized the genius and integrity of the folk soul or the myths of political nationalism which made a divinity out of the sovereign nation. He was a disciple of Bentham interested in the liberty, happiness, and prosperity of his people. Irish nationalism promised to be the best means to these goals, but in 1835 O'Connell gave British politicians another opportunity to demonstrate that the Union could promote the welfare of the Irish people.[3]

For five years O'Connell loyally kept his commitment to the Whigs, but the Melbourne ministry fell short in its effort to satisfy the expectations of Irish nationalists. The tithe question was settled, if not completely to Catholic satisfaction, and Irish municipal government was opened to Catholic participation, but nothing was done to expand the Irish parliamentary franchise or to increase Irish representation in the House of Commons.[4] The Irish poor law bill was offensive to O'Connell's laissez faire convictions and contradicted his knowledge of the Irish economy.[5] Irish Catholics were also disappointed with the Whig reluctance to place them on equal footing with the Protestant ascendancy in the competition for government office. In 1838 O'Connell decided that it was time to warn Melbourne that his continued support must be earned by further concessions to Irish needs. He organized the Precursor Society as a prelude to the revival of Repeal and again demanded reform legislation from the Whig administration.

By 1840 it was clear that Melbourne had done all for

3 O'Connell's willingness to abandon Repeal for concessions to Irish reform demands is discussed in Tierney (ed.), *Daniel O'Connell*, 162-64.

4 The tithe act of 1838 "commuted the tithe from a toll upon the annual product to a rent charge whose amount was fixed and guaranteed by the state at 75 per cent of the value of the uncommuted tithe." (Élie Halévy, *A History of the English People, 1830-1841* [London, 1949-52], 208. O'Connell wanted the bill to include a clause providing that Church surpluses be used for the education of all the Irish people but did not push his case for fear that it might defeat the bill. Irish Catholics claimed that Irish landlords raised rents to cover the tithe payments and insisted that disestablishment was the only satisfactory solution to the tithe question.

5 O'Connell's views on the poor law will be discussed later in this chapter.

Ireland that he was going to do, and O'Connell decided to carry out his threat of 1838. In April 1840 the first public meeting of the National Association of Ireland, rechristened the Loyal National Repeal Association in 1841, was held at the Corn Exchange, Burgh Quay, Dublin. Only a hundred people attended this meeting, and only fifteen of them joined the Association. This apathetic response to O'Connell's new summons was an indication that many Irish nationalists were convinced by the Lichfield House Compact and the subsequent close relations between O'Connell and the Government that their leader was insincere concerning Repeal and was only forging another weapon to blackmail the Whigs.

T. M. Ray, an energetic and thorough Dublin clerk who enjoyed the full confidence of O'Connell, was appointed secretary of the Loyal National Repeal Association while the Liberator, as chairman of all committees, dictated Repeal strategy and policy. The new organization was modeled on that paragon of Irish popular movements, the Catholic Association. Members contributed annual dues of one pound. Those who sent in ten pounds to the Repeal treasury were called Volunteers and could display a uniform similar to the one worn by the Irish Volunteers in 1782 when they forced concessions from the British Parliament. O'Connell was most interested in obtaining the support of the Irish masses. He invited tenant farmers, agricultural laborers, and the urban proletariat to put their names on the Association books for the modest dues of a shilling a year, a penny a month, or a farthing a week. In urban and rural parishes Repeal Wardens (men selected by the clergy and approved by the Repeal leaders in Dublin) supervised the collection of dues (the Repeal rent), sent the money and the names of the contributors to Dublin, encouraged Repeal enthusiasm on the local level, kept people in touch with events taking place at the Corn Exchange, and set up Repeal reading rooms stocked with nationalist pamphlets and newspapers. The

Repeal Warden performed all the functions of the modern precinct captain and was considered by O'Connell as the main cog in the machinery of Repeal.

For the first three years of its existence the Loyal National Repeal Association made little progress in capturing the affection and loyalty of the Irish people. Most of the bright and energetic young Catholic lawyers who helped O'Connell carry Catholic emancipation were now established in their profession or were loyal allies of the Whigs in the House of Commons, and some even held government office. They were not going to risk their hard earned prosperity and respectability for the sake of an agitation so unlikely to succeed in its goal. Even the Catholic hierarchy seemed indifferent to the fortunes of Repeal. O'Connell was left with those attached to him through personal loyalty, like his court jester Tom Steele, or through the ties of family connection.[6] He would have to find a new group of lieutenants from a new generation of discontented young men.

Lord Stanley's Irish registration bill, which never became law,[7] the inclusion of disestablishment of the Irish Church as a plank in the Repeal platform, and the Tory victory in the general election of 1841 combined to win a few more recruits for the Repeal movement. But in 1842 the agitation was practically suspended while O'Connell concentrated on his duties as first Catholic Lord Mayor of Dublin.

In January of 1843 Repeal seemed to be an insignificant factor in Anglo-Irish affairs. The little group of men that

[6] Steele was a Protestant landlord from Clare and an important figure in the Clare election in 1828. He was an idealist who fought as a volunteer in the Republican revolution in Spain. He spent most of his fortune in the struggle for Catholic emancipation. Steele worshiped O'Connell, and O'Connell was fond of him. O'Connell enjoyed the companionship of his flamboyant friend and gave him the fantastic title of Head Pacificator.

[7] Stanley's bill would have reduced the small landholder suffrage in Ireland. Only by clever parliamentary manipulation did the government prevent passage of the registration bill.

met weekly at the Corn Exchange in Dublin had not won the confidence of Irish nationalists, and the British press and periodicals scornfully described the Repeal agitation as the last attempt of a washed up old demagogue to keep his name before the people, Repeal rent in his pocket, and his reputation for mischief alive. One important Tory periodical put it this way: "What can you any longer do, or affect to do old gentleman to earn your honorable wages? Is there not (as the lawyers would style it) a failure of consideration? If you go on any longer collecting "the rent" may you not be liable to an indictment for obtaining money under false pretences? Poor old soul, his cuckoo cry of Repeal grows feebler and feebler, yet he must keep it up or starve."[8]

However, this Tory optimism that O'Connell was slowly but surely fading from the Irish scene overlooked the continued existence of Irish discontent. As long as O'Connell retained his genius for channeling the many sources of Irish frustration into organized and disciplined agitation he would remain a formidable obstruction to British rule in Ireland. True, most of the outstanding Irish grievances had been the subjects of parliamentary legislation since 1829: Catholics were now permitted to sit in Parliament, to hold Government office, and to obtain the rewards of the legal profession; the tithe had been commuted to a land tax paid by the landlord; economies had been made in the established church by reducing the number of bishoprics; and the municipal corporations had been opened to Catholic participation. But not one of these reform measures completely satisfied the aspirations of Irish Catholics.

The emancipation act, while it conceded a number of Catholic political rights, attempted to restrict Catholic political influence by disfranchising the forty shilling freeholder, and a few years later the reform bill eliminated

8 *Blackwood's Magazine*, 53:142.

the Irish working class suffrage. Irish nationalist leaders complained that British governments never honored the spirit of Catholic emancipation. Certainly during the Peel administration of the 1840's Lord DeGrey, the Lord Lieutenant, and his staff in Dublin Castle refused to appoint Catholics to positions of prestige or responsibility. Although the Irish municipal corporation bill of 1840 appeared to present the Catholic urban population with an opportunity to destroy Protestant domination in municipal government, franchise restrictions maintained Protestant influence out of proportion to the Protestant population.

The tithe commutation act removed some of the heat from the controversy involving the established church but did not come to grips with the principal Catholic objection to the Establishment. The Catholics were not mainly concerned with the question of who should pay the tithe, the landlord or the tenant farmer. They argued that the tithe should not be paid by either the owner or the occupier of the land. They could not accept the proposition that a church ministering to the spiritual needs of a small minority of the population should be supported in comparative luxury by the whole populace while the church holding the allegiance of the vast majority of Irishmen should depend on the voluntary contributions of a poverty-wracked peasantry. And the Church of Ireland was supported by the whole population. The landlord might pay the tithe but he paid it out of rents collected from Catholic and Nonconformist as well as Protestant tenant farmers. Irish Catholics did not ask for the establishment of their own church. They followed O'Connell's lead and demanded the complete separation of Church and State.

The contrast between the material prosperity of the Protestant Church and the poverty of the Catholic Church created a unique situation in western Europe during the

age of Metternich—a Catholic hierarchy and clergy sympathetic to and allied with a radical reform and nationalist
movement. Catholic bishops and priests, the best educated
and the most respected and influential class in Irish
Catholic society, were antagonistic to the Government and
were prepared to lend their support to movements threatening the status quo of Irish society.

The most important Irish problem, the relationship
between landlord and tenant, was left untouched by
Parliament because British politicians considered it a
matter more of "morals than legislation." The Irish
agrarian question was a dreary history of eviction and
outrage. A typical Irish tenant farmer held just enough
land to raise a few potatoes for his own use and some
grain to sell so he could meet his obligations to the
landlord. Often through motives of greed, financial need,
or the responsibility to provide a living for the families of
his children, he subdivided the small farm he occupied,
became something of a landlord himself, and created a
large class worse off than himself. Land hunger meant
excessive rents. Irish families were large—the Irish fer-
tility rate was the highest in Europe and Irish men and
women married young—and there were no industries to
employ the surplus population. This situation permitted
the landlord to determine the rent since he could always
find a tenant willing to meet his demands. Often a tenant
farmer agreed to a rent that he knew was beyond his
means. Once in possession of his farm he had either to
reduce his living standard to the lowest subsistence level
or sublet part of his land to another farmer, who also must
pay an excessive rent or suffer the fate of eviction.

Another grim facet of the Irish agrarian problem was
the tradition of short term leases between landlord and
tenant and the absence of any obligation on the landlord's
part to compensate the tenant for improvements made on
the productive potential of the farm. This situation

injured both tenant and landlord because it encouraged sloppy agricultural methods which limited Irish agricultural production. Since any initiative shown by the tenant tended to increase his rent payments, he contented himself with subsistence farming, and consequently the real property value of land decreased every year.[9]

The Irish land system was also cursed by the burden of absentee ownership. It would be difficult to prove that absentee proprietors were not as kind or as interested in their tenants as resident landlords, but they did deny to Ireland the income they derived from their estates, which was spent in Britain, and they demonstrated little interest in the welfare of Ireland. These nonresident Irish proprietors were more British than Irish in point of view, and the loss of such a large proportion of the aristocracy retarded the development of a vital, intelligent, and influential Irish political and economic opinion.

While it is true that the complaints against the inadequacies of the Irish reforms enacted by the British Parliament were expressed long before 1843 without producing an energetic Repeal agitation, they must be taken into consideration in any attempt to understand O'Connell's strategy and success in reviving national enthusiasm. He would use these grievances in his effort to recreate the popular enthusiasm of Catholic emancipation days, but he needed other issues more current, more controversial, even more passionate, to get Repeal off the ground. He found such an issue in the poor law.

In 1833 the Whig Prime Minister, Lord Grey, appointed a commission to investigate the extent and depth of

9 The relationship between landlord and tenant in Ulster was more satisfactory for the latter than in Leinster, Munster, and Connacht. In Ulster the tenant had a customary stake in the land he occupied. This custom was called Ulster tenant right. It was enforced by public opinion and "gave the tenant an interest in his holding, secured him as long as he paid his rent, and on his quitting possession enabled him to sell his interest in the farm." E. Curtis, *A History of Ireland* (London, 1950), 375.

poverty in Ireland and to submit recommendations to alleviate the problem. The Government expected the commissioners' report to justify the establishment of a poor law system in Ireland. Leading Irish clergymen, Catholic, Protestant, and Presbyterian, served on the commission along with several prominent laymen. The commission spent two years carefully gathering testimony and evidence and submitted its findings and its recommendations to the Government in 1835. In their report the commissioners rejected the poor law system as practiced in Britain as a solution to Irish poverty. They emphasized that such a system violated the temperament and religious feelings of the Irish people, particularly the Catholics.[10] In Ireland poverty was not an unfavorable reflection on the character and ambition of the mendicant. The pauper played a valuable role in Irish society. He traveled the country and brought entertaining stories into the cabins of the peasantry, and he provided Christians with the opportunity to practice their most important virtue, charity. Irish Catholics would consider the workhouse a penal institution and would continue to support the poor voluntarily, completely destroying the objectives of the poor law system.[11]

The commissioners also argued that Ireland with its low tax potential and its exceptionally large pauper population—there were always two and a half million on the verge of starvation—could not afford a poor law. It would overburden the financial resources of the country without meeting the need it was designed for.[12]

As an alternative to the poor law the commission recom-

[10] Remarks on the evidence contained in appendix D, E, F, *Poor Inquiry Commission Report* (London, 1836), 41.

[11] *Ibid.*, appendix H, 1:3.

[12] R. Barry O'Brien, *Fifty Years of Concessions to Ireland, 1831-1881* (London, 1883-1885), 1:555ff. O'Brien argues that it would have cost £5 million a year to operate the Irish poor law, and the revenue of the Irish landlords was only £6 million. O'Brien used the *Poor Inquiry Commission Report* for these figures.

mended an increase in the number of voluntary relief agencies, the establishment of Government financed public works projects, a Government sponsored emigration program, and an agricultural education scheme directed to the improvement of the weaknesses and inefficiency of the existing land tenure system.[13] The commissioners tended to agree with the politicians that agrarian reform was more a problem of education than legislation since the issue was moral rather than political.[14]

Lord John Russell had evidently made up his mind that Ireland was to have a British modeled poor law system, so he completely ignored the report of the Irish poor law commission. What was good for England was, according to his utilitarian logic, also good for Ireland. Russell sent George Nicholls to Ireland for a six week survey of Irish poverty. Nicholls had done a great deal to establish the British poor law system, but he knew nothing about Ireland and he did not overcome his ignorance in six weeks. But his recommendations provided the nucleus of the Irish poor law enacted by Parliament in 1838.

Under the Irish poor law bill Ireland was divided into unions, each with a workhouse, and the unions were subdivided into electoral districts. The workhouse test was established as the basis of relief and no aid was to be given outside the workhouse. No residence clause was included in the bill to determine admittance to workhouses. A central board of commissioners in Dublin supervised the operation of the law. Local boards of guardians collected the poor rate and managed the local workhouses under the supervision of the Dublin authorities. Members of the local boards were elected by ratepayers with a franchise restriction not to exceed thirty pounds. All magistrates were eligible to serve as exofficio guardians, but their

---

13 *Poor Inquiry Commission Report*, Remarks on evidence, 40ff.
14 *Ibid.*

number was not to exceed one third of the total membership of the local boards.[15] George Nicholls took up residence in Ireland to direct the operations of the poor law.

The Irish poor law bill contained one clause which
indicated a Government attempt at agrarian reform. Only
those tenants who paid five pounds in annual rent could
be rated, and one half the sum paid for poor relief could
be deducted from each pound of rent paid to the landlord
"whether such rent shall be greater or less than such net
annual value."[16] This meant that holdings were evaluated
by the poor law board and that the poor rate was based
on this evaluation. If the landlord overcharged his tenant
some compensation was given, since the latter could
deduct one half the poor rate from the excess rent demanded by the former. The landlord also received some
consideration since he was permitted to deduct his poor
rate contribution from his tithe payment.[17]

The Irish poor law was put into operation in the middle
of 1842, and it encountered immediate opposition from the
Irish masses. In many parts of Leinster, Munster, and
Connacht the people organized a resistance to the payment
of poor rates. This resistance strongly resembled the tithe
war of the 1830's and forced the Government to resort to
the use of troops and the confiscation of cattle to collect
the rates. This often meant that the expense of collecting
rates exceeded the amount collected. O'Connell did not
organize the resistance to the poor law, but he quickly
perceived that the militant opposition to paying rates
encouraged anti-British sentiments that could be exploited
by the Repeal movement. O'Connell attacked the poor
law as an example of the kind of Irish legislation passed
by the British Parliament and argued that only Repeal
would protect Ireland from further misgovernment.

15 This summary of the Irish poor law is a condensation of the bill
as presented in *Pickering's Statutes* (London, 1838), 274ff.
16 *Ibid.*, clause LXXIV, 296.
17 *Ibid.*, clause LXXVI, 297.

Resistance to the payment of poor rates was not the only agitation stimulating the Irish mind in the 1840's. Father Theobold Mathew, a simple Capuchin friar, rivaled O'Connell in the public's affection. In 1838 he had taken charge of the nonsectarian Temperance Society, and through the force of his saintly personality had made temperance the most important influence in Irish life. Father Mathew traveled all over Ireland holding enormous outdoor temperance meetings on Sunday afternoons. Thousands of people turned out to hear Father Mathew preach total abstinence, to take the temperance pledge, and to receive a temperance medal from the apostle of sobriety. Well organized temperance societies appeared in almost every Irish village with reading rooms and flashy costumed bands. The decrease in the use of liquor and in crimes associated with overindulgence testified to Father Mathew's healthy influence over the Irish masses. His success in Ireland brought him fame in England and the United States and he was invited to plead his cause in both these countries.[18]

Father Mathew never expressed any political opinion; in fact, he seemed indifferent to Irish nationalism. He won the respect of nationalists, Orangemen, Tories, and Whigs. His sole objective was the elimination of a vice he considered responsible for most of the misery and misfortune of the Irish people. On several occasions he refused to entertain O'Connell's suggestion that the causes of temperance and Repeal should be united. He said that he did not wish to endanger his sacred mission by tarnishing it with the bitterness of Irish politics. But Father

[18] Two books have been published on the career of Father Mathew: John Francis Maguire, *Father Mathew* (London, 1863), and Patrick Rogers, *Father Theobold Mathew: Apostle of Temperance* (Dublin, 1943). Both books chronicle the life of Father Mathew, but neither gives satisfactory insights into his personality and his appeal to the Irish masses. Father Mathew lectured in England in 1843 and in America the following year. He was praised by Protestant leaders and politicians in both countries and apparently won many converts for temperance.

Mathew's polite refusal to associate temperance with Repeal did not discourage the master agitator. O'Connell considered temperance a valuable ally for Repeal, and he meant to exploit the movement with or without its leader's blessing. Father Mathew's crusade had maintained the tradition of large scale agitation and public meetings while O'Connell was fraternizing with the Whigs. Temperance also fostered the type of discipline so essential to O'Connell's method of agitation. Sober Repealers were more likely to obey the commands of their leaders and avoid conflicts with authorities than men made mad by the influence of drink. The anti-poor law campaign created enthusiasm, and temperance promoted discipline. The results of these two movements channeled into the stream of Repeal under O'Connell's direction would produce a formidable nationalist agitation.

O'Connell attacked the poor law and he cultivated the friendship and support of the temperance men. He described himself as a teetotaler, he flattered Father Mathew and his followers, he praised their cause, he asked for their support, and he credited them with the discipline of the Repeal movement: "It is the temperance that will give us the Repeal. Temperance will give it to us; for now I can trust in every one of you; as I am not afraid that any drunkard will, in his haughtiness, refuse to obey my commands. I have you by temperance. I defy your enemies. Yes, the moral miracle of temperance has rendered the cause of Ireland irresistable. Those who have overcome their vice cannot be conquered by any enemy.[19] . . . For I believe that Father Mathew was sent by God to bless Ireland with virtue, in order that she might be then fit for freedom. Liquor brings false courage. Oh I tell you that there is not an enemy in the world that could fight with my Irish teetotalers. Teetotalism therefore is a foundation

19 Speech given at Kilkenny, June 8, 1843, *Nation*, June 10, 1843.

stone of the edifice of Irish liberty, and I call on you all to think of that as you go home."[20]

O'Connell's strategy and his blarney quickly paid dividends. Although Father Mathew personally shunned any association with nationalist politics, he could not control the political conduct or opinions of his followers. Soon nationalist newspapers, particularly the *Nation,* were in every temperance reading room and temperance bands were an important part of Repeal demonstrations. British newspapers, once warm in their praise of Father Mathew and his work, gradually cooled and became critical of the abstinence movement.[21]

The conquest of temperance by Repeal was a natural event. Overindulgence was and is a characteristic of Irish life. It is probably a compensation for poverty, insecurity, and boredom. When a man frees himself from the liquor habit he is still left with the problems that made him drink—poverty and insecurity. So another outlet for discontent and frustration becomes necessary. The Repeal agitation with its promise of a more prosperous and exciting Ireland under an Irish parliament provided another means of expression. The pride, the self-respect, the discipline, the enthusiasm, and the extra money that temperance gave the Irish masses they would now lay at the feet of O'Connell and Repeal.

In addition to the anti-poor law activity and the mass appeal of the temperance movement, O'Connell was

[20] Speech given at Roscommon, August 20, 1843, *Nation,* August 26, 1843.

[21] *Times,* March 15, 21, 1843. Sir Robert Peel viewed Father Mathew "with suspicion and distrust" after temperance bands were used at Repeal meetings and Repealers recruited members at temperance meetings (Peel to Lord Eliot, November 4, 1843, Peel Papers Add. MSS 40480, British Museum; all subsequent references to MSS in the British Museum are to these papers). Eliot assured Peel that the political opinions and actions of temperance Repealers were not approved or sanctioned by Father Mathew. He said: "They love Father Mathew but obey O'Connell" (Eliot to Peel, November 16, 1843, Add. MSS 40480, B.M.).

presented with another powerful weapon to be used for Repeal. On October 15, 1842, the first issue of the *Nation* appeared. This weekly newspaper was the product of the combined talents of three remarkable young men— Thomas Osborne Davis, John Blake Dillon, and Charles Gavan Duffy. They gave Irish nationalism its most powerful newspaper voice and traditions and doctrines that were permanently to shape its character.

Thomas Davis was born in 1816 at Mallow, County Cork, where his father, James Thomas Davis, was serving as a surgeon in the Royal artillery. James Davis' family was English with Welsh roots. His wife, Mary Atkins Davis, was an Anglo-Irish Protestant. James Davis died the same month that his son Thomas was born, and Mrs. Davis moved the family to Dublin. Thomas Davis attended Trinity College, received his B.A. in 1836, and was called to the bar two years later. However, he never practiced law. From 1838 to 1840 he was an observant and thoughtful traveler on the Continent. His reading and his continental experiences focused his attention on the problems of nineteenth-century European politics and economics, and he identified himself with the liberal and democratic points of view. In a speech that he delivered before the Trinity College Historical Society in 1840 Davis declared himself an Irish nationalist. At the same time he revealed his sympathy for peasant proprietorship and his hope for friendly relations between Irish Catholics, Protestants, and Nonconformists. Anxious to indoctrinate the Irish people with his own nationalist convictions Davis teamed with his friend, John Blake Dillon, to edit the Dublin *Morning Register*. The *Morning Register's* new national editorial policy failed to attract either new readers or advertisers, and the proprietor, Michael Staunton, let his young editors go after a four months' experiment. Davis was not discouraged; he maintained his nationalist convictions and joined the Loyal National Repeal Association in April of 1842. O'Connell graciously welcomed the young Protestant intellectual to the ranks of Repeal and encouraged his enthusiasm.

John Blake Dillon was born in 1816 of a prosperous Catholic middle class Connacht family. He attended Trinity College and was called to the bar in 1841. Study of Irish affairs attracted him to nationalism, but he tended to concentrate on the economic rather than the political problems of his country. Dillon was a keen student of Bentham and DeTocqueville and came to the conclusion that a transfer of the ownership of Irish property from the landed aristocracy and gentry to the peasant masses was necessary for economic progress and prosperity in Ireland. His interest in the land question concentrated his legal studies on the Irish land codes. After the failure of the *Morning Register* experiment Dillon followed Davis into the Loyal National Repeal Association.

Charles Gavan Duffy was born in Monaghan town in 1816. His father John was a prosperous middle class shopkeeper. Duffy's youthful experience as a Catholic in the North of Ireland made him a strong advocate of Irish nationalism. In 1836 he came to Dublin and began a career of journalism. Two years later he was invited to Belfast to become editor of a new Catholic newspaper, the *Vindicator*. From the beginning Duffy was a conscientious journalist with a brilliant style. He used the columns of the *Vindicator* to promote an interest in Irish folksongs and poetry and his pet project, mass education. Duffy advised the temperance leaders to sponsor educational projects which would instruct artisans in the latest mechanical techniques and farmers in the newest methods of agriculture.

In 1839 Duffy decided to become a barrister and enrolled at King's Inn, Dublin. On a visit to Dublin during the first term of his legal training he met Dillon, who introduced him to Davis. Since the three young men shared an interest in Irish nationalism, law, and journalism they soon became close friends. Often they discussed the need for an Irish newspaper which would serve the cause of nationalism and still maintain high standards of writing and criticism. Finally they decided to translate their hopes into reality. Duffy resigned his position in Belfast, established residence in Dublin, and became the proprietor and editor of the *Nation*.

Duffy, Davis, and Dillon founded the *Nation* to create a cultural nationalist opinion in Ireland: "To create and foster public opinion and make it racy of the soil." They insisted that "a nation is a spiritual essence." The Young Irelanders, as the writers of the *Nation* came to be called, developed the ideology of modern Irish nationalism. Romantic and cultural Irish nationalism was defined in the *Nation* and eventually conquered Irish opinion. The writers of the *Nation* emphasized the spiritual qualities of peasant Ireland and ridiculed the materialism of industrial England. They argued that Ireland must be free to protect its cultural integrity from contact with British materialism. Since the British-planned Irish education system was designed to deprive Irishmen of their cultural heritage and make them subservient to alien values the writers of the *Nation* undertook the crusade of making Irishmen proud of their own history and culture and conscious of the perfidy of Britain.

The *Nation* attracted talented young writers like Thomas MacNevin, Daniel Owen Madden, John Mitchel, John O'Hagan, and Thomas Meagher. They informed the Irish reading public about the high standards of early Christian Irish culture, the monks from Ireland who brought Christianity and civilization to British and Continental barbarians, the patriots who fought Danes, Normans, and Englishmen for Irish freedom, and the Irish exiles who fought for the liberty of other countries. The editors of the *Nation* also tried to encourage a rebirth of Irish culture. They printed the best in contemporary Irish writing —James Clarence Mangan and William Carleton among others contributed to the *Nation*—and they encouraged readers to submit essays, poems, and patriotic ballads for publication. Many of the nationalist songs still enjoying favor among the Irish in Ireland, America, and throughout the Commonwealth first appeared as ballads in the *Nation*. A number of Young Irelanders were champions of the Irish language and tried to convince the Irish that it should be preserved.

Duffy, Davis, Dillon and their associates also attempted to divorce Irish nationalism from its close association with Catholicism. They wanted to end sectarian strife and emphasized the common nationality of all Irishmen. In the columns of the *Nation* the contributions of Protestants and Presbyterians to Irish culture and history received the same attention and praise as the work of Catholics. The *Nation* emphasized the common grievances shared by Irish Protestants, Catholics, and Nonconformists and the mutual profit to be gained from the liberation and progress of their common country.[22]

The *Nation's* news coverage was of secondary importance to its creative and propaganda efforts. It usually borrowed its news items from other Irish and British newspapers and periodicals. The Young Irelanders concentrated their energy on poetry, historical essays, biographical sketches, reviews, and spirited editorials. The editorials championed cultural nationalism, sectarian co-

[22] The biographical information concerning Davis, Dillon, and Duffy, the analysis of the objectives of Young Ireland, and the description of the contents of the *Nation* are taken from the following sources: Sir Charles Gavan Duffy, *Young Ireland* (London, 1896), *Four Years of Irish History* (London, 1883), *Thomas Davis: the memoir of an Irish patriot* (London, 1890), *My life in two hemispheres* (London, 1898), P. S. O'Hegarty, *A History of Ireland under the Union, 1801-1922* (London, 1952), Helen Mulvey, "The Young Ireland Nationalist Movement, 1842-1848" (unpublished manuscript); and the columns of the *Nation*. Kevin M. MacGrath published a valuable index to the writers in the *Nation* in *Irish Historical Studies*, 6:189-223.

operation, Repeal, Ulster tenant right for all Ireland, increased and improved educational facilities on all levels, and other reforms consistent with liberalism and democracy. The patriotic ballads, the historical essays, and the dynamic editorials made such an immediate and favorable impression on the Irish mind that the *Nation* was soon a topic of conversation in Parliament. British M.P.'s were forced to concede the talent of the Young Irelanders but condemned the revolutionary content of their writing.[23]

O'Connell and the Repeal agitation profited by the impact the *Nation* had on Irish opinion, but the Liberator was always a little suspicious of his militant young allies. Because O'Connell's Irish patriotism was conditioned by a Benthamite concern with the bread and butter issues of politics rather than the passion of cultural nationalism, he had a hard time understanding the minds and the goals of men like Duffy, Davis, and Dillon. O'Connell never hesitated to tell Irish audiences that they were the most virtuous, courageous, intelligent, chaste, and industrious people in the world and that the English were low, treacherous, barbarian Saxons. But this was campaign blarney used to stimulate the enthusiasm of impoverished, depressed, and illiterate peasants badly in need of a little flattery. O'Connell sincerely loved his country and his countrymen, and he was proud of his position as "uncrowned King of Ireland"; however, he had little time for sentimental excursions into the Gaelic past. His utilitarian views are well illustrated in his attitude toward the Irish language. He knew it and occasionally used it in public speeches—sometimes as a joke to confuse police reporters—but he had no interest in preserving it or spreading it. In fact he considered the Irish language a barrier to progress, a symbol of inferiority, and he thought Irishmen would be much better off if they knew and perfected English. O'Connell looked to the future rather

[23] *Hansard* 69: 1142ff.

than the past. He wanted Irishmen to have full civil, political, and religious rights and he wanted them to enjoy all the economic advantages the nineteenth century could offer. He believed that a native parliament could best achieve these objectives, but he could live with the Union if that proved the best road to Irish progress.

Since cosmopolitan O'Connell did not understand the assumptions or the appeal of the cultural nationalism spreading over Europe and now entering Ireland, he distrusted the militant tone of the *Nation* and on occasion ridiculed its literary efforts. On the other hand, the Young Irelanders were often impatient with O'Connell's inconsistencies, his political pragmatism, his flirtations with the Whigs, his willingness to compromise Repeal for reform, his despotic control of the Repeal Association, and the arbitrary manner of his favorite but untalented son John. The *Nation* and O'Connell held opposing views on the Chartists, corn law repeal, and federalism. Young Ireland viewed the Chartists as representatives of the British democracy and therefore natural allies of Irish nationalists since both groups were oppressed by the British aristocracy. O'Connell condemned the Chartists, and particularly his old enemy Fergus O'Connor, for methods of agitation which tended to encourage violence. He was true to his utilitarian and free trade principles in supporting the repeal of the corn law, while the *Nation* argued that protection was necessary for the welfare of the Irish agrarian economy. Young Ireland was willing to cooperate with Irish federalists in a common attack on British rule in Ireland, but it condemned the limited legislature advocated by federalists as inadequate for Irish needs. O'Connell was willing to accept federalism as a settlement of the Irish question if he could rally Irishmen to support it and if British politicians were inclined to make such an offer. Despite their differences in temperament and in policy, the young men realized that O'Connell had the allegiance of the Irish masses and that without him the national movement would collapse. Therefore they were gentle in their criticism of the old man and submitted to his leadership in the Loyal National Repeal Association.[24]

O'Connell and Young Ireland shared a fallacy—an exaggerated faith in the efficacy of constitutional methods of agitation. Although this confidence in the ultimate peaceful triumph of Irish opinion proved the weak link in the Repeal agitation, people were conditioned by the success of O'Connell's methods in winning Catholic emancipation. They could not be blamed too much for emphasizing the superficial similarities between the situations in 1829 and 1843 and for their failure to understand that legislation unanimously opposed by British parliamentary and public opinion could not be carried even if supported by a unanimous Irish opinion unwilling to take up arms in its defense.

It is extremely difficult to evaluate the significance of a newspaper in political agitation, but the *Nation* certainly played an important role in creating vital nationalist opinion. Shortly after the first issue appeared it had the largest circulation of any Dublin newspaper, and it was widely read in the provinces. It was in most of the temperance reading rooms and was the favorite literature for Repealers. In many peasant cottages throughout the country, those unable to read gathered around the fire to hear the local scholar read the poems, the historical essays, and the editorials of the *Nation*. There was a new voice in Ireland—a voice introducing a dynamic era in Irish nationalism.

After completing his duties as Lord Mayor of Dublin, O'Connell left Dublin for his home at Derrynane Abbey

24 The differences between O'Connell and the Young Irelanders are discussed in the sources listed in n. 22.

in Kerry. He spent most of the autumn and early winter there enjoying the affection and conversation of friends and relatives and his favorite diversion, hunting hares in the Kerry mountains with his well trained and beautiful pack of beagle hounds. But he also took time to consider the future of the Repeal movement. In January of 1843 O'Connell issued a manifesto *To the Irish people* outlining the platform of the Repeal Association and the plan of campaign for 1843. The first part of the manifesto was written on January 1 and read by John O'Connell to the Repeal Association on January 5. Part two was completed on January 12 and read by the Liberator's son to the Association on January 19.

In his manifesto, O'Connell promised the Irish people that "This is, therefore, emphatically the repeal year."[25] He said that Britain faced serious international conflicts with an aggressive American republic and a confident Louis Phillipe and that her imperial interests were challenged in the East Indies, India, China, and Syria. Hostile tariffs against British manufacturers in Russia, Portugal, France, Belgium, the United States, and the German League indicated hostility to Britain throughout the world. Added to foreign and imperial problems, Britain was confronted with a sagging domestic economy producing internal discontent bordering on revolution. Facing these foreign, imperial, and domestic challenges, British politicians would not dare to refuse the demand of a powerful Irish opinion insisting on Repeal.

But the combination behind Repeal must represent a great body of Irish opinion determined to succeed within the framework of constitutional agitation: "There must be no riots, no violence, no tumult, no breach of the peace, there must be submission to every legal authority; but

25 On January 2, 1843, the *Pilot* printed a letter from O'Connell to the editor, Richard Barrett. In this letter 1843 was again referred to as the Repeal Year.

ardent, continuous, and persevering exertion within the strict limits of the law and the Constitution." Once Ireland was united behind the demand for Repeal, victory was certain. O'Connell promised that when there was a Repeal warden in every parish and three million Repealers on the Association books there would also be an Irish parliament in College Green. He said that recent history demonstrated the invincibility of moral force exhibited in mobilized and disciplined public opinion: "by that system we carried Catholic emancipation despite the king—despite a very powerful, and then armed faction in Ireland—despite the great majority of the English people; and not only in spite of, but in fact through the instrumentality of our bitterest enemies, Wellington and Peel, who had actually formed their administration on the basis of, and for the purpose of resisting our claims."[26]

In the first segment of his manifesto O'Connell proposed "five great measures" as a basis for uniting all Irishmen behind Repeal. These five measures would "constitute the great national compact upon which I call on Irishmen of every persuasion to rally together in order to obtain national independence and prosperity for their native land." He insisted that only an Irish parliament would enact these reforms: 1) the total extinction of tithes, 2) fixity of tenure for the occupiers of the land, 3) legislative "encouragement and protection" to Irish manufacturers,[27] 4) a

[26] O'Connell also pointed to the reform bill as another public opinion victory and argued that the Anti-Corn Law League, modeled on the Catholic Association, was another monument to moral force.

[27] But on September 10, 1843, John O'Connell at a Repeal Board of Trade meeting denied that an independent Irish Parliament would construct a tariff wall against British goods. The only Irish duties would be for revenue to reduce the tax burden (*Pilot*, September 11, 1843). The Repeal Board of Trade was composed of representatives of the Dublin trades and it met Sunday afternoons at the Corn Exchange with John O'Connell in the Chair. The Repeal Board of Trade discussed the decline in various Irish trades and the need for a revitalized Irish economy. Many resolutions were passed at these Sunday meetings praising Repeal and presenting it as the only alternative to the heavy taxation and absentee ownership of property destroying the Irish economy.

democratic suffrage by secret ballot, and 5) abolition of the poor law and substitution of more effective public charity.

The second part of the manifesto guaranteed Irishmen that when there were three million Repealers and a Repeal warden in every parish "the Union will be repealed and Ireland will be free." This would mean the end of tithes, poor rates, the grand jury cess, the achievement of a peasant proprietorship consistent with landlord rights, universal male suffrage by ballot, free education, free religious consciences, and a flourishing Irish economy.[28]

On January 5, 1843, John O'Connell delivered another important message from his father to the Loyal National Repeal Association. The Liberator once more assured his colleagues that 1843 would be the Repeal Year. He also told them that he had decided not to attend the parliamentary session at Westminster because nothing worthwhile could be accomplished for his country in the British Parliament and because he had "enough to do in Ireland agitating Repeal."[29]

On January 22, 1843, O'Connell spoke to a large outdoor Repeal meeting at Newcastle, County Limerick. In his speech he denounced Saxon rule in Ireland and described the Union as a compact which brought Ireland "distress, destruction, and robbery." He objected to a system that forced Catholics to support a religion they did not profess, and he attacked the grand jury cess, the poor rates, and absentee landlords. He then praised the physical energy of the Irish people and their strong religious faith and said that a nation that was so superior could not long remain without the benefits of self government.

At a banquet following the Newcastle meeting O'Connell told the local Repeal leaders that constitutional agitation would bring victory. He reminded them how similar tactics resulted in Catholic emancipation when the King, the House of Lords, a considerable element in the

---

[28] *Freeman's Journal*, January 6, 20, 1843.   [29] *Ibid.*

House of Commons, and British opinion opposed it, when Wellington the great British hero headed a Cabinet dedicated to the defeat of the Catholic agitation, and when Ireland lacked the support of strong foreign friends. O'Connell insisted that the moral force of Irish opinion forced Wellington and Peel to reconsider their opposition to Catholic claims for justice, and he expressed confidence that a Britain facing many foreign and domestic challenges would be even more willing in 1843 to concede Repeal than she was to grant Catholic emancipation in 1829. He argued from history that Ireland never received consideration from Britain unless the latter faced foreign and domestic dangers.[30]

As his Newcastle speech indicated, O'Connell expected to exploit Irish hostility to the poor law. In late December 1842 he wrote a letter to the poor law guardians of County Cork which was an appeal to the Irish gentry to join him in his opposition to the poor law. He said that the safety and the permanence of the "social state in Ireland" was menaced by the continued existence of the poor law. It presented the "utmost danger to the lives, as well as the fortunes of the landlords of Ireland." Unless the poor law was modified or repealed, the discontent that it produced would lead to violent revolution "and an insurrection which, I strongly apprehend will, at least in its commencement, be to a considerable extent successful, perhaps permanently so."[31]

The letter to the poor law guardians of County Cork received considerable publicity in the Irish press, and O'Connell followed it up with a letter to a Cork newspaper. In this letter he linked the fortunes of Repeal to the anti-poor law agitation. "There is nothing more likely to promote the Repeal than allowing the present poor law system to work out many more mischiefs; and to aggravate by personal sufferings the dislike we naturally entertain to

30 *Pilot*, January 23, 1843.   31 *Nation*, January 7, 1843.

English legislation. No. If I could abolish the present poor law, I should deprive myself of a powerful weapon which I otherwise could, and which (if left to me) I candidly confess I will use, in every legal and constitutional way to promote the interests of the Repeal."[32]

And he did use it. The Loyal National Repeal Association appointed a committee to study the operation of the poor law and to submit recommendations for its amendment. John O'Connell, chairman of this committee, submitted a report on January 16, 1843. The report listed the major grievances that the Irish people held against the poor law: 1) the arbitrary power of the central board of commissioners and their reluctance to consider suggestions submitted by local boards of guardians, 2) the ruinous expenditures involved in operating the workhouses, 3) the failure of the law to diminish poverty, and 4) the excessive rates which forced many ratepayers into the pauper ranks.

The committee then made several suggestions designed to eliminate poverty in Ireland and to improve the existing poor law: 1) legislation establishing fixity of tenure for Irish farmers, 2) the revival of Irish manufacturing, 3) a reduction of the power of the central board and an expansion of authority for local boards of guardians, 4) outdoor poor relief with guarantees against abuses, 5) a transfer of the burden of poor rates to the property owning classes, 6) an act of settlement, 7) a clause in the poor law limiting relief to the aged and infirm, 8) and a public works program to employ the able bodied on projects to improve the economic potential of the country.

A majority of the committee demanded a total repeal of the poor law because it "tended to weaken the spirit of industry" and to encourage "indigence." But a minority favored a retention of the poor law modified by suggestions recommended by the committee. The minority argued that the poor law, despite its weaknesses, had re-

[32] *Ibid.*, January 14, 1843.

duced the consequences of poverty for the Irish poor and
that it was erroneous to argue, as the majority did, that
the poor law taxed the industrious for the sake of the idle.
Many people in Ireland needed poor relief due to economic situations beyond their control and not because
they were lazy or shiftless. The minority report also attacked the majority assumptions that private charity would
be able to cope with the needs of the paupers and that
workhouse confinement was more demoralizing than mendicancy. Supporters of the minority report emphasized one
positive result of the poor law—the obligation to pay poor
rates forced Irish landlords, particularly the absentees, to
face the reality and extent of poverty in Ireland, and the
need to reform the system of land tenure responsible for
that poverty.[33]

The majority report was consistent with the economic
philosophy endorsed by O'Connell and his son John and
was accepted by the Repeal Association, but the *Nation*
recommended the minority position. Thomas Davis was
indignant that John O'Connell had committed the Association to a definite anti-poor law stand. He and the other
Nation editors agreed that the law needed amendment but
rejected the notion of its repeal. They argued that the
poor law transferred some of the burden of supporting the
needy from the financially pressed citizens of the towns to
the wealthy gentry and that an effective residence clause
would complete this process. They also claimed that the
poor law transferred some of the burden of supporting the
ants in rents. The *Nation* placed itself on record as favor-
ing amendments to the poor law which would establish a
public works program, restrict workhouse confinement to
the aged and infirm, limit the power of the central board,
raise the minimum on property valuations for paying the
rates to ten pounds, and permit members of the clergy to
have places on local boards of guardians.[34]

[33] *Ibid.*, January 21, 1843.   [34] *Ibid.*, January 7, February 4, 1843.

In January a typical Dublin Castle blunder gave O'Connell fresh ammunition in his attack on the poor law. Dr. Phelan, one of the two Catholic poor law commissioners, was dismissed from his post without explanation. This strange and undiplomatic move by the Government resulted in protests from the nationalist press and the Loyal National Repeal Association. O'Connell, in denouncing the Government for dismissing Phelan, again warned that the poor law, if not repealed, would produce a revolution in Ireland.[35]

O'Connell's warning of revolution had a basis in fact. Every day the newspapers reported failures in the operation of the poor law and incidents of resistance to the payment of poor rates. The Enniskillen workhouse was forced to shut down because of a shortage of funds. In the course of one week the Waterford Union managed to collect only sixteen shillings in rates, one half of the amount going to a bank to help repay a forty thousand pound advance for the construction of the workhouse. The Kilkenny Union had difficulty collecting rates, and the bank refused further loans for operational expenses. In Castlebar the local board of guardians could not recruit a poor rate collector since that occupation was a risk to life and limb, and the guardians voted to close the workhouse. In Tipperary the authorities impounded the cattle of those who refused to pay rates but no one would purchase them at public auction.[36]

---

[35] *Ibid.*

[36] *Times,* February 4, 21, 27, March 11, 1843. The *Times'* Irish correspondent was thorough in his coverage of the anti-poor law campaign in late 1842 and early 1843. The *Times* considered the poor law the main source of Irish discontent and warned that O'Connell was using resentment against the poor law to strengthen Repeal (January 25, 30, May 16, 1843). The *Edinburgh Review* also considered the poor law a key to Irish unrest and advocated a stronger mendicancy law as the answer to the problem (77:391ff.). The Peel correspondence indicates that until May 1843 the Government was more concerned with the potential dangers of the anti-poor law campaign than the Repeal agitation (Sir Robert Peel to Sir James Graham, April 14, 1843, Add. MSS 40448, B.M.).

County Waterford, particularly the Gaultier district, was the center of the anti-poor law agitation. In early March, 1843, the Waterford Union turned to the government for help in collecting the rates. A hundred and fifty policemen were sent to Waterford from neighboring counties to assist local rate collectors. The extra police help did not do much to increase the amount collected for poor rates. In the city of Waterford a series of demonstrations were held to protest against the poor law and thousands of marchers participated in the protests. The Irish correspondent of the *Times* (London) commented on the orderly manner of the demonstrators marching with cudgels in hand and credited the temperance movement with the sober demeanor of the protestors, adding that temperance had many implications in Ireland. Finally, in April, the Government sent in cavalry and artillery to collect the poor rates in the Gaultier district. This also proved a futile gesture. While the soldiers were occupied in their unpleasant task the people barricaded themselves in their cabins, laughed as the soldiers marched off with their cattle, and refused to participate in efforts to auction off the confiscated livestock.[37]

This resistance to the payment of poor rates spread from Waterford to the neighboring counties of Cork, Wexford, Tipperary, and Limerick, and even in Ulster there were examples of anti-poor law feeling.[38] By the time the anti-poor law campaign had lost some of its steam the Repeal agitation was going at full blast. There can be little doubt that O'Connell drained off the opposition to poor rates into the Repeal movement and that the energy of the former agitation was transferred to the self-government cause.

Throughout the months of January and February O'Connell continued to assure his followers that Repeal

37 *Times*, March 13, 17, 1843. From March until well into May 1843 the *Times* reported in detail the efforts of troops to collect poor rates in the Gaultier district.
38 *Ibid.*, April 24, 1843.

would mean the dawn of a new and prosperous era for Ireland, that the Irish people "had a double barrelled gun in their hands—England's disasters—and their own combination," and that no Irishman should vote for any man who was not a Repealer. At a Repeal meeting in St. Patrick's Ward, Dublin, he said "I would not be here today if I did not believe I was working out my salvation by working to obtain the freedom of my country."[39]

In its editorials the *Nation* continued to advocate amendments to the poor law, tenant-right legislation, and the study of Irish history and the Irish language to counter the anti-national bias of the national education system. The *Nation* praised the temperance movement as "the first fruit of deep-sown hope, the offering of incipient freedom." While the writers of the *Nation* enthusiastically endorsed democratic economic, social, and political reforms, they questioned the inclusion of such objectives in the Repeal platform because they might antagonize the Protestant gentry. They argued that a commitment to Repeal should be the sole qualification for admission to the Repeal Association. When Ireland won her own parliament, then the representatives of the Irish people could settle other issues.[40] But O'Connell, a genius in the art of agitation, knew that a mass movement must rest on a broad basis. It must embrace a wide range of discontent in order to attract mass support.

Although O'Connell was throwing all his energies into the Repeal agitation, powerful members of the Roman Catholic hierarchy like Archbishop MacHale decided to lend their support to the cause, and the *Nation's* circulation continued to expand; Repeal never caught the public fancy until it was debated in the Dublin Corporation.

On February 28 O'Connell asked the Corporation to petition for a Repeal of the Union. He spoke four hours

39 *Freeman's Journal*, February 14, 15, 1843; *Pilot*, February 22, 1843.
40 This summary of the *Nation's* point of view is based on an analysis of editorials published in January, February, and March 1843.

and ten minutes in defense of his motion and witnesses
agreed that his presentation of the Repeal case was one
of his finest performances—a perfect balance of logic and
passion. He first argued that Ireland had the "capacity
and capability" for self government. She had a favorable
geographic position for a vital commercial economy, water
power to move the wheels of industry, and nine million
brave, generous, temperate, religious, and moral people.[41]
Ireland's population and her natural resources exceeded
those of such independent states as Portugal, Bavaria,
Saxony, Hanover, the Papal States, Tuscany, Denmark,
Greece, Holland, and Belgium.

O'Connell told the Dublin aldermen and town councillors that Repealers were loyal subjects of the Crown and
wanted to maintain a permanent connection with Britain
based on a common allegiance to the monarchy. He insisted that Repeal would heal the wounds of sectarian
strife and promote the prosperity of all classes. He pointed
to the consistency of his Repeal loyalty and how he had
always maintained that it was more important than even
Catholic emancipation.[42]

Then O'Connell defended Ireland's claim to self government by appealing to history and traditional British
political theory. He said that the Irish Parliament was

[41] "I appeal to the reports of the English House of Commons, the
result of the evidence brought before it, that a more moral people than
the people of Ireland does not exist; and in all the private relations of
life—in those of husband, wife, sister, mother, parent, children—I ask
if in all those relations do they not evince an equality with, if not a
superiority over, the other nations of Europe."

[42] He recalled that in 1800 he had said that he would prefer a
reenactment of the Penal Code to the loss of the Irish Parliament and
that "he would rather confide in the justice of his brethren the Protestants
of Ireland, who have already liberated him, than lay his country at the
feet of foreigners," and he repeated a statement that he had made in
1810: "I trample under foot the Catholic claims if they can interfere
with the Repeal. I abandon all wish for emancipation if it delays the
Repeal. Nay were Mr. Percival to-morrow to offer me a Repeal of the
Union upon the terms of re-enacting the entire penal code, I declare it
from my heart, and in the presence of my God, that I would most
cheerfully embrace his offer."

as ancient as the British legislature and had developed spontaneously among the Anglo-Saxons in the Pale. But now Ireland was the only country under British domination without some form of local government, and this denial of self determination violated the inherent right of all men to administer their own affairs. Britain had conceded this right to Ireland in 1782, and the Irish Parliament had no authority to surrender it in 1800. Arguing from Locke's principle of delegated authority, O'Connell insisted that sovereignty rested with the Irish people and that the Irish Parliament with its delegated powers lacked moral justification to transfer this sovereignty into alien hands. Therefore, the Act of Union was in conflict with the whole revolutionary settlement of 1688.

This discussion of the question of popular sovereignty led O'Connell into a lengthy attack on the integrity of the Irish Parliament which passed the Act of Union. He said that the Irish M.P.'s surrendered the liberty of the Irish people during a period of coercion when the expression of anti-Union sentiment was severely restricted. He also reminded his Corporation colleagues that many members of the Irish Parliament were bribed by the British to assent to the Union. Since the Act of Union was then clearly illegal, the Irish Parliament still existed in theory if not in fact.

After disposing of the legal status of the Union, O'Connell described its evil consequences: overtaxation, an increased national debt, declining trade and manufacturing, absentee landlords spending Irish money abroad, foreign control of Irish affairs, and second class citizenship for Irish people in a sham Union.

O'Connell promised the members of the Corporation that Repeal could be achieved by peaceful means of agitation "without the violation of law, and without the destruction of property or life." If the Irish people of all

classes and sects were united behind Repeal, the British
would have to bow to the legitimate demand of Irish
opinion; if "Father Mathew's five million teetotalers were
all Repealers do you think we would not succeed?" All
that was necessary for victory in 1843 was the resolution,
the courage, the unity, and the discipline that achieved
Catholic emancipation in the 1820's.

O'Connell closed his speech with a prediction of the
consequences of Repeal. As the leader of the Irish Catholic nation he assured Irish Protestants that Repeal would
not result in a Catholic ascendancy. Irish Catholics were
tolerant people, ready to forget past persecutions, and
anxious to cooperate with Protestants in constructing a
free and prosperous Ireland. In addition to concluding
sectarian hostility, Repeal would result in prosperity,
national pride, the end of absenteeism, the restoration of
Dublin as a major European capitol, and all of the other
benefits that come from free initiative and energy. Then
referring to the histories of the United States, Switzerland,
Belgium, Venice, and Norway, O'Connell asked "do you
know any country that has submitted to slavery that has
not purchased poverty along with it—and do you know
any country that has risen to liberty without achieving
prosperity at the same time?"

The Corporation debate lasted three days, and many
aldermen and councillors spoke to the motion, but Isaac
Butt, the bright young man of no-Popery, Tory Ireland,
the founder of the *Dublin University Magazine,* former
professor of political economy at Trinity College and now
a successful Dublin barrister, entered the lists against
O'Connell as the champion of Unionism. It had all the
ingredients of an exciting contest—the wily, battle tested
old demagogue versus the polished, clever, and articulate
champion of Protestant ascendancy.

Butt began his presentation of the anti-Union argument
by moving the following amendment to O'Connell's mo-

tion: "That believing the question of Repeal of the Legislative Union between England and Ireland, in the
Corporation of the City of Dublin is calculated to produce
political dissension, prevent all cordial co-operation between persons of different political opinions, and to prevent this body from exercising its municipal functions for
the good of the citizens at large, this assembly repudiates,
in the strongest manner, the introduction of this question;
and that, therefore, the consideration of the question be
adjourned sine die."

Then Butt went on to argue that O'Connell's plea for
the restoration of the independent Irish parliament was
based on a historical myth. No bill passed by the Irish
Parliament from 1782 to 1800 could become law unless it
received the assent of the Crown under the Great Seal of
England. The Seal was controlled by the English Chancellor who was responsible to the British but not the Irish
Parliament. Butt said that O'Connell in demanding the
Irish Constitution of 1782 as a final settlement of Anglo-
Irish differences was asking for provincial rather than
national status. The revived Irish Constitution would
have a Lord Lieutenant and a Chief Secretary appointed
by a British Prime Minister and responsible largely to the
British Parliament. Ireland would not have an army or a
navy or foreign ambassadors. She would lose the power
and the privilege of influencing imperial decisions, but she
would still be bound by the imperial commitments made
by the British Parliament. Butt said that complete separation from Britain would make more sense than this
request to return to a previous provincial status.[43]

Butt then used the platform of the Loyal National
Repeal Association to demonstrate that O'Connell did not
really want to restore a previous state of affairs. No one

---

[43] Butt's constitutional arguments were ably refuted by Councillor
Staunton who pointed out that under the Union Ireland was a province
with no influence over her own destiny. He concluded that any kind of
legislature would be an improvement over existing conditions.

could join the Repeal Association unless he accepted separation of Church and State, fixity of tenure for Irish farmers, universal male suffrage by ballot, and three year Parliaments.[44] This was not an attempt to restore an old constitution: "Repeal was a revolution . . . an untried and wild system of democracy." O'Connell clearly wished to destroy existing institutions. His Ireland would be a secular state deprived of the counsels of religion and with a House of Commons without property and aristocratic influences. Butt predicted that the British Parliament would never make concessions to O'Connell's revolutionary program or surrender to his methods of agitation. Repeal would never triumph without violence and bloodshed. Butt pleaded with Repealers to abandon agitation and to cooperate with Irish Unionists so that their common country "could have peace from political agitation," the main factor which had "retarded her prosperity."

The Unionist champion claimed that Repeal was an artificial agitation. He said that the good sense of Ireland rejected it. For thirteen years O'Connell had failed to light a Repeal fire. He was trying to lead the Irish people into a fight they could not win because "they had against them the whole English people—the Parliament—the Irish gentry—the property of the country, Roman Catholic and Protestant—a great proportion of the population." Butt warned his listeners that the Repeal issue would revive sectarian hatreds, and he begged Repealers to give up their ambition to dominate Irish Protestants— "the real object of Repeal." Since Catholics had achieved their goal of civil rights let them now "vindicate their character by resting contented as they were."

Butt spoke well and his arguments were clever, but the leading Unionist newspapers, the Dublin *Evening Mail*, said that he made an indifferent presentation of his case.[45] By this the editor probably meant that Butt should have

---

[44] O'Connell interrupted to say "no, no."
[45] *Evening Mail,* March 10, 1843.

defended and praised the Union rather than have concentrated on weaknesses in the Repeal position. But O'Connell praised his opponent's speech as an excellent effort in a bad cause. He described Butt as a man of genius who "must have some yearnings for his native land," and correctly predicted: "Depend upon it that Alderman Butt is in his inmost soul an Irishman, and that we will have him struggling with us for Ireland yet."[46]

On March 2, after the third day of debate, the members of the Corporation rejected Butt's amendment and passed the Repeal motion forty-one to fifteen, a majority of twenty-six. A large crowd had assembled outside the Corporation chambers and the news of O'Connell's victory brought a great cheer. O'Connell spoke to the crowd from a window and asked them to disperse quietly and not to molest any of the gentlemen who voted with the minority.[47]

The consequences of the Corporation victory were immediate. Other municipal corporations, town councils, and public bodies in Leinster, Munster, and Connacht petitioned Parliament for a Repeal of the Union;[48] the weekly Repeal rent began to climb; John Cantwell, Nicholas Foran, and Michael Blake, Roman Catholic bishops in the diocese of Meath, Waterford, and Dromore, renewed their membership in the Repeal Association;[49] and many aldermen and councillors joined the movement.

[46] Comments made by O'Connell at a Repeal Association meeting, March 6, 1843, *Nation*, March 11, 1843.

[47] This account of the Corporation Debate is taken from the *Nation*, March 4, 1843. Butt's speech was published in pamphlet form; *Repeal of the Union: The Substance of a Speech Delivered in the Corporation of Dublin on the 28th of February, 1843, on Mr. O'Connell's Motion to Petition for a Repeal of the Legislative Union* (Dublin, 1843).

[48] The corporations of Cork, Waterford, and Limerick, and the town councils of Sligo, Drogheda, Galway, Longford, Clonmel, and Athlone were quick to follow the Dublin example.

[49] At a Repeal Association meeting on March 20, 1843, O'Connell said that most of the Catholic bishops had joined the Association and that some had become Volunteers (*Pilot*, March 22, 1843). Volunteers paid a £10 life subscription in the Repeal Association. They could wear a uniform modeled on the one worn by the men of 1782.

Repeal prosperity was also evident in the large numbers attending the weekly meetings at the Corn Exchange. In fact, these meetings had become so long with the reading of the names of new members and reports on Repeal progress that they were often adjourned until the next day, and sometimes a third day was necessary to complete the week's business. Since the Repeal rent was increasing and the Corn Exchange could not accommodate all those wishing to attend meetings, O'Connell in mid-March announced plans to construct a new meeting place designed to accommodate three thousand people. The new headquarters, to be called Conciliation Hall, would be next door to the Corn Exchange. When Repeal was won Conciliation Hall would serve as the Irish House of Commons and the Corn Exchange would be used as the House of Lords until the old Parliament building in College Green could be re-purchased from the Bank of Ireland.[50]

O'Connell proved sensitive to the criticism of Butt, shared by the *Nation*, that only Irishmen sympathetic to economic and political Radicalism were eligible to be members of the Loyal National Repeal Association. At the March 6 meeting of the Association he moved that anyone who believed in Repeal could join the movement, "but no one shall be admitted who is not an entire Repealer." He said that the economic and political differences that divided Irish nationalists could be resolved in an Irish parliament, but he also made it clear that his new membership policy would not deter him or other Repealers from advocating reforms to improve the political, social, and economic environment of the country. The motion passed unanimously.[51]

A week later O'Connell again demonstrated his flexi-

[50] *Nation*, March 18, 1843. The cornerstone of Conciliation Hall was laid April 29. Progress on the building was rapid, and it was completed in the fall of the year.
[51] *Ibid.*, March 11, 1843.

bility on the question of membership in the Repeal movement. On this occasion he supported the request of Patrick Kennedy, Roman Catholic bishop of Killaloe, to be accepted as a member of the Association. Since Bishop Kennedy was a well known federalist, O'Connell's recommendation contradicted his statement of the previous week. But he wanted and needed the cooperation of this articulate man who believed that the British Parliament would never concede Repeal but might consent to a federal arrangement between the two islands. The Repeal Association without a dissenting voice welcomed Bishop Kennedy to its midst. In his speech recommending Kennedy as a member of the Association, O'Connell touched on the question of federalism. He said that he personally could not endorse a subordinate and dependent Irish legislature as a final solution to the Irish Question, but if the Government made him such an offer he would accept the same form of government for Ireland then enjoyed by Canada.[52]

In April one of the committees of the Loyal National Repeal Association presented the results of its investigation into the land question. Two plans for agrarian reform had been submitted to the committee. William Conner, an agrarian radical who had served a prison sentence for his views, recommended that all rents should be based on the value of holdings, the value to be determined by compulsory arbitration, and permanent leases be given to tenant farmers. William Sharman Crawford, M.P. Rochdale, an important tenant-right advocate from Ulster, argued that if landlords were forced to compensate tenants for improvements to the farm on eviction, it would discourage arbitrary evictions and promote security of tenure. O'Connell objected to Conner's proposal because it would transfer monopoly control over the land from the landlord to the tenant and because it did not guarantee

52 *Ibid.*, March 18, 1843.

an equitable income to the owners of property. He urged the Association to accept Crawford's recommendation that the tenant be compensated for improvements with an amendment advocating twenty-one year leases. Crawford's plan as amended by O'Connell was accepted by the Association as its official agrarian policy.[53]

During the first week of April Irish newspapers began to report the latest Government blunder concerning Irish policy. Peter Purcell, a Dublin Catholic and a Whig Unionist, had the Government contract for carrying the mail in Ireland. Purcell operated a factory in Dublin which manufactured the mail coaches and employed about two thousand men. When the mail contract came up for renewal in early 1843, Croal Brothers, a Scottish concern, underbid Purcell and received the contract. The Croals were able to submit a lower bid because they bought up at cheap prices English coaches made obsolete by the advent of the railroad. When Purcell heard of the Croal bid he immediately matched it but was informed that the contract had already been awarded to the Croals.

This new arrangement meant two thousand unemployed workers in a city already short on job opportunities and the transfer of more Irish money to Britain. The mail contract affair seemed to demonstrate O'Connell's argument that Ireland could never prosper as long as her welfare was in the hands of British politicians. Meetings protesting the Croal contract were held in Dublin and in other parts of the country. Even the Tory *Evening Mail* expressed the opinion that the Government's mail contract decision proved the necessity for an independent Irish party in Parliament.[54]

There was a note of irony in the mail contract affair. Purcell was one of the fifteen opposing O'Connell's motion

53 *Ibid.*, April 15, 1843.
54 *Evening Mail*, April 17, 19, 21, 26, 1843.

in the Corporation debate. He had argued that Ireland would prosper if only nationalists would cease their agitation for Repeal. O'Connell wouldn't be human if he did not feel that his enemy had been taught a painful lesson, but he did not permit his animosity for a man he considered a turncoat to stop him from protesting the injustice of a Government decision which would produce much economic distress in Dublin.

On April 27 O'Connell announced an important innovation in Repeal strategy. He said that as soon as three million Repealers were enrolled on the Association books he would frame an act of Parliament for an Irish House of Commons and summon a Council of Three Hundred, to be called the Preservative Society, to meet in Dublin and to serve as a pre-Parliament. The three hundred members of the Preservative Society would match the number of M.P.'s in the future Irish House of Commons. They would come from the same constituencies that would elect the future Irish M.P.'s. The local Repeal leaders in the areas to be represented in the Irish House of Commons would select their representative to the Preservative Society and entrust him with one hundred pounds for the cause of Repeal. O'Connell assured the Association that the Preservative Society would not conflict with the convention act because there would be no elections and the Society would meet in Dublin under the guise of such social functions as Repeal banquets.[55]

As the weather began to turn warm O'Connell could view the past winter's work with satisfaction. He had revived Irish national spirits, leading public bodies had endorsed his agitation, the Catholic hierarchy and clergy were beginning to display the same enthusiasm for Repeal that they once gave to Catholic emancipation, and the pounds and the dollars flowed in from Ireland, England,

[55] *Pilot*, April 28, 1843.

Scotland, and America. Now was the time to demonstrate to the British Parliament, Government, and public opinion the extent and depth of Repeal strength. Once more he would make Bobby Peel and the Duke shake in their shoes. Once more he would force them to come to terms with the leader of the Irish masses.

2

Course of the Agitation

IN APRIL, O'CONNELL began to hold a series of outdoor meetings to petition Parliament for a Repeal of the Union. But gathering names for petitions was not the sole or even the primary purpose of these meetings. They were designed to indicate to British political leaders and their constituents that the Irish masses supported Repeal with the same intensity that they rallied to the Catholic emancipation cause in the 1820's. They were also intended as a warning of the dangers involved in frustrating the self-government demand of an organized and disciplined Irish national opinion. And they also implied a threat of civil war if the Government attempted to suppress the Repeal agitation by coercive legislation or by military force. In short, the outdoor Repeal meetings were an effective method of constitutional intimidation. O'Connell described their purpose in the following manner: "It may be asked why I should take the superfluous trouble of attending those other meetings, but I attend them not to convince myself or you that Ireland is with me, but to convince our enemies—to convince the British statesmen—to make the Duke of Wellington aware of it, bothered as the poor old man is (loud laughter). I want to make all Europe and America know it—I want to make England feel her weakness if she refuses to give us the justice we require—the restoration of our domestic parliament . . . but do not imagine that I intend to stop calling those meetings. If those meetings don't procure something, I am bound to do something substantial, and the basis of the movement to effect that object is to be found in those meetings. They are satisfying both friends and foes that the nation is with me—man for man with me—aye, and ready if it were necessary, to perish to the last man (the entire company arose, and continued cheering for several minutes)."[1]

The outdoor meetings were successful even beyond O'Connell's expectations. Newspapers estimated crowds attending them in the hundreds of thousands, and it was reported that a million were present on the Hill of Tara in August, 1843.[2] There can be no doubt, however, that nationalist newspapers exaggerated the numbers attending the outdoor meetings in the effort to prove the mass support behind Repeal, and British and Irish Unionist newspapers did the same to frighten British opinion so that it would put pressure on the government to suppress the Repeal agitation. The *Times* (London) was most disturbed about the sober and disciplined Irish masses traveling miles to hear O'Connell preach the doctrines of

[1] Remarks made by O'Connell at Drogheda, June 29, 1843, *Freeman's Journal,* July 1, 1843.

[2] Here are newspaper estimates of the size of some of the crowds: Limerick, April 19, 120,000; Kells, April 23, 150,000; Charleville, May 19, 200,000; Cork, May 21, 500,000; Cashel, May 23, 300,000; Nenagh, May 24, 500,000; Kilkenny, June 8, 300,000; Mallow, June 11, 500,000; Ennis, June 15, 500,000; Skibbereen, June 22, 500,000; Donnybrook, July 3, 200,000; Waterford, July 9, 500,000; Enniscorthy, July 20, 400,000; Tuam, July 23, 300,000; Castlebar, July 30, 400,000; Tara, August 15, 1,000,000.

Repeal and described the outdoor demonstrations as "Monster Meetings." O'Connell accepted this as an appropriate description of meetings that were gigantic in their display of pure spirit, innocent conduct, respect for law and order, and determination to achieve Irish self government.[3]

The Monster Meetings usually took place on Sunday afternoons, and the leading cities and towns of Leinster, Munster, and Connacht took turns playing host to them.[4] Late Saturday night and early Sunday morning the roads leading to the meeting place were alight with the torches of people coming long distances to hear and see their Liberator. As dawn broke the hillsides were alive with those hearing Mass said by priests on outdoor altars or eating their simple breakfasts of bread and potatoes cooked over turf fires. Late in the morning the leaders of the community—shopkeepers, aldermen and town councillors —riding in coaches or on horseback, temperance bands in their brightly colored uniforms carrying banners, and a large number of pedestrians would leave the town to meet O'Connell's coach on its way in from Dublin. As soon as the Liberator's coach appeared the horses were detached, and the Repealers pulled the carriage by hand. The procession then escorted O'Connell in glory to the meeting place. These parades preceding the Monster Meetings were often five miles long and took several hours to pass a given point. Multitudes stood along the road as the procession passed and the women and children threw flowers at O'Connell's carriage.

When O'Connell reached the meeting site—usually a large field on the outskirts of town—he found the speaker's platform already crowded with Catholic priests, some-

---

[3] Remarks made by O'Connell at Donnybrook, July 3, 1843, *Pilot*, Supplement, July 5, 1843.

[4] As the summer progressed meetings became more frequent. Sometimes O'Connell would hold three meetings a week in a particular part of the country.

times a bishop or two, and other local leaders. Before his own speech, O'Connell had to listen to a number of local nationalists, clerical and lay, pledge their allegiance to him and Repeal and their determination to stand behind him to the day of victory. When he finally spoke the Irish masses heard him at his demagogic best. The parade, the cheers, and the multitude before him gave O'Connell the vigor, the passion, and the confidence of his youth. He played on the emotions of his audience like an accomplished musician on his instrument. They laughed when they were supposed to laugh, they cried when they were supposed to cry, they cheered when they were supposed to cheer and when he wanted quiet it was like a church at Consecration. Since the crowds were large and the meetings outdoors, probably only a small proportion of the audience could hear even O'Connell's powerful voice. But the ones who could only see their hero from a distance were orderly and united in spirit with those privileged to be close to the platform.

O'Connell's Monster Meeting speeches all followed a similar pattern. First he flattered his audience. He told them that they were the most virtuous, religious, intelligent, loyal, brave, and strongest people in the world and that they lived in the most beautiful and potentially most productive country in the world. He assured them that such a noble race of people and such a marvelous country deserved the benefits of self determination. And they would have their own parliament if they followed him, obeyed the laws and his commands, and refrained from violence. But he was confident of their obedience and patience because they were teetotalers. Father Mathew was the precursor of Repeal. He had given Ireland a disciplined army of Repealers. With the sober and determined Irish masses behind him the "poor old Duke" and "crafty spinning jenny" Peel would have to surrender to the Irish national will. The victory of 1829 had conclusively demonstrated the invincibility of the moral force of organized public opinion. He promised that as soon as three million Repealers belonged to the Loyal National Repeal Association he would summon the Preservative Society to Dublin and Ireland would have the nucleus of her future House of Commons.

Then O'Connell described all the benefits that would flow from Repeal. The poor law would be repealed, the tithe rent abolished, and the Protestant Church disestablished. There would be separation of church and state with perfect religious liberty and equality. Tenant farmers would have security in their holdings, and their landlords would be protected in their property rights. Irish agriculture would flourish, absentee landlords would return home, Irish money would be spent in Ireland, Irish manufactures and commerce would revive, and there would be employment for the workers in the cities.

O'Connell never failed to warn the Government, the Parliament, and British opinion of the dangers involved in ignoring or frustrating the ambitions of the Irish democracy. He said that he would obey the law and that he personally would not initiate a violent course of action, but he also insisted that Repealers would defend their constitutional right to petition. Following the same tactics that he used during the Catholic emancipation agitation, O'Connell embraced the principles of nonviolence and constitutional agitation but always suggested the possibility of war. He emphasized his unwillingness to take the responsibility for the consequences that would follow government action directed against the Repeal movement. He said that more violent men might push him aside, seize the reins of the nationalist organization, enlist the support of the Irish masses disillusioned with constitutional methods, and plunge the British Isles into a tragic civil war. And he never denied the probability that he would lead the Irish masses in a defensive war against a

tyrannical government that initiated military action in
Ireland. He praised his disciplined army of Repealers as a
better body of men than those who gave Wellington the
verdict at Waterloo and as troops capable of victory against
trained soldiers if war was forced upon them. O'Connell
also courted the sympathy and good will of British troops
stationed in Ireland. He praised the enlisted men, particularly the sergeants, attacked the class privileges of the
officers, and suggested that the common soldier shared
grievances with the oppressed Irish democracy. He said
that he was certain that the enlisted men, many of them
Irish, would never turn their guns on people demanding
legitimate political rights.

O'Connell always had a great deal of praise for the
Queen. She was a paragon of virtue in love with her Irish
subjects. She would never abandon them. If her wicked
and unscrupulous Tory Ministers obstructed the parliamentary road to Repeal, Victoria would take the question
out of Peel's hands and use the Royal Prerogative to
revive the Irish Parliament. No doubt O'Connell was a
loyal monarchist, but he wasn't a fool. After fourteen
years in the House of Commons he couldn't have believed
that the Queen would dare insult her Government, the
Parliament, and British opinion by employing moribund
prerogatives to reestablish the Irish Parliament. No man
who defended the cause of Repeal on the principles of
1688 could be so naive. This constant assurance that the
Queen would personally grant Repeal if Parliament refused to do so must have been a tactic to maintain Repeal
morale and maintain an affection for the Crown among
the Irish masses.

The Monster Meetings were followed by banquets attended by the local Catholic bourgeoisie and members of
the Catholic hierarchy and clergy. Ladies attended these
banquets but sat in the gallery. Banners with Repeal
slogans covered the walls of the banquet halls: "God Save

The Queen," "Repeal," "Whoever Commits a Crime
Gives Strength To The Enemy," "See The Conquering
Hero Comes, Cheered On By Erin's Temperate Sons,"
"Repeal And Order Will Conquer," "The Modern Moses
Has Burst Asunder The Saxon Chains We Long Stayed
Under." During the meal temperance bands entertained
the diners with patriotic tunes. After everyone had finished
eating the toasts began: the Queen, Prince Albert, the
Duchess of Kent, the Royal infants, the Catholic clergy,
the people of Ireland, old Ireland, the Repeal, and finally
O'Connell. Each toast meant a long speech by a priest, a
bishop, or a local lay Repeal leader. O'Connell's speech
was in reply to the toast in his honour. His postdinner
statement usually repeated the sentiments of his afternoon
address but in a more cautious and subdued manner.
Following the banquet O'Connell would spend the night
at the bishop's palace or in the home of one of the leading
citizens and then depart early the next morning for
Dublin.[5]

The Monster Meetings were by far the most dramatic
feature of the Repeal agitation in 1843. They focussed
attention on O'Connell and his cause in Britain, America,
and on the European continent.[6] Even the anti-Repeal
British press paid tribute to the sobriety and discipline
of the Repealers (both virtues were attributed to temperance). The only violence associated with a Repeal
meeting occurred in Clones, County Monagahan, when a
group of Orangemen attacked and killed a cobbler named
McCaffrey as he walked home from a small local Repeal

5 This description of the activities at the Monster Meetings is a
composite picture based on the reports published in the *Pilot, Freeman's
Journal,* and *Nation.*

6 Lord William Russell wrote his brother Lord John Russell on July
10, 1843, from Hungary that even the remote villages of Hungary,
Croatia, and Slavonia were interested in news of O'Connell and Repeal.
To the people of the Balkans he was the great democratic leader of the
times, the "triumphant tribune of the people." (Lord William Russell
to Lord John Russell, July 10, 1843, Russell Papers, Public Record Office,
London)

demonstration.[7] The Monster Meetings certainly impressed the British government and the British public with the strength and depth of Repeal sentiment in Ireland and with the potential dangers presented by the agitation.

As soon as O'Connell made it clear that he was going to concentrate his energies in 1843 on the Repeal agitation, the Unionist press demanded that the government take notice of this threat to the Union. In the spring of the year, when O'Connell began to attract the enthusiasm of the Irish masses for Repeal and when the municipal corporations and other public bodies in Leinster, Munster, and Connacht endorsed the Repeal program, Unionist editors insisted that Peel take action to suppress the Loyal National Repeal Association. But until late April Irish Government officials in Dublin Castle paid little attention to the progress of Repeal. They seemed convinced that O'Connell would not succeed in relighting the fire of Repeal and that he was only pushing nationalism to encourage the generosity of the Irish masses when it came time for them to donate something to the O'Connell tribute. The tribute was an annual gift of money from the Irish people to O'Connell for his own personal use. British politicians and journalists liked to make sarcastic comments about the tribute. They argued that it reduced O'Connell to the position of a beggar who was constantly forced to agitate to earn his keep. Irish nationalists replied that since O'Connell had sacrificed his legal practice to the welfare of his people he was entitled to compensation for his services. They insisted that the Liberator was the advocate of the Irish people and the Irish nation and had more than earned his public salary.

During the late winter and early spring of 1843 the

[7] McCaffrey was killed in May. There was a hearing but no one was convicted and punished for the murder.

Castle crowd was far more concerned about the real and potential dangers of the anti-poor law campaign in Munster than it was about the ravings of an ancient and declining demagogue at the Corn Exchange. However, the masses attending the Monster Meetings and the consistent rise in the weekly Repeal rent finally convinced the Viceroy, Lord DeGrey, that O'Connell had succeeded in diverting the many channels of Irish discontent into the Repeal reservoir.

In early May the Lord Lieutenant informed the Prime Minister that Ireland was on the brink of disaster. The Irish Catholic masses led by bishops and priests had given their enthusiastic support to Repeal. Thousands of people were attending large outdoor Repeal meetings where they listened to O'Connell promise them Repeal before the year was out. And they demonstrated their confidence in this promise by contributing their farthings and pennies to the Repeal treasury. Irish Protestants were in a panic. They feared that Repeal might lead to a class and religious war which would threaten their property and their lives or that Peel might come to some arrangement with O'Connell, as he did in 1829, which would compromise the basic interests of the ascendancy. Irish Catholic magistrates supported the Repeal agitation by their attendance at the Monster Meetings and many Irish M.P.'s, ignoring their Westminster obligations, remained in Ireland to help O'Connell fan the fires of discontent.

After completing his pessimistic description of the Irish political situation, DeGrey recommended to Peel that he ask Parliament for emergency legislation to put down the Repeal agitation or, at the very minimum, that he announce the Government's determination to preserve the Union. He thought that a strong statement by the Prime Minister in Parliament might convince Irish Unionists that they still enjoyed the confidence of the Conservative Government and it would provide Irish officials with the necessary authority to deal with magistrates sympathetic to Repeal.[8]

On May 9, 1843, in response to the request of the Lord Lieutenant and the demands of Irish unionist peers and M.P.'s for government action to suppress the Repeal agitation, Peel in the House of Commons and Wellington in the House of Lords pledged that the Government would employ every means at its disposal to preserve the Union and would not even shrink from civil war if necessary.[9] On May 25, using the Peel-Wellington statements as his authority, Sir Edward Sugden, the Lord Chancellor of Ireland, dismissed Lord Ffrench and six other Irish magistrates. In his letter to Lord Ffrench, Sugden did not question the technical legality of the Repeal Association or its meetings to petition for a Repeal of the act of Union, but he insisted that the Monster Meetings violated "the spirit of the Constitution" and that they posed a danger "to the safety of the State." He argued that since Her Majesty's Government had declared its intention to maintain the Union "it becomes the duty of the members of the Government to support that declaration." And since the Monster Meetings could lead to violence and civil disorder the Government "should be able to place a firm reliance on the watchfulness and determination of the magistracy to preserve the public peace." But a "magistrate who presides over or forms a part of such meetings can neither be prepared to repress violence nor could he be expected to act against a body for whose offense he would himself be responsible." Now that the Prime Minister had made the Government's position on Repeal clear to everyone, Sugden wrote Ffrench, he could no longer tolerate the delegation of police and judicial powers to those sympathetic to the dissolution of the Union. "To allow such persons any longer to remain in the commission of the peace would be to afford the power of the

8 DeGrey to Peel, May 6, 7, 1843, Add. MSS 40448, B.M.
9 *Hansard* 69:7-10; 23-25.

Crown to the carrying of a measure which her Majesty has, like her predecessor, expressed her determination to prevent."[10]

The Lord Chancellor's dismissal of the Repeal magistrates created controversy both in Britain and Ireland. A considerable number of peers in the House of Lords and M.P.'s in the House of Commons condemned his act as a violation of the constitutional right to petition for a repeal of legislation passed by Parliament. They also argued that since Sugden had not questioned the legality of the Repeal meetings he had no legitimate authority for dismissing those magistrates who attended them. They reminded the Government that statements made by Ministers in Parliament did not have the force of law, and they resented the use of the Queen's name in support of Sugden's conduct. Since she had not made a public statement on the Repeal agitation the Lord Chancellor had no right to invoke her authority.[11]

In private Peel agreed with the critics of Sugden that the Irish Lord Chancellor had presented a poor case in defense of his decision to dismiss the Repeal magistrates, and he censured Sugden for his lack of tact and judgement.[12] But in Parliament Peel and the other members of the cabinet supported Sugden's position that Repeal magistrates could not be depended on to maintain law and order in Ireland and that the Government could not

[10] The next of Sugden's letter is given in William J. O'Neill Daunt, *Personal Recollections of the Late Daniel O'Connell, M.P.* (London, 1848), 2:159. Before his letter of May 23 Sugden wrote to Lord Ffrench on May 17 asking if it was true that Ffrench intended to chair a Repeal meeting at Caltra on May 21. On May 19 Ffrench replied that he had not agreed to chair a meeting at Caltra, but he had consented to preside at Athlone. He added: "And I have further to state, that it is my intention to attend the meeting at Caltra, as well as that which is to be held at Athlone, both being for the legal and constitutional purpose of petitioning for the repeal of the Legislative Union." (*Freeman's Journal*, May 26, 1843)

[11] *Hansard* 69:1064-66, 1067, 1068, 1074-78, 1081-82, 1084-89, 1094, 1289, 1293-94; 70:1099, 1130-33, 1156ff., 1184-87.

[12] Peel to Sugden, June 1, 4, 1843, Add. MSS 40529, B.M.

retain in its service men who were hostile to its declared intention to preserve the Union.[13] Once the precedent was set the government could do nothing but continue the policy initiated by Sugden. During the following weeks every magistrate in Ireland who was directly or indirectly associated with the Repeal agitation lost his commission of the peace. A number of other magistrates, including William Smith O'Brien, M.P., resigned their commissions in protest against the denial of constitutional liberties in Ireland.[14]

In Ireland the dismissal of the Repeal magistrates proved a boon to the Repeal cause. From the beginning of its existence the Loyal National Repeal Association lacked the respectability enjoyed by the Catholic Association in the 1820's. In the struggle for Catholic emancipation O'Connell was able to enlist the talents of the Catholic gentry and the Catholic middle class, but only the

[13] *Hansard* 69:1072 ff.; 70:113 ff.

[14] On May 29 William Smith O'Brien, M.P. Clare, resigned his Commission of the Peace for the Counties of Limerick and Clare. In his letter to Sugden he said that it was no crime "to seek the repeal of an act of parliament, which history tells us was obtained by the basest means, and by the foulest corruption; and, though anxious to exhaust every hope of good government through every means before I unite with them (Repealers) in soliciting the repeal of that act, I cannot consent to retain any office which compels me to forego the acknowledged right to hold and propagate opinions not at variance with moral and statute law, which belongs to every British subject." He went on: "Nor am I sorry to be relieved from the responsibility of acting in any capacity under a government which, while it forbids the expression of national indignation, loses no opportunity of exciting well-founded discontent." Smith O'Brien said that as long as his fellow countrymen abstained from violating any moral law he would "feel it a privilege to participate in whatever indignities or sufferings may be inflicted upon them by their anti-Irish rulers." He concluded: "Being desirous to perform my duties as a free citizen of a free state without infringing any established law, I may be permitted to ask your lordship who are the chief interpreters of the laws of Ireland, not more for my own guidance than for that of others, with what number of loyal, peaceful, and well-disposed persons, I am at liberty to associate myself in an opening meeting, in case I should be driven by continued misgovernment to ask from the British legislature a Repeal of the Act of Union? Is the legal maximum 100, 1,000, 10,000, or 100,000? Does the law as interpreted by your lordship apply equally to England?" (*Freeman's Journal*, May 31, 1843)

peasant and proletarian masses rallied to Repeal. The dismissal of the Repeal magistrates forced some members of the legal profession to take a fresh look at Repeal. Petition was a basic right of the Constitution, and Sugden's letter to Lord Ffrench indicated that this right did not exist in Ireland. Immediately following the dismissal of the magistrates and Peel's support of Sugden in the House of Commons, the Loyal National Repeal Association received applications for membership from many members of the legal profession. Many of the future greats of Irish politics made their initial commitment to Irish nationalism at this time—Sir Colman O'Loghlen, James O'Hea, Francis Brady, Thomas MacNevin, Michael Joseph Barry, Denny Lane, Thomas O'Hagan, John Ferguson, and McCarthy Downing.[15]

The decision of the leading Catholic solicitors and barristers to support Repeal meant that O'Connell had achieved an Irish Catholic front; the agrarian masses, the city proletariat, the shopkeepers, the lawyers, and most important of all, the Catholic bishops and priests, were united in demand for an Irish parliament.

As soon as O'Connell announced the formation of the Precursor Society in 1838 he solicited the support of the Catholic hierarchy and clergy for the new organization.[16]

---

[15] O'Loghlen played an active role in Irish politics through the 1850's, 60's and 70's and was a member of the first Home Rule party in the House of Commons. Francis Brady, as Sir Francis Brady, later became Chief Justice of Newfoundland. Thomas MacNevin became a prominent member of the Young Ireland group and a distinguished contributor to the *Nation*. Michael Joseph Barry, like MacNevin, also supported Young Ireland and won a reputation as an orator. Thomas O'Hagan joined the Loyal National Repeal Association as a Federalist and later, as Baron O'Hagan, became Lord Chancellor of Ireland. Denny Lane remained an active nationalist and was one of the first Home Rulers in the 1870's. John Ferguson in the 1870's led the Home Rule cause among the Irish in Scotland, and McCarthy Downing was a member of the first Home Rule party at Westminster.

[16] In the following discussion of the Repeal activities of the Catholic bishops and priests, my principal authority is John F. Broderick, S.J., *The Holy See and the Irish Movement for the Repeal of the Union with England, 1829-1847* (Rome, 1951). Father Broderick has made excellent use of the archives in Rome.

Archbishop William Crolly, Armagh, the Primate, and a number of other bishops encouraged O'Connell in his effort to secure reforms for Ireland by threatening a resumption of the Repeal agitation.[17] But in March 1839 Philip Fransoni, Cardinal Prefect of Propaganda, wrote Crolly a letter expressing Vatican disapproval of the nationalist activities of Irish bishops and priests, particularly the anti-Government pronouncements of Archbishop John MacHale, Tuam. Fransoni asked Irish clergymen to ignore politics and to concentrate their energies on spiritual matters: "it must be seriously considered that Ministers of Christ recollect that they have not been sent to pursue eagerly the ways of the world and the activities of political parties, but to weep without remission between the porch and the altar in the misfortunes, so many and so great, of the persecuted Church, and by prayers and works of penance to implore aid from on high. Therefore I entrust the whole matter to your most noble excellency, and as soon as possible I earnestly desire that you take care to send me a reply."[18] No doubt Crolly circulated Fransoni's message among the members of the hierarchy, but it was kept a secret from the laity. Even O'Connell did not know about the directive from Propaganda until 1845 when another message from Fransoni with the same sentiments provoked a bitter controversy over the political role of the Catholic bishops and priests. Propaganda's request influenced Crolly to abstain from further political activity, but most of the hierarchy apparently ignored it.

When the Loyal National Repeal Association opened its doors in 1840, it quickly received the endorsement of MacHale and other Catholic prelates—John Cantwell, Meath; George Browne, Galway; James Keating, Ferns; Michael Blake, Dromore; William Higgins, Ardagh; Nicholas Foran, Waterford and Lismore; and Thomas Feeney,

---

17 Broderick, 109-11.
18 *Ibid.*, 102.

Killala. Early in 1843 Bishops Edmund Ffrench, Kilmac-
duagh and Kilfenora, and Thomas Coen, Clonfert, joined
the Loyal National Repeal Association. And as previously
noted, in March 1843 Patrick Kennedy, Bishop of Killaloe,
a Federalist, was accepted into the Association.[19] By January of 1844 fourteen bishops and two archbishops (Michael Slattery, Cashel, and MacHale) were members of the
Repeal Association, while two archbishops (Crolly and
Daniel Murray, Dublin) and nine bishops remained aloof
from the national movement.[20]

During the first four months of 1843 MacHale, Browne,
and Cantwell were the most active prelates in the Repeal
cause, but when Higgins returned to Ireland in May from
a visit to France he exceeded them in his enthusiasm for
an Irish parliament. Early in May, at a Monster Meeting
in Mullingar, Westmeath, Cantwell and Higgins made
militant Repeal speeches, and the Bishop of Ardagh's
words received a great deal of publicity. Higgins told the
many thousands gathered at Mullingar that "every Catholic bishop in Ireland, without an exception, is an ardent
Repealer," and he defied Peel—"that foolish minister
who presides over the fatal destinies of our country"—to
put down the nationalist agitation: "If they attempt, my
friends, to rob us of the daylight, which is, I believe,
common to us all, and prevent us from assembling in the
open fields, we will retire to our chapels, and we will
suspend all other instruction, in order to devote all our
time to teaching the people to be Repealers in spite of
them. If they beset our temples, and mix our people with
spies, we will prepare our people for the circumstances:
and if they bring us for that to the scaffold, in dying for

[19] The list of bishops active in the Repeal agitation was compiled
from newspaper reports on Repeal activities. At a Loyal National Repeal
Association meeting on March 20 O'Connell said that a majority of the
hierarchy were members of the Association and several were enrolled as
Volunteers (*Pilot,* March 22, 1843).
[20] Broderick, 135.

the cause of our country, we will bequeath our wrongs to our successors (The entire assembly here rose and continued cheering for several minutes). Let them try that experiment if they will . . .No, they would not do it; and therefore I am justified in saying that the bishops of Ireland and the people who co-operate with them, despite . . . all the malignity of British councils, have within their grasp the power . . . to carry out Repeal in spite of every possible resistance. I am but an humble man . . . I not only belong to the people, but I am proud to proclaim it. I belong to the very humblest class of the people. I do not speak it without pride, for to no aristocrat on earth do I owe anything, save the unbounded contempt that I have for the whole class (deafening shouts of applause) . . . I may speak officially, and without exaggeration say, that not only are they (bishops of Ireland) Repealers, but that they participate with ardour in every statement that has fallen from me. . . . You may draw to the utmost extent on us until our country has not one single grievance to complain of."[21]

Higgins' belligerent challenge to the Government, his threat to use the influence and the power of his Church to subvert any effort by Parliament and Peel to suppress Repeal, and his insult to the Irish aristocracy created a stir in the House of Lords and in the inner councils of the Vatican. Lord Beaumont, a prominent English Catholic peer, told the House of Lords that Higgins' Mullingar speech did not reflect official Irish Catholic opinion. He described it as a disgraceful exhibition that should be repudiated by the rest of the Irish hierarchy. He warned Irish Catholic leaders that if the bishops gave support to Repeal they would lead Ireland into a blood bath of greater dimensions than previous religious persecutions in their unfortunate country.[22] Lord Brougham claimed to have

21 *Ibid.*, 132-33.
22 *Hansard* 69:570-72; 752-53.

reliable information that the Irish Catholic clergy as a
body was not hostile to the Union, and the Earl of
Wicklow told his fellow peers that Archbishop Murray
did not endorse the demand for Repeal.[23]

On May 23, 1843, Irish newspapers published a letter
from Archbishop Murray to the Catholic clergy of his
diocese. The distinguished spiritual leader of Dublin's
Catholic population denied the statement of his old foe
Higgins that all the Catholic bishops stood behind the
demand for an Irish parliament. He said that he had
never participated in the national movement and that he
had never given anyone reason to believe that he had or
that he would.[24]

Following his letter to the priests of his diocese, Murray
wrote Paul Cullen, Rector of the Irish College in Rome,
a man of considerable influence in Vatican circles, and
later his successor as Archbishop of Dublin, suggesting that
Cullen ask Propaganda to issue a statement requesting
the Irish hierarchy to refrain from further involvement in
the Repeal agitation. He expressed the fear that Repeal
would lead to civil war and that many bishops through
mistaken motives and ignorance of the consequences of
their words and actions would bear the responsibility for
the violence and bloodshed which would certainly follow
a confrontation between armed and disciplined British
soldiers and the unarmed Repeal masses.[25]

On May 28, 1843, at another Monster Meeting, this time
at Longford, Higgins replied to Murray and to the attacks
of British and Irish peers. He expressed admiration for

---

23 *Ibid.*, 753.

24 "In January, 1843, I concurred in the resolution unanimously passed
at our general Episcopal meeting, recommending our clergy to abstain
in future from taking any prominent part in proceedings of a merely
political character. To the spirit of that resolution I strictly adhere;
and I have not, by any act or word of mine, set an example at variance
with it." (Part of the Murray letter published in the press and quoted
in Broderick, 134)

25 Broderick, 136.

the spiritual qualities of the Archbishop of Dublin, repeated his pride in his humble origins and his contempt for the aristocracy, and asked the multitude to join him in a sacred pledge never to abandon Repeal and its leader —a request enthusiastically endorsed by the thousands surrounding the speaker's platform.[26] At the banquet following the outdoor meeting Higgins repeated his promise to "make every chapel in Ireland a Repealing place" if Peel attempted to suppress the national movement. "I will," he said, "if necessary, go into the very sanctuaries, and there I shall denounce those who will force us there as conspirators against the Constitution of my country." Higgins then said that he had "one of the most respected clergymen in the kingdom ready to verify that he heard the Most Reverend Dr. Murray declare himself to be a Repealer before a large company of priests." He closed his comments with an emotional declaration of loyalty to the Queen and Constitution.[27]

Bishop Cantwell spoke after Higgins and endorsed the sentiments of his colleague. He said that his enthusiasm for the Liberator and Repeal was shared by 150 priests and 250,000 laymen in his diocese. Cantwell insisted that he and the other Catholic bishops had a moral obligation to identify themselves with the Irish people in a struggle

---

[26] *Pilot,* May 31, 1843. Higgins could not refrain from giving Murray a little dig in typical Irish fashion. He mentioned that Murray was a frequent visitor at Dublin Castle. But he assured his Repeal audience that Murray went to the Castle for noble and charitable purposes. Of course, Higgins said, a humble man like himself, not far from the grave and ready to give his all for his country, never would frequent the Castle.

[27] *Ibid.* The animosity displayed by Higgins toward Archbishop Murray on the Repeal question originated in the bitter controversy that divided the hierarchy on the issue of national education. MacHale and Higgins vehemently denounced Murray in Ireland and at Rome for a friendly attitude toward the national school system which was based on the principle of mixed or nondenominational education. For an interesting discussion of the education controversy see Emmet Larkin, "The Quarrel among the Roman Catholic Hierarchy over the National System of Education in Ireland, 1838-41," *The Celtic Cross,* ed. by Ray B. Browne, William John Roscelli, and Richard J. Loftus (West Lafayette, 1964), 121-46.

against oppression and poverty—evils represented and caused by the Union, "that accursed measure that entailed misery and starvation in our country."[28]

When Higgins learned that his Mullingar speech created a sensation in Rome, he wrote Cullen proclaiming his loyalty to the Queen and Constitution. He argued, like Cantwell, that Irish bishops had a moral obligation to stand with the Irish people in their effort to establish an Irish parliament. Repeal was a just cause. It would relieve the Irish masses from oppression and poverty— the obvious results of foreign domination. Irish bishops and priests were of the people, and to merit the loyalty of the people they must demonstrate their sympathy with the legitimate aspirations of Irish nationalism. Repeal was a conservative movement which channeled discontent into a legal effort to amend the Constitution, thereby frustrating more violent forms of agitation. If Catholic bishops took the lead in agitating Repeal it would guarantee that Irish nationalism would continue to follow the path of constitutional agitation.[29]

A few weeks later Higgins sent a second letter to Cullen. This time he advised him to warn the Vatican against interfering in Irish politics. He argued that since the oath of allegiance in the Catholic relief bill forbade Catholic subjects of the Crown to accept Papal jurisdiction in temporal matters, any condemnation of the Repeal activities of bishops and priests would invite them to violate this oath. He suggested that Cullen recommend that the Vatican fall back on the Oath of Allegiance as an excuse not to condemn the participation of bishops and priests in the national movement. In this letter, and one that he wrote in September, Higgins repeated his conviction that Repeal was a constitutional agitation preventing violent men from seizing the reins of the nationalist movement.

28 *Pilot*, May 31, 1843.
29 Broderick, 137-38.

And for that reason, he argued, O'Connell should be supported by the hierarchy. By encouraging O'Connell, the bishops would be in a position to shape the destiny of their country.[30]

Archbishop Murray was the only Catholic prelate publicly to declare himself a non-Repealer, but other bishops refused to lend their influence to the progress of the agitation. In May 1843 John Murphy, Bishop of Cork, pleaded ill health as an excuse not to attend a Monster Meeting in his city and added his determination not to become involved in politics. Bartholomew Crotty, Bishop of Cloyne and Ross, also rejected an invitation to the Cork meeting on grounds of ill health. Crotty admitted a sympathy for Repeal but argued that an Irish parliament would not eliminate all of the economic and social problems confronting the country. In June William Kinsella, Bishop of Ossory, refused to sign a requisition for a Monster Meeting in Kilkenny. He confessed to Repeal sympathies but also expressed determination to avoid politics.[31]

Although Higgins obviously exaggerated Repeal enthusiasm among the hierarchy, he was more accurate in his estimate than Lords Brougham and Beaumont who rejected the claim that Catholic clerical opinion favored nationalism. Most of the bishops, with varying degrees of energy, continued to support O'Connell. Some went so far as to collect the Repeal dues of their clergy and forward the money to the Association in Dublin. The most important cogs in the Repeal machinery on the local level were the priests. They organized and participated in Repeal meetings, and they selected the parish Repeal Wardens.[32] On Sunday morning many Catholic chapels

---

30 *Ibid.*, 138-39.
31 *Ibid.*, 140.
32 *Ibid.*, 129; *Pilot*, March 15, 1843. At a Repeal meeting July 18 John O'Connell said that Repeal Wardens were appointed on the same basis that Wardens were selected by the Catholic Association. They must have

served as the schools of Irish nationalism. Priests preached Repeal in their sermons. They demanded that members of their congregations join the Loyal National Repeal Association and pay the Repeal rent. One priest advised the young ladies in his parish to wed only Repealers, and another handed out Repeal Association membership cards at the altar rail of his church.[33] The British Government took notice of the Repeal activities taking place in Catholic chapels and instructed army officers to march their men out of any place of worship where the priest used the pulpit to preach Irish nationalism. One officer anxious to comply with this instruction was confused when the priest in his district often resorted to the Irish language in his sermons.[34]

No one examining the events of 1843 can overestimate the role of the Catholic hierarchy and clergy in cultivating and preserving Repeal enthusiasm, but Repeal also received strength from the support it received from Irishmen who had emigrated to Britain, various parts of the Empire, and the United States. The sentimental love for Ireland and the bitter hate of Britain entertained by these exiles was passed on to their descendents and often grew in intensity among Irishmen who never saw Ireland. Even before the famine considerable numbers of Irishmen sailed for Britain, Canada, and the United States to seek economic opportunities unavailable in their own country. As soon as the news of the Repeal enthusiasm in Ireland

clerical approval. That is why a Repeal Warden in Athlone was dismissed "because one of the rules of the Association was, that in any locality where the parish priest is a Repeater, no person that he certifies against can be a Repeal Warden; and the Association cannot enter into the question whether the reasons given in his certificate are satisfactory or not." (*Pilot*, July 19, 1843)

33 Broderick, 124-25.

34 Lt. Col. Greaves, Military Secretary to the Under Secretary, to Edward Lucas, the Under Secretary, June 29, 1843, Kilmainham papers, National Library of Ireland.

reached the ears of transplanted Irishmen in the commercial, industrial, and transportation centers of Britain and the New World they rallied to the cause of Irish freedom and contributed hard earned pounds and dollars to the treasury of the Loyal National Repeal Association. Money came in from English and Scottish Repeal organizations in Manchester, Birmingham, Leeds, Liverpool, London, Preston, Glasgow, and Edinburgh, and from Repeal associations in Halifax, Nova Scotia, New York, Boston, Philadelphia, Baltimore, Charleston, Savannah, New Orleans, Natchez, St. Louis, Cincinnati, and Pittsburgh. Even the small towns of the American South, East, and Midwest—wherever there was a factory, railroad, or canal to use the surplus unskilled labor of Ireland—produced local organizations to collect pennies, nickles, dimes, quarters, and dollars for the cause of Repeal.[35]

Repeal stimulated such an emotional response among Irish-Americans that state and national politicians found it expedient to endorse O'Connell's objectives. William Seward, one of the most promising young men in New York state politics, became an active champion of Repeal, and Robert Tyler, the son of the President of the United States, was a frequent speaker at Repeal functions in the eastern states. Finally in July, 1843, his father John Tyler gave an unqualified endorsement to the demand of the Irish masses for their own parliament: "I am the decided friend of the Repeal of the legislative Union between Great Britain and Ireland. I ardently and anxiously hope that it may take place, and I have the utmost confidence that Ireland will have her own Parliament, in her own capital in a very short time. On this great question I am no half-way man."[36]

Shortly after the dollars began to flow into the Repeal

[35] O'Connell placed British and Canadian Repealers on the books of the Repeal Association since they were subjects of the Crown.
[36] *Pilot*, July 21, 1843 (quoted in the Philadelphia *Ledger*).

treasury from American sources O'Connell decided to make it clear that while the Loyal National Repeal Association welcomed and appreciated financial contributions from Irish-American slave states, Irish nationalism was completely and resolutely opposed to slavery as an institution. He said that he would rather give up the Repeal cause than have it used to encourage the continuation of a disreputable and anti-Christian social and economic system. As a Catholic he could not conduct an agitation that supported the proposition that the end justified the means.[37]

On many occasions during the spring and summer of 1843 O'Connell continued to attack slavery and contrast the principles of American democracy with the reality of human bondage existing in the South. Many Repeal leaders in the slave states complained that O'Connell's continued attacks on their way of life hampered the organization of Irish-Americans in the Southern and Border states and frustrated the effort to collect money for the Repeal cause.[38] O'Connell replied that he would not sacrifice his Christian zeal for human freedom and the moral principles of his religion in order to win the support and the dollars of the defenders of slavery.

In the fall of 1843 the Executive of the Irish Repeal Association of Cincinnati wrote to the Loyal National Repeal Association in Dublin condemning the antislavery position of O'Connell and denying his right to criticize an institution valued by many Irish-Americans. The Cincinnati Repealers argued that slaves were legal property and that slavery was supported by the United States Constitution, that it was a natural condition for Negroes

37 Nation, April 15, 1843.
38 Freeman's Journal, September 28, 1843. O'Connell's antislavery views were denounced by Repeal organizations in Savannah, St. Louis, and Cincinnati. The Savannah group claimed that O'Connell's antagonism to slavery caused the collapse of Repeal associations in Charleston, South Carolina, and Natchez, Mississippi.

since they were physically, morally, and intellectually inferior to whites, and that it had the support of many Catholic clergymen in the United States.

O'Connell replied that no man could be the property of another man and that no law or constitution could deprive a man of his rights or dignity as a human being. All men were equal before their Creator, and the apparent intellectual and moral inferiority of Negroes was the result of a brutalized and degraded environment. He denounced Catholic priests who supported slavery as holding views contrary to the spirit of the religion they preached and the pronounced antislavery position of the Vatican.

O'Connell described Irish-Americans as among the most notorious anti-Negroes in the American community. He asked them to look into their depraved hearts and to recognize how far they had departed from the tolerant and humane spirit associated with the Irish people. He pleaded with them to support the egalitarian principles of the Declaration of Independence of their adopted country. He advised them to join with the abolitionists in the effort to free their Negro brothers in Christ. And once the Negro walked in freedom, he urged Irish-Americans to do everything in their power to guarantee that they would be granted full citizenship in the American community.[39]

O'Connell's defense of the dignity and equality of the Negro led to a bizarre incident at the October 2, 1843, meeting of the Loyal National Repeal Association. According to the Repeal press, after the meeting had adjourned, a Negro stepped on to the Speaker's platform and made the following little speech: "I am vera glad to see Massa Dan O'Connell, for he save the life of black people (cheers and laughter). I hear of him when no bigger than that (placing his hand within a foot of the surface of the

[39] Reply of Daniel O'Connell to the Executive Committee of the Irish Repeal Association of Cincinnati, October 11, 1843, O'Connell MSS, University College Library, Dublin.

table), and though I was brought up a Protestant, I am now a Catholic, and will die in that religion for the sake of Massa Dan O'Connell (loud laughter, in which the Liberator heartily joined, followed this burst of eloquence)."[40]

Irish-American nationalists often took a more belligerent tone in discussing the British Government and Irish Freedom than did Repealers in Ireland. They recommended that Ireland should imitate the example of the American colonies and win her independence by rebellion if constitutional agitation failed to achieve the desired goal. The Irish-American confidence in revolution was shared by French Radicals, who, like men of the left in all countries, were fascinated and inspired by events in Ireland. Ledru-Rollin, articulate radical spokesman in the Chamber of Deputies and later a leader in the successful effort to depose Louis Phillipe, sent O'Connell a letter expressing his hope for the triumph of the Repeal cause. He reported that the French people shared his enthusiasm for the effort of the Irish people to obtain political liberty and economic security. He said that the French and Irish peoples had always been allies in the cause of freedom against a common foe, the British aristocracy. Rollin promised O'Connell that if the British Tories attempted to crush the Repeal movement Irish nationalists could rely on French military aid in their resistance against despotism. He expressed a desire to come to Ireland so that he might witness the birth of Irish freedom, and he asked O'Connell to extend him an invitation.[41]

O'Connell was not pleased with the militant tones of American and French sympathizers. He wanted to discourage influences that might stimulate Irish hotheads to abandon constitutional methods of agitation and thereby provide British authorities with a justification for coercion.

40 *Pilot*, October 4, 1843.
41 *Ibid.*, August 4, 1843.

He thanked Americans and Frenchmen for their pro-Repeal sentiments but reminded them that Repeal was a constitutional agitation which repudiated militarism and violence. He conceded that Americans won their freedom by revolution, but he insisted that times had changed. The successful Irish Catholic campaign for emancipation had demonstrated that organized public opinion firmly committed to a just cause could not be defeated. He would win Repeal the same way that he had won emancipation —without shedding a drop of blood.[42] He asked Ledru-Rollin not to come to Ireland during the Repeal crisis because his presence would be misinterpreted by the British press as a military alliance between French Radicals and Irish Repealers.[43]

No matter how often O'Connell insisted that even precious liberty was not worth a drop of human blood or that organized and disciplined public opinion was a more effective instrument of reform than revolution, he knew as well as the British Government that the strength of the Repeal Association rested on the possibility of revolution if the demand for an Irish parliament was frustrated by British authorities. In 1843 O'Connell spoke with the same two voices he used in conducting the Catholic emancipation agitation in the 1820's. With one voice he talked peace, the Constitution, public opinion, and law and order; with the other he threatened resistance to any Government effort to suppress Ireland's right to petition for a redress of grievances. He insisted that Ireland would not initiate any contest with the British but he warned

---

[42] O'Connell in reply to a pro-Repeal statement by Robert Tyler (*Nation*, April 15, 1843). The Repeal agitation also attracted the attention of James Gordon Bennett of the New York *Herald*. He attended a meeting at the Corn Exchange on August 7. At this meeting O'Connell described him as the editor "of the vilest gazette that ever disgraced the press in any country . . ." and asked him to leave. Bennett promptly left the room (*Pilot*, August 7, 1843).

[43] *Pilot*, August 7, 1843.

that the Repeal army was disciplined by temperance and would not respond as cowed slaves to any challenge to its courage. And he reminded the British Government of the large number of Irishmen serving in the British army sympathetic to the political, economic, social, and religious misfortunes of their parents, brothers, and sisters. If Peel insisted on civil war as an answer to Repeal, could he rely on Irish soldiers to shoot down their own flesh and blood?

O'Connell, in advertising his pacifism and his confidence in constitutional methods of agitation, notified British politicians that there were many nationalists in Ireland who believed that the pike was the only message that the British understood. He said that he was the only man who could restrain the forces of violence in Ireland. If Peel would not make terms with him, someday he would have to bargain with men less amenable to reason and far less friendly to the British connection.[44]

Shortly after May 9, when Peel and Wellington told both houses of Parliament that they would preserve the Union at all costs, O'Connell told the Loyal National Repeal Association that the Government's first response to the Repeal agitation probably meant a coercion bill. He said that he would go to Westminster to resist such a bill with all the legal and parliamentary resources at his disposal, and he pledged never to abandon the constitutional movement for self government: "Let him (Peel) take his choice, and extinguish, in the blood of the Irish people, the last remnant of their liberties (vehement applause and waving of hats and handkerchiefs for several minutes). Friends may desert me—foes may threaten; but I will never forsake the path that I have proposed to myself. I will violate no law. I will outrage no ordinance of man nor of Heaven; but as long as there remains to me one inch of the Constitution on which I can plant my

---

44 O'Connell expressed these opinions in many speeches at the Corn Exchange and at the Monster Meetings.

footstep, I will find some archimedian point, whereon to plant the lever with which I will still uphold the fainting liberties of my country."[45]

O'Connell could be a dogmatic pacifist in the halls of the Corn Exchange, but at the Monster Meetings he was the general of the Repeal army and therefore for the sake of national morale had to reply more violently to Peel's threat of civil war to maintain the Union. At a Monster Meeting at Kilkenny O'Connell dared the Government to make war on the Irish people. He promised that Ireland would not strike the first blow but she would defend her rights and her honor. He scorned the threats of Peel and Wellington. He said that the British army in Ireland was on good terms with the Repeal masses and would hesitate to make war on its friends. O'Connell assured his audience that they would win the final victory in any contest with the Government because they were disciplined by temperance. Because he had this disciplined and obedient army at his disposal and because he enjoyed the good will of enlisted men in the British army he could ignore the enemies of Ireland in Whitehall. But do not worry, he told the Kilkenny Repealers, the Queen supported Ireland's demand for an independent legislature. She did not share the anti-Irish opinions of her Prime Minister. In an emergency she could and she would restore the Irish Parliament: "it is not dead—it only sleeps."[46]

At the banquet following the afternoon meeting, O'Connell sustained the militant mood of his afternoon address: "We stand at the head of a body of men that, if organized by military discipline would be quite abundant for the conquest of Europe. Wellington had never such an army as we saw today. There were not at Waterloo on both sides so many stout, active, energetic men as we saw here today. Oh! but it will be said, they were not disciplined!

45 *Nation,* May 20, 1843.
46 *Freeman's Journal,* June 10, 1843.

If you tell them what to do you will have them all disciplined in an hour (great and continued cheering). Do you not think that they were as well able to walk in order after a band as if they wore red coats, and that they would be as ready to obey their Repeal Wardens as if they were called sergeants and captains?"[47]

While O'Connell was cautioning his friends in France and America to go slow on the revolution talk and rejecting their offers of military aid, the Young Irelanders in the columns of the *Nation* took the opposite point of view. They argued that a war in defense of "truth, country, and freedom" was moral and brought credit and honor on those who fought it—win or lose.[48] The Young Irelanders also insisted that Ireland needed a foreign policy which would encourage firm alliances with those countries ready and willing to support Ireland's struggle for freedom. Repealers should encourage the overtures of friends in France and America. They should ignore anti-French propaganda fostered by the British Government and planted in the columns of a bought British press. France was Ireland's oldest friend and ally. France represented culture and freedom. Britain symbolized materialism, barbarism, and slavery.[49]

Although O'Connell responded in a militant manner to the Peel and Wellington declarations in Parliament, he still indicated that he was willing to reach an honorable compromise with the Government. He repeated his consistent position that he would be willing to abandon Repeal if the British Government could demonstrate that the Union would bring prosperity, individual freedom and opportunity, and religious equality to Ireland. On May 16, in an interesting speech in the Corn Exchange, O'Connell issued an invitation to Peel to destroy Repeal

47 *Ibid.*
48 *Nation,* June 10, 1843.
49 *Ibid.,* April 22, 1843.

by conferring justice on Ireland. He estimated that thousands would desert Irish nationalism for every demand of the Repeal platform conceded by the Government. If Ireland was given equal status with Britain within the United Kingdom, the Irish masses would cease to demand their own parliament.[50]

Peel's and Wellington's pledge to resist Repeal even to the point of civil war might have maintained, and in some instances restored, the confidence of British and Irish Unionists, but it did nothing to restrain Repeal enthusiasm in Ireland. Perhaps the best way to measure that enthusiasm is by the weekly rent collected by the Loyal National Repeal Association from its supporters. This rent rose from £185, 4s, 5½d on February 27 to £287, 17s, 3d on March 27 to £464, 7s, 4½d on April 24, to £2,205, 16s, 3d on May 29. O'Connell argued that the constantly increasing Repeal rent demonstrated the determination and extent of Repeal opinion. Since it was clear that the great majority of the Irish nation was with him and that the Government could not for long resist the onslaught of this disciplined, determined, yet constitutional opinion, he thought it necessary before final victory to spell out in some details the objectives of the Repeal agitation.

On June 6 the Loyal National Repeal Association issued a manifesto "To the People of Ireland" which was published in the Irish press. According to the manifesto Repeal would mean the establishment of an Irish parliament composed of sovereign, lords, and commons which would make all laws for Ireland and an Irish court system to handle domestic litigation. But the restoration of the Irish parliamentary and legal systems would not completely satisfy the needs of the country. Ireland must have the benefit of all the constitutional changes conferred on Britain since 1832 and other reforms necessary for

50 *Ibid.*, May 20, 1843.

economic security and a government responsible to the pressures of public opinion. This would mean the enactment of tenant right, household suffrage by secret ballot, and a reform of the old Irish House of Commons. The manifesto insisted on separation of church and state in a free Ireland but assured Protestants that their religious, property, and political rights would remain intact.[51]

This manifesto was an effort by O'Connell to attach the Protestant clergy, aristocracy, and middle class to the Repeal movement. He also appealed to the "Lords of Patriotic Tradition" (the Duke of Leinster, the Earl of Charlemont, the Marquis of Kildare, and Lord Cloncurry) to return to the Irish nationalism their families once embraced and take their rightful place in the front lines of the march to freedom. He constantly promised Irish Protestants that the disestablishment of their church would not be followed by a Catholic establishment and ascendancy. Separation of church and state would follow Repeal and that would mean complete freedom of religious expression and conscience for all Irishmen. Ireland, he said, needed the contributions of all of her sons and daughters—Catholic, Protestant, and Dissenter. However, he warned, if Irish Protestants turned their backs on their Catholic fellow countrymen during this great struggle for independence, it would be difficult to protect Protestant rights in an Irish parliament achieved in the face of Protestant hostility.[52] But O'Connell's pleas for Protestant collaboration fell on deaf ears. A prosperous class which enjoys political, economic, social, and religious ascendancy because it persecutes and exploits another class is not likely to expect great kindness, morality, justice, and reason from its victims.

When O'Connell attended the Monster Meeting at Mallow, County Cork, on Sunday, June 11, he had knowl-

[51] *Freeman's Journal*, June 7, 1843.
[52] *Ibid.*, May 31, July 15, 1843.

edge that the cabinet was in emergency session to devise a strategy in regard to Repeal. And he had every reason to think that Peel would decide on coercion. At the afternoon meeting O'Connell seemed relatively calm as he told his audience, estimated at 400,000, that they had the attention and the sympathy of enlightened opinion on the Continent and in America and that their discipline and temperance would be rewarded with the control of their political and economic destiny. But at the evening banquet, O'Connell decided to issue his defiance to the Government. He said that he was not in the mood for making speeches because a time of action was approaching. Irishmen would soon have to choose between living as slaves or dying as freemen (the audience responded with a shout, "We will die freemen"). He told his listeners about the cabinet meeting and warned that Peel might try to halt Repeal with coercion. He reminded them that Ireland had no friend at the cabinet table. Wellington had been born in Ireland but at heart he was no Irishman: "If a tiger cub were dropped in a fold would it be a lamb? (hisses and groans)." O'Connell promised that he would lead a resistance movement in defense of Irish liberties if the British Government sent troops to crush Repeal: "Oh," he said, "they shall never trample me at least (tremendous cheering that lasted for several minutes)." "I was wrong," he continued, "they may trample me under foot (cries of 'no, they never shall'). I say they may trample me, but it will be my dead body they trample on, not the living man (hear, hear and the most tremendous cheering that lasted for several minutes)."

Stimulated by his own emotions and by the enthusiastic reception his fiery words received from the audience, O'Connell went on to describe Peel and Wellington as "second Cromwells" who might imitate the work of their master and send Repealers to the West Indies to replace emancipated Negro slave labor. And then he pointed to the ladies gallery and said that Peel and Wellington might follow another Cromwell precedent and slaughter in cold blood the women of Ireland: "When Cromwell entered the town (Wexford) by treachery, three hundred inoffensive women of all ages and classes were collected around the Cross of Christ, erected in a part of the town called the 'Bull Ring'; they prayed to heaven for mercy, and I hope they found it—they prayed to the English for humanity, and Cromwell slaughtered them (oh, oh, and great sensation). I tell you this: three hundred of the grace, and beauty, and virtue of Wexford were slaughtered by the English ruffians. Sacred Heaven! (tremendous sensation and cries of 'oh, oh.'). I am not at all imaginative when I talk of the possibility of such occurences anew (hear, hear); but yet I assert there is no danger for the women, for the men of Ireland would die to the last in their defense. (Here the entire company rose and cheered for several minutes!) We were a paltry remnant then, we are nine million now (renewed cheering)." Yes, continued O'Connell, Cromwell, Peel and "old buccaneering Wellington," aided and abetted by the "maniac disposition of Stanley" and the "bigoted prejudices and disposition of Sir James Graham," might decide to make war on the Irish people. He would try to prevent this with every available constitutional weapon but if necessary he would resist force with force. Let Peel "the Cromwell of the present day commence his murder if he desires." Ireland would initiate no violence, but Irishmen would gladly surrender their lives in defense of dignity and freedom. O'Connell told Repealers to expect war but to exercise prudence and caution. They should respect the Constitution and obey their leader. There was always a possibility that Peel and his associates would not loose the Saxon horde. Perhaps they would realize that Britain was despised in the civilized world and that any attack on Ireland would give the French, the Russians, and the Americans the excuse and the opportunity to attack and crush her.[53]

O'Connell at Mallow made perhaps the most militant speech of his career. Irish nationalists considered it a pledge by their leader to command an armed resistance to any British Government effort to crush Repeal by military force. His stirring words soon became known as the Mallow Defiance, and their effect on the nationalist masses was demonstrated by a Repeal rent of £3,103, 7s, 6½d for the week beginning June 11. The members of the Loyal National Repeal Association were so impressed with the Mallow Defiance that the Association commissioned John Hogan, the leading Irish sculptor, to perpetuate the memory of O'Connell challenging the Government at Mallow. Hogan's likeness of O'Connell at the height of his national reputation now stands in the City Hall in Dublin, once the Royal Exchange.

O'Connell soon realized that the British Government was not going to meet the Repeal challenge either with coercive legislation enforced by British troops or with the same concession techniques that it used to solve the Catholic emancipation crisis in 1829. This seriously upset the strategy of the Irish leader because his 1843 tactics were based on the precedents of the 1820's. Once again he had successfully channeled the many streams of Irish discontent into a single agitation, and, aided by the temperance movement, he had mobilized and disciplined the forces of Irish nationalist opinion. Following the paths of the 1820's he had strengthened the cause of constitutional nationalism by holding out the threat of armed resistance to any British effort to crush the expression of Irish opinion through the instruments of coercive legislation and military force.

O'Connell often told Repeal audiences in 1843 that the present agitation was more powerful than the movement

[53] *Ibid.*, June 14, 1843.

for Catholic emancipation. Perhaps he was right. Certainly the 1829 success had increased public confidence in his leadership and the validity of his methods. The effort of the *Nation* to create an Irish cultural nationalism added a powerful, articulate, and emotional voice to the popular movement. And the British Government's clumsy handling of the mail coach contract, the Dr. Phelan affair, and the dismissal of the Repeal magistrates seemed to confirm O'Connell's claim that Ireland could obtain justice only in an Irish parliament.

But while the strength of organized Irish opinion was at least as formidable in 1843 as it was in 1829, Repeal sentiment in Britain, except among Irish immigrants and some Chartists, had little strength. In the 1820's proponents of Catholic emancipation in the House of Commons were numerous and sometimes commanded a majority. Even several members of the Tory cabinet supported the Catholic cause. There was also an enlightened, though small, pro-emancipation British opinion outside Parliament. In the critical years of the late 1820's, Peel and Wellington knew that British support for Catholic emancipation in and out of the House of Commons made a civil war in support of Protestant ascendancy a dangerous alternative to concessions and therefore they bowed to expediency. But in 1843 British parliamentary and public opinion was almost unanimous in the conviction that Repeal was not a satisfactory solution to the Irish Question. The Irish connection was considered necessary to British defense and the preservation of the Empire and a moral commitment to Irish Protestants fearing a Catholic ascendancy in an independent Ireland. Therefore Peel was free to employ any tactic he believed necessary to preserve the Union. This canceled out O'Connell's threat to resist coercion by armed force.

There is no way to prove that O'Connell really believed that he would obtain Repeal in 1843 or that he used the

agitation to force lesser concessions from the Government
or from the Whigs at some future date. He was a politician
who believed that it was always necessary to ask for more
than he expected to get, and during the course of the
1843 Repeal agitation O'Connell often suggested that he
was prepared to abandon the demand for an Irish parliament if the British Government could demonstrate that
the Union would guarantee to Irish Catholics political
liberty, religious equality, economic security, and an equal
share in the government of the United Kingdom and the
Empire. This was a position consistent with O'Connell's
previous statements on Repeal. He was a realist, and he
must have known that his old enemy Peel might never
make the concessions necessary to justify the abandonment
of Repeal. But he could hope that the Repeal agitation
would lead to the downfall of the Conservative administration, a Russell-Palmerston Government, and a new Irish-
Whig alliance on terms favorable to the former.[54]

But by midsummer O'Connell knew that his strategy
had failed, and he found himself the leader of an agitation
that could easily slip out of his control into the hands of
young hotheads. Ireland was mobilized, probably in excess of his January expectations, but Peel was not going
to make any concessions to Irish nationalist opinion to

[54] There is evidence that O'Connell would have welcomed a new Whig
alliance as an escape from the dead end of the Repeal agitation. On
September 9, 1843, he wrote Lord Campbell, a Whig peer, suggesting
that Lord John Russell should come out publicly for disestablishment,
tenant right, an expanded Irish suffrage, more Irish M.P.'s in the House
of Commons, and an extension of municipal reform: "In short, why does
he not prove himself a high-minded, high gifted statesman, capable of
leading his friends into all the advantages to be derived from conciliating
the Irish nation and strengthening the British Empire?" W. J. Fitzpatrick,
Correspondence of Daniel O'Connell (London, 1888), 2:308-309). On
January 9, 1844, in a remarkable letter to Charles Buller, O'Connell said
that the Whigs could destroy the Repeal movement by a program
involving tenant right, disestablishment, franchise and municipal reform,
and expanded Irish representation in the House of Commons. However,
in this letter O'Connell expressed doubts that the anti-Catholic Russell
would adopt such a program and if he did that he could carry it through
in the face of British anti-Irish, no-Popery opinion (Russell papers).

appease O'Connell, and the success of Repeal had stimulated anti-Irish sentiments in Britain and strengthened the
position of the Peel Government in its opposition to an
Irish parliament. The Irish leader also realized that Peel
had devised a clever strategy to relieve the Government
permanently of the O'Connell nuisance. The Prime Minister was going to ignore Repeal and attempt to prove that
O'Connell was a fraud. Soon the Irish masses would be
forced to recognize that 1843 was not going to be the
Repeal year. Then in disgust and frustration they might
abandon their leader, and they might also reject constitutional nationalism and embrace physical force. This
choice would give Peel the legal justification to crush Irish
nationalism by the use of British troops. This would leave
the work of O'Connell's life in a shambles and permit the
British Government to deal with the Irish Question on
its own terms.

In the summer of 1843 O'Connell's leadership over the
Catholic masses faced its greatest challenge. He would
need to utilize all of his experience and his unmatched
genius as a democratic agitator to retain the loyalty of his
followers and preserve the unity of Irish nationalism. He
must continue the effort to force concessions from the
Tories, and failing that, the overthrow of the Peel Government and its replacement by a Whig administration
anxious to come to terms with the forces of Irish discontent. But the situation did not encourage hopes for
Repeal, reform, or the defeat of the Tories. Peel's position
was even milder than the anti-Irish, no-Popery sentiments
of British opinion, and the Whig leaders sensitive to this
opinion were timid and cautious in approaching the Irish
Question. The Prime Minister could sit back and watch
an enraged and frustrated Irish nationalist opinion lose
heart and retreat from Repeal, or in anger devour its
leader. And if Irish nationalism decided to repudiate
constitutional methods for insurrection, Peel would have

the justification to crush the machine so carefully constructed by O'Connell.

O'Connell would not win Repeal or reform or a friendly Whig Government in 1843, but perhaps he could defeat Peel's effort to destroy him by retaining the allegiance of his supporters and by keeping the Repeal forces intact, ready to fight future battles. And he devised a bold, imaginative, yet constitutional strategy to obtain these goals. Ireland would not see a parliament in College Green before January 1844, but perhaps she could have a provisional government. O'Connell began to place more emphasis on the Preservative Society (the Council of Three Hundred). Three hundred men representing Repealers from every section of Ireland, each entrusted with one hundred pounds from nationalists in his district, would meet in Dublin and plan the future of Ireland. He was vague on the date for calling the Preservative Society into session. Sometimes he said it would meet when three million were enrolled on the books of the Loyal National Repeal Association. On other occasions he said it would meet before January 1, 1844.[55]

On August 22 O'Connell indicated that the Preservative Society might be more than just an idle promise to boost national morale. On that day he presented his plan for an independent Irish government. Victoria and her successors, protected in their ancient prerogatives, would remain on the Irish throne. The Irish House of Lords would be restored with its old privileges, but Catholic bishops would take their place alongside the Protestant hierarchy. The House of Commons would retain its 300 pre-Union membership but it would be a reformed House reflecting population shifts and Catholic emancipation; 173 county representatives and 127 from towns and cities, including two from Dublin University, would constitute the Irish House of Commons. O'Connell based his detailed scheme

[55] *Nation*, April 29, 1843; *Freeman's Journal*, August 23, 1843.

for parliamentary representation upon the census returns of 1831. He hinted that membership in the Preservative Society would be based on his scheme for parliamentary representation and that Repealers selected for the former would in most cases be the first elected M.P.'s in the reformed Irish House of Commons. This would mean that the Preservative Society, in fact if not in theory, would be a provisional government commanding the allegiance of the Repeal masses.

In presenting his plan for the revived and reformed Irish parliament, O'Connell pledged that the connection between Ireland and Britain through joint allegiance to the Crown "to be perpetual, and incapable of change, or of any severance or separation." Once more he appealed to the Protestant gentry to join him in this great constitutional effort to restore the national sovereignty of their country. He argued that his plan guaranteed a large Protestant representation from Ulster in the Irish House of Commons and predominate Protestant and property influence in the Irish House of Lords. Then the Liberator addressed an appeal to Peel, Wellington, Graham and "every sane man in the Cabinet" (according to O'Connell this excluded Stanley) to grant Ireland her modest demand for a parliament before it was too late. He warned them to avoid the same stupidity that lost Britain her American colonies. He said that he "was now willing to make terms with Peel and Wellington too, and scornfully as his overtures might now be treated he would remind Peel and Wellington of them when the day of entreaty would be past and gone, and when triumph of Ireland would be inevitable (great cheers)." The Repeal Association unanimously approved O'Connell's proposal for the future Irish parliament.[56]

On July 11 O'Connell projected a brilliant plan to

56 O'Connell requested local Repeal Wardens to take surveys of eligible voters in their districts. This information would be used to draw up final plans for the Irish parliament.

supplement his proposal for a provisional Irish parliament. On that day he announced that the Repeal Association would establish a system of arbitration courts to supersede the British legal system. The dismissed magistrates would serve as judges in the arbitration courts, and the people would be able to present their legal problems to men they trusted rather than to alien and anti-Irish judges. O'Connell insisted that the arbitration courts would be constitutional because the people would voluntarily use their services and voluntarily accept their decisions. Dr. John Gray, proprietor of the *Freeman's Journal,* was appointed chairman of a committee to organize and draw up rules for the arbitration courts.[57] On August 23 Gray submitted the first report of his committee. Each Irish county would be divided into arbitration districts based on the petty session districts already familiar to the people. Three or more arbiters would be assigned to each district, and sessions would be held at least once every two weeks. Arbiters would arrive at decisions by a majority vote. In case of a tie, the chairman would have an extra vote. Those magistrates dismissed by the Government and those magistrates who resigned their commissions in protest against the dismissal of their colleagues would be appointed arbiters. The remaining arbiters would be nominated by Repeal Wardens, the Repeal clergy, and the Repeal gentry and would be appointed to their positions by the Loyal National Repeal Association. People using the arbitration courts could use the services of solicitors and barristers, but they would not have to pay fees to the court. While use of the court was voluntary, those who went before the courts but then refused to abide by the decisions of the arbiters would be dismissed from the Repeal Association.[58]

On September 12 Gray reported that Repeal Wardens

[57] *Pilot,* July 12, 1843.
[58] *Freeman's Journal,* August 24, 1843.

and Catholic priests were sending in their nominations for arbiters. He said that some had already been appointed and that the system would soon begin to function.[59] In late October, he published the rules for the arbitration courts and people began to take advantage of the national tribunals. Since the Irish masses used the arbitration courts they served as an effective threat to British rule in Ireland. Arbitration courts were first used during the Catholic emancipation agitation and later were effectively employed during the 1919-1922 struggle for freedom. They were one of the most significant contributions made by O'Connell to the tactics of nationalist agitation.

As summer blended into fall O'Connell waited anxiously for the results of his strategy to counter Peel's policy of calculated indifference. Would the promise of a provisional parliament and the reality of an independent legal system satisfy the expectations of the Irish masses? Or would the long, cold, damp winter nights breed despair and violence? Would Peel retain his aloofness in the face of a possible effective Irish provisional government making a mockery of existing British institutions? Or would O'Connell's brilliant new tactics force the Prime Minister to make concessions to Irish demands or to adopt a policy of coercion? If Peel chose the latter course, would O'Connell, knowing the inability of the unarmed Irish masses to resist well equipped British troops, be forced to redeem his Mallow pledge?

59 *Ibid.*, September 13, 1843.

3

Unionist Reactions to Repeal

SHORTLY AFTER O'CONNELL issued his January Repeal manifesto the Dublin *Evening Mail*, most influential of the Irish ascendancy newspapers, responded to the Liberator's call for national action. Much of the *Mail's* reply to O'Connell consisted of personal abuse, but there were detailed comments on the various planks in the Repeal platform. To the *Mail* Repeal simply was treason—the first step on the path to an eventual collapse of the British Empire. O'Connell's pledge to abolish the tithe and separate church and state was a threat to destroy the Protestant Church, his promotion of the fixity of tenure cause menaced the rights of Protestant property, and his support for universal manhood suffrage and the ballot was an attempt to substitute a wild system of democracy for aristocratic government. *Mail* editorials piously implored O'Connell to place the interests of his country before his private lust for political power and to desist in his efforts to whet the Catholic appetite for religious ascendancy and to stimulate the Catholic desire for Protestant property. According to the *Mail* it was politically unrealistic to assume that these appetites and desires could ever be satisfied and cruel to encourage the peasant masses to retain fanciful dreams. O'Connell's political agitations against the Union only discouraged British capital investment in Irish industry and agriculture, thereby perpetuating poverty and unemployment for the Irish agricultural and urban proletariat.[1]

Since the editor of the *Mail* had witnessed the rise and fall of several other Repeal agitations it is unlikely that he really believed that O'Connell had much chance of arousing national enthusiasm. But the Repeal agitation presented him with a convenient opportunity to needle Sir Robert Peel. As the leading newspaper spokesman for Irish Tory opinion the *Mail* insisted that the Irish policy of any truly Conservative Government should be directed to the maintenance of Protestant ascendancy in Ireland. Like most Irish Protestants, the editor of the *Mail* assumed that the vast majority of Irish Catholics were inherently disloyal and that the British connection and Irish Protestantism were dependent on the traditional loyalty of the Protestant garrison. The Union and the Protestant Church could exist only as long as the garrison was strong, and the strength of the garrison rested on its confidence that the British Government would continue to support its religious, property, and political interests. To insure the Unionist causes in Ireland the Government must reserve all administrative, judicial, and police appointments as a monopoly of the Protestant ascendancy.

By January of 1843 Irish Tory leaders suspected that Peel was not as committed to the principle of Protestant ascendancy as previous Conservative party leaders. Peel was a devout Protestant, a champion of the established church, a stanch defender of the Union, and by instinct,

---

[1] *Evening Mail*, January 6, 1843.

background, and intellectual conviction a Conservative, but his six years' experience as Irish Chief Secretary had convinced him that Ireland could not be successfully administered from the narrow, venal, and bigoted viewpoint of the self-conscious, introverted Protestant garrison. Peel indicated a willingness to face all the implications of the emancipation act when he appointed two proponents of Irish reform to important posts in the Irish administration. Lord Eliot was selected as Chief Secretary, and Sir Edward Sugden was appointed Lord Chancellor.

The *Mail* detested Eliot and accused him of having pro-Whig and pro-Papist leanings. The editor constantly attacked the Chief Secretary for supporting the Irish municipal reform bill in 1843.[2] The reformed municipal corporations were described by the *Mail* as "normal schools" for treason, and when the Dublin Corporation decision to support Repeal in March of 1843 was endorsed by the other municipal bodies in Munster, Leinster, and Connacht, the *Mail* held Eliot responsible for this Repeal victory.[3]

As the Repeal agitation gathered momentum in the late winter and early spring of 1843 and it became clear that the movement rested on the strong foundation of a unified and increasingly enthusiastic Irish Catholic opinion, the *Mail* stepped up its criticism of the Government's Irish policy, and the editor did not hesitate to criticize Peel as well as Eliot. The Prime Minister was described as a chameleon changing his political colors to fit shifting political trends. When out of power Peel was the bold Protestant champion castigating the Whigs for their in-

---

[2] The *Mail* also accused Eliot of donating money to a Whig newspaper, and it condemned his choice of Whigs and Catholics for Irish administrative and legal positions, his opinion that justice had long been denied the lower classes in Ireland, his sympathy with Liberal Irish policies, his alleged antagonism to Protestant ascendancy, and his rumored support for a federal arrangement between Ireland and Britain (*Evening Mail*, January 4, 1843).

[3] *Evening Mail*, March 6, 1843.

trigues with O'Connell and their cowardly attacks on the Irish Church. But in office, the once bold champion became quite timid in his Protestantism. He rejected Irish Protestant appeals for a state supported system of religious education at the elementary school level, and he maintained the godless national school system established by his Whig predecessors. Irish Protestants who had most loyally supported the Conservative party in defeat were now denied the fruits of victory. The enemies of the ascendancy had the Prime Minister's ear, and Papist sympathizers like Eliot were now in charge of the Government's Irish policy.[4]

The *Mail* asked if Irish Protestants must continue their support of this ungrateful Conservative Government. Must they always have to choose the lesser of two evils— a Conservative Government, panting for their support but indifferent to their interests and scornful of their loyalty to the British connection, or a Whig administration, anxious to appease O'Connell and his seditious followers by sacrificing Protestant religious, property, and political interests? "No!" said the editor. Irish Protestants were not the captives of the Conservative party. There were other possibilities: they could work for a reform of the Conservative party which would eliminate the influence of political adventurers like Peel and Eliot, or, more practically, they could take the initiative in forming an Irish party in Parliament. Irish Protestants, learn from your enemies, recommended the editor of the *Mail*. See how O'Connell used the threat of Repeal to extort concessions from the Whigs. Why couldn't Irish M.P.'s committed to the Union, whether Whig or Tory, combine to maintain the British connection and work for legislation beneficial to Irish economic interests? An Irish party, independent of all British influences, would be strong enough to court the attention of British political leaders.

4 *Ibid.*, March 20, 24, 27, April 10, 1843.

The British Parliament and public opinion must be made
to recognize the existence of Irish Protestant and Unionist
points of view.[5]

Through the remainder of the Repeal crisis the *Mail*
continued to advocate the Irish party as a feasible alternative to Irish dependence on either Whigs or Tories, but
when the Repeal agitation came into full bloom in the
summer of 1843 the editorials occasionally went beyond
the Irish party policy. Peel was warned that if his ministry
continued to ignore the dangers of Repeal and to slight
the interests of Irish Protestants, the latter might be forced
to seek some sort of accommodation with O'Connell.
Irish Protestants might have to reconsider their commitment to the Union; they might decide that an Irish
parliament, with Protestant interests protected by a Protestant dominated Irish House of Lords, was a more attractive alternative than a British legislature where those
interests were often compromised to political expediency
and neglect.[6]

The Irish party proposal and the threat of an alliance
with Catholic nationalism were clubs that Irish Protestants
of the *Evening Mail* variety frequently held over the head
of the Conservative party in the course of the nineteenth
century. But events during the century demonstrated
that they were merely threats arising from fears of a
Catholic ascendancy rather than soberly considered policies. When the chips were down and Catholic nationalists
opened their arms to Protestants, suspicion of the Catholic
democracy was too strong to permit the risk of abandoning
even a disappointing ally for an uncertain journey down
the road of nationalism with a despised and dangerous
old enemy.

[5] The Irish party policy was advocated in editorials published on March
20, 27, April 10, 17, and 19. In fact, the *Mail* never abandoned the Irish
party idea during the Repeal crisis.

[6] *Evening Mail*, April 17, June 14, 1843.

On May 20 the *Mail* praised Peel and Wellington for declaring their intention to maintain the Union even at the risk of civil war, but warned that statements made in the House of Commons were not adequate weapons to silence O'Connell and his stable of demagogues. The success of the Repeal Monster Meetings in stimulating nationalist opinion among the Catholic masses demonstrated that the Repeal Association should be suppressed, public meetings outlawed, Repeal magistrates relieved of their commissions, Repeal leaders prosecuted for sedition, and the Protestant yeomanry mobilized to defend the Union and Protestant lives and property. No new coercive legislation was necessary. The nature of the Repeal agitation permitted the Government to cope with the crisis under existing laws. Repeal was treason and should be treated as such.

When the Government adopted one of the *Mail's* suggestions and dismissed the Repeal magistrates, the reaction of the editor was critical rather than complimentary. Sugden was accused of compromising the Government's case against Repeal when in his letter to Lord Ffrench he conceded the legality of the Repeal meetings. Sugden must go, demanded the *Mail*. "Neither the Government nor the country can go on with such a man at the most important branch of the executive."[7]

After roasting the Lord Chancellor for a fortnight on the coals of scathing criticism, the *Mail* suddenly redirected its fire at Peel. His Irish policy was dismissed as a feeble attempt to maintain the Union by appeasing Whigs, Radicals, and Papist Repealers. Peel, said the *Mail*, was preparing to sacrifice Protestant property and religious interests to conciliate O'Connell and the parliamentary Opposition. The editor did not hesitate to remind his readers that the Prime Minister was the same man who

[7] *Ibid.*, May 26, 31, June 2, 1843.

sold out the ascendancy in 1829 when O'Connell waved the sword of treason.[8]

When Peel told the House of Commons that property had its duties as well as its rights, the *Mail* became obsessed with the fear that the Prime Minister was ready to concede tenant right claims. This fear was encouraged by editorials in the *Times* (London) suggesting that landlord-tenant relations in Ireland deserved the attention of Parliament. To balance what the *Mail* described as a growing anti-Irish landlord opinion in Britain, the editor recommended the formation of a Protestant Association to defend the reputation and interests of the Irish gentry. Protestants, led by the aristocracy and gentry, should meet and devise strategy to defend the ascendancy. But the Orange order was advised not to hold any public demonstrations, particularly on the first and twelfth of July, since in adopting the intimidation techniques of the Repealers, Protestants would destroy their case against O'Connell and injure their standing with British opinion.[9]

The Queen's speech, which closed the session and repeated the Government's intention to preserve the Union, temporarily restored the *Mail's* confidence in British intentions to preserve the Union. According to the editor Her Majesty had taken the helm from her weak and indecisive ministers and had made it clear that she would sail the ship of Union through the Repeal storm. It was now clear to all that O'Connell's hopes for a constitutionally achieved independent Irish parliament were without substance. What reason could he have to persist in his folly? But when the Repealers ignored Victoria's majestic pronouncement condemning Repeal the editorials of the *Mail* returned to a mood of gloomy foreboding. No doubt about it, Ireland was on the verge

---

[8] *Ibid.*, June 5, 12, 14, 19, July 5, 7, 1843.
[9] *Ibid.*, June 9, 23, July 14, September 18, 20, October 2, 1843.

of insurrection. O'Connell was a coward and would not fight but could he control the hotheads in the Repeal ranks? The "arch demagogue" was a pathetic figure. His Repeal balloon had burst, but he dare not confess this to his ignorant followers. Such an admission would mean a loss of power, his very nourishment. What would this wily politician do to divert attention from his failure? The editor knew the answer. He would start an anti-rent campaign to exploit the tenant right leanings of his peasant following and the rising anti-Irish landlord sentiment in Britain. William Conner's motion in the Repeal Association asking that the Repeal movement should adopt a no-rent, no-tithe campaign of passive resistance to British rule was used by the *Mail* as evidence to support its prediction of an anti-landlord agitation. When the Repeal Association denounced Conner's motion and expelled him from the organization, this was also exploited by the *Mail* to support its attack on O'Connell. Conner's expulsion from the Repeal Association only meant that the Kerry fox was too shrewd to telegraph his attack on private property.[10]   *133063*

The Dublin University Magazine, the intellectual voice of Irish Protestant conservatism, shared most of the *Evening Mail's* opinions concerning Repeal. O'Connell and his supporters intended "the dismemberment and the destruction of the greatest empire in the world," "a sweeping confiscation of property," the "recovery of forfeited estates," and "a redistribution of them among the victorious armies of Repeal." In the view of the editor Repeal prospered because the Government ignored Irish Protestant interests and gave Irish policy making posts to men antagonistic to the Ascendancy. *The Dublin University Magazine* also revealed the fear that the Government might attempt to appease O'Connell and conciliate

10 *Ibid.,* August 28, September 18, 20, 1843.

the Opposition benches by an Irish policy that would
further curtail the influence and wealth of the Irish
Church and restrict the rights of Protestant property.
Peel was told that any such action would violate the
contract made between the British Government and the
Irish Protestant Parliament in 1800 and that this breach
of contract would free Irish Protestants from all bonds of
loyalty to the British connection. Like the *Mail, The
Dublin University Magazine* did not scruple to appeal to
the no-Popery passions of British public opinion. The
Catholic priests were credited with manipulating the
strings of the Repeal agitation while O'Connell and the
Corn Exchange crowd danced to the tune of the pup-
peteers. The Repeal platform was a disguise for the real
ambitions of the Catholic hierarchy and clergy—a Catholic ascendancy in Ireland.

On two points *The Dublin University Magazine* did
take issue with the *Evening Mail*. The former did not
share the latter's view of Peel and did not believe that the
existing relationship between landlord and tenant was
completely satisfactory. The Prime Minister's response
to the Repeal agitation, while not dramatic, was reasonable. It was designed "to baffle these daring aims by
affording the freest scope to the devices for their accom-
plishment, and it is hoped that the integrity of the British
empire can be ensured by affording such latitude of in-
dulgence to its enemies." This strategy of calculated indifference to the Repeal bombast had many risks, but it was
a more honorable course than suppressing an agitation
that fulfilled the qualifications of legality with a coercive
policy that might prove more of a danger to the Constitution than the agitation it intended to crush. *The
Dublin University Magazine* supported the Irish Protestant thesis that Parliament had no right to interfere with
the settlement of property in Ireland but conceded that
the Irish peasant masses had many just complaints against

their landlords. As long as these just complaints lasted, Ireland would not enjoy the social peace necessary for economic prosperity.

The Dublin University Magazine endorsed the view that Irish Protestants should organize a confederation to argue their case and defend their position. The Protestant confederation should have a central executive in Dublin to plan defensive strategy in case of a religious or civil war, to organize assistance for those Protestants dwelling in Catholic areas, and to prepare a Unionist brief for presentation to the jury of British opinion. This Protestant confederation should be considered a supplement rather than a substitute for the Government's Irish policy and perhaps an insurance against its failure. Leaders of the Protestant confederation could take another constructive step in the effort to pacify Ireland and preserve the Union. They could arrange a settlement, on a voluntary basis, with Irish tenant farmers, an arrangement which would erase all the vestiges of agrarian discontent and class animosity.[11]

There is substantial evidence to indicate that the *Evening Mail* accurately represented the Irish Protestant majority opinion on the menace of the Repeal agitation and the Government's ineptitude in meeting O'Connell's challenge. Comments made by the Irish Protestant peers in the House of Lords and their fellow countrymen and coreligionists in the House of Commons, Irish Protestant appeals addressed to the Lord Lieutenant and other members of the Irish Executive, and the waves of rumors sweeping over the country indicated that by the summer of 1843 a large segment of the Irish Protestant population was in a state of hysteria. Repealers were going to despoil the Protestant Church, confiscate Protestant property, and

11 *The Dublin University Magazine* discussed Repeal in the following essays: "The Repeal Agitation—Policy of the Movement and the Ministry," 22:356-78; "The Do Nothing System," 22:240-52; "Ireland—Repealers and Landlords," 21:156-67; "The Irish Grievance Debate," 22:177-84.

satisfy their blood lust by murdering Protestants in their beds or any place they could find them. Put down the Monster Meetings, suppress the Loyal National Repeal Association, prosecute the demagogues, increase the size of the army in Ireland, give us guns and ammunition to defend ourselves, pleaded the ascendancy. But the Government seemed deaf to its cries of anguish. Pleas for coercive action against Repeal and for protection against the designs of the Repealers, when ignored, turned into bitter recriminations against the Government. Peel has deserted us, he plans to make a deal with O'Connell at our expense, and we must prepare for our own defense, were opinions frequently heard in Irish Protestant circles. Sensible Protestant peers like Lords Farnham, Clare, and Clancarty tried to convince fellow Protestants that the Government knew what it was doing and tried their best to discourage the revival of Orange activity that could result in a religious war. But the majority of the Protestant aristocracy and gentry, led by the no-Popery fanatic, Lord Roden, and his son Lord Jocelyn, remained estranged from Peel and continued to agitate for independent Irish Protestant action to put down Repeal.

In early summer Protestant leaders began to organize a Unionist opposition to the Repeal Association. On June 17 nine Irish peers met at the Earl of Wicklow's Dublin house to discuss the Repeal crisis. They agreed to resolutions condemning Repeal as a menace to the public peace and as a distraction interrupting the economic life of the country. They notified the Government that the public mind in Ireland was excited by the dangerous words uttered by O'Connell, but assured the Ministers that they could depend on the support of the loyal aristocracy of Ireland in any effort to uphold the law, to preserve the Union, or to put down sedition in Ireland.[12]

July 26 was the day for an important Protestant meeting

12 *Evening Mail,* June 19, 1843.

in Belfast. Lord Donegal was in the chair, and the cream of the Ulster Protestant aristocracy, gentry, clergy, and middle class was in attendance. This meeting passed resolutions describing Repeal as a plot to dismember the Empire, exterminate the Protestant religion, destroy Protestant property rights, and ruin the Protestant people of Ireland. The Union was praised as the source of Irish prosperity and Repeal damned as a threat to that prosperity because it distracted the Catholic masses from their economic responsibilities and fostered a state of anarchy which discouraged capital investment in Irish agriculture and industry. The resolutions of the meeting also called the Government's attention to the rebellious mood of the Catholic masses. They claimed that the inflammatory speeches delivered in the Corn Exchange, from the pulpit, and from the public platform were all designed to encourage this excitement. These speeches, plus the seditious newspapers circulating in Ireland, promised the tenant farmers agrarian reforms contradictory to established property rights and encouraged Catholics to hate Saxons and Protestants. The delegates to the Belfast meeting demanded protection against the possible results of the Repeal agitation. They said that Repeal had reached the stage where it was doubtful if the leaders of the movement could restrain the passions of the rank and file. It was also suggested that Protestants take the necessary steps to insure their own survival and the maintenance of their religious and economic interests. These Ulster Protestant leaders decided that they had a responsibility to the other Irish Protestants living in areas where they were a minority. Before adjourning the delegates agreed to hold a large Protestant meeting in Belfast on September 7 to complete arrangements for forming a Protestant confederation.[13]

On September 1 Lord Donegal, chairman of the com-

---

[13] *Ibid.*, July 26, 1843.

mittee preparing for the September 7 Belfast meeting, announced cancellation of the great Protestant convention. He said that Protestant leaders had decided to place their confidence in the Queen's announced determination to maintain the Union and to avoid the charge that they were encouraging the continuation of political agitation in Ireland. But in this announcement Lord Donegal and his colleagues again voiced their anxiety concerning the menace of the Repeal movement and their conviction that O'Connell was out to destroy Protestant institutions and property rights.[14]

The editorials of the Evening Mail, articles in *The Dublin University Magazine,* and the opinions of Protestant leaders indicate an Irish Unionist consensus concerning Repeal. The agitation was a dangerous threat to the Union, the Empire, the Protestant Church, Protestant property, and Protestant lives. However, when it came to evaluating the effectiveness of Government policy in handling the Repeal crisis this consensus broke down. A sober and responsible minority of Protestant leaders was content to trust Peel and to put faith in his hope that the Repeal agitation would collapse as a result of inherent weaknesses. A larger portion of the Protestant community was convinced that Peel had no policy for dealing with Repeal and that the Prime Minister was a political adventurer who would attempt to appease O'Connell and the Whigs by compromising Protestant interests and rights. The hostility of this Irish Protestant majority to the Government endangered the Prime Minister's policy of calculated indifference to O'Connell's threats. Peel had to face the discouraging possibility that the Irish Protestants, motivated by hysteria, would initiate a religious war to protect their position in Ireland. A struggle between Irish Catholics and Protestants would force a

14 *Ibid.,* September 1, 1843.

Conservative Government to intervene on the latter's side, widening the class and religious chasms that prevented the assimilation of Ireland within the British system.

In the early months of 1843 British newspapers and periodicals treated O'Connell and Repeal either with contempt or with indifference. The *Times'* Irish correspondent reported that the anti-poor law agitation was the only significant activity in Ireland and that the Loyal National Repeal Association had very little influence on Irish opinion.[15] The ultra-Tory *Blackwood's Magazine* confidently told its readers that O'Connell was a political has-been who was forced to continue his "cuckoo cry for Repeal" in order to collect the Repeal rent.[16]

On March 8, in commenting on the results of the debate in the Dublin Corporation, the *Times* supported Isaac Butt's argument that Repeal was a reactionary proposition. It would reduce Ireland from a state of equality with England, Scotland, and Wales to the degrading position of a conquered and dependent province. But the editorial writer advised his readers not to take Repeal too seriously. It was a "hopeless and miserable delusion" propagated by an arch-demagogue solely to keep his name before the public for mercenary reasons. All intelligent Irishmen and Englishmen knew that the two countries shared a common history and mutual interests. The common good of both islands determined the permanency of the bonds of Union.

Two months later the *Times* returned to the subject of Repeal, still discussing it in a dispassionate manner. The editorial admitted that Ireland had legitimate complaints concerning her treatment by the Parliament at West-

15 From March of 1842 until the spring of 1843 the *Times* concentrated its Irish reporting on the resistance to the poor law and the payment of poor rates. As late as mid-May of 1843 the *Times* seemed to think that the anti-poor law agitation deserved more attention than Repeal activities.

16 *Blackwood's Magazine,* 53:141.

minster: the poor law was "a false and unnatural system," and the property settlement in Ireland was unjust to the peasant masses. As long as Parliament continued to pass ill-advised and inappropriate legislation such as the poor law and to ignore the Irish tenant farmer's need for security Irish discontent would feed the Repeal agitation. However, the *Times* cautioned Irishmen not to expect Repeal, even if it could be carried, to solve the basic problems besetting their country. In fact, they had more hope for beneficial reforms from the British Parliament than from an Irish legislature. If O'Connell's scheme for an Irish parliament was put into operation the Protestant gentry in the Irish House of Lords would never consent to any legislation emancipating the Catholic masses from the chains of economic insecurity.[17]

By late May the *Times* was no longer able to discuss the Repeal agitation in a cool and detached manner. Readers were now told that they must not regard O'Connell's movement as essentially either nationalist or Catholic. At its core, Repeal was a "democratic or, to speak more accurately, an anarchial movement." The Irish demagogue wished to return to the wild lawless system that prevailed in Ireland before the Union. If O'Connell succeeded he and his friends would reap a financial profit, but the poor peasant masses would have retrogressed a hundred years. The *Times* insisted that "Repeal is madness and no English ministry will grant it."[18]

By July the editor of the *Times* was not so sanguine concerning the sanity of the Peel ministry. Ireland was obviously on the brink of rebellion. Vast multitudes attended Monster Meetings with almost military discipline in their conduct, they listened to harangues designed to fill them with hatred for the Saxon and his system of government, and there was evidence to indicate that "the

17 *Times,* May 16, 1843.
18 *Ibid.,* May 27, 1843.

cowardly braggadocio who had been entrapped by his own sordid selfishness" was losing control of the monster he had created. While Ireland did have legitimate complaints, this was not the time for remedial legislation. Any attempt by the Government to remedy Irish grievances would be considered appeasement by the Repealers and would encourage them to intensify the agitation. Instead of negotiating with agitation, the Government should outlaw these illegal and dangerous mass meetings before Ireland was in the grip of civil war. No doubt Peel's cautious response to the ferment in Ireland resulted from good intentions. He probably wanted to avoid an outbreak of violence that might result from an attempt to suppress the Repeal movement. But, asked the *Times,* wouldn't it be kinder to nip the agitation in the bud, even at the risk of some violence, before it exploded into a rebellion which would engulf Ireland in a blood bath?[19]

In August the *Times* reached the same conclusion as the *Evening Mail:* O'Connell was prepared to lead the Irish tenant farmers in a no rent campaign. One had only to see the way peasant eyes lighted up when Repeal agitators promised fixity of tenures at fair rents to know that these radical agrarian doctrines enlisted mass support for Repeal. At some future time Parliament should concede justice to Irish tenant farmers but not until the current agitation was smashed.[20]

By late summer it became evident that the editor of the *Times* no longer believed that Peel was motivated by good intentions in his approach to Repeal. Like many of the Irish Unionists he concluded that the Prime Minister was afraid of O'Connell and that his refusal to employ coercion in Ireland was the result of feebleness and indecision. On many occasions the *Times* warned the Government that its policy of appeasement would produce a rebellion

19 *Ibid.,* July 10, 1843.
20 *Ibid.,* August 1, 1843.

in Ireland that would take all the might of the British Empire and many lives to put down.[21]

The two leading conservative periodicals, the ultra-Tory *Blackwood's* and the more moderate *Quarterly Review,* had similar reactions to the Repeal agitation.[22] They agreed that Britain's interests would not tolerate an independent and potentially hostile Ireland. The laws of nature—"moral," "political," and "physical"—clearly demonstrated that "the greatest body shall overbalance and control the lesser." Ireland could no more have separate status within the British system "than the moon could abandon the earth and set up for herself as an independent planet." There could be no doubt that Repealers intended complete separation from Britain and once this was accomplished they would proceed to their ultimate objective: the elimination of the Protestant religion—the extermination of the Protestant race—the confiscation of Protestant property.[23] In an independent Irish nation the Unionist minority would be defenseless; Catholic bishops would be influential in an Irish House of Lords and Catholic demagogues would dominate an Irish House of Commons. Protestants would either have "to fly the country, or be crushed on the spot."[24] If they made

21 In an editorial published on August 23 the *Times* claimed that Irish peasants were drilling at night and that the failure of the Government to deal with Repeal resulted in "the absorbtion of the Protestants and Orangemen in the Repeal vortex." The editor credited the Government with good intentions in its attempt to conciliate the Repealers "by neutrality and inactivity." But he warned "that there is too much reason to fear lest the deliberate moderation may turn to involuntary cruelty; and that this disaffection which might have been cut short by early severity, will require an iron arm and a stern purpose to crush it in its season of vigour and audacity." And on September 7 the *Times,* again on the editorial page, insisted that firmness by the Government in the early stages of the Repeal agitation would have averted "the necessity of future cruelty and bloodshed."

22 *Blackwood's,* 51:509-10; 53:14; 54:264-74, 679-86; *Quarterly Review,* 72:561-93.

23 *Ibid.,* 75:221, 222-92.

24 *Blackwood's,* 51:144-45.

a stand against the tyranny of the Catholic controlled Irish parliament, Ireland would once more become the battleground for the Papist and Protestant forces of Europe and the Irish people would again experience the destructive anarchy of the seventeenth century.

The *Quarterly Review* and *Blackwood's* also shared a hatred and contempt for O'Connell. Both attributed unworthy motives to the Repeal leader. They said that he was too intelligent to believe that the British Government would ever agree to his mad scheme to destroy the Union and that he would never endanger his position as the leader of Irish agitation by engaging in a futile war against the might of the British Empire. Therefore it was obvious that he was motivated by financial greed and the lust for power. His main source of income was the Repeal rent, and his control over the Irish people depended on his exploiting their discontent by ceaseless agitation against the British connection. Once he stopped waving the flag of Repeal he would find himself an impoverished and rejected old man.[25]

These two Tory periodicals would not criticize the way Peel responded to the Repeal agitation. He had refused to yield to intimidation and he had made it clear that he was prepared to wage war to preserve the Union. John Wilson Croker, confidant of Peel and the *Quarterly Review's* Irish expert, described Peel's reluctance to ask for coercive legislation as a reasonable precaution to forestall Whig and Radical support for O'Connell in the House of Commons.[26] Croker and the writer in *Blackwood's* blamed the existing state of anarchy in Ireland on the policy of the previous Melbourne administration. The Whigs had capitulated to O'Connell's threats in the past and by forming an alliance with the Repealers had surrendered "that fair

[25] *Quarterly Review*, 72:564; 79:226. *Blackwood's*, 51:509-10; 53:14, 54:264-67.
[26] *Quarterly Review*, 72:553-93.

portion of the empire into the hands of a political repro-
bate and imposter."[27] These two Tory voices of opinion
also charged the Whig leaders with encouraging the
present Irish agitation by opposing the passage of the
arms bill.

The leading Whig periodical, the *Edinburgh Review,*
also considered Repeal an impossible proposition but
emphasized the potential danger of Irish separation to the
economic progress of Ireland rather than its disadvantages
to Britain. The writer described O'Connell as an unscrupulous demagogue agitating Repeal to maintain his
control over the Irish masses. This power-mad politician
had frustrated all efforts to achieve a permanent settlement
between Ireland and England for fear that such a settlement would deprive him of his control over Irish Catholic
opinion.[28]

The *Edinburgh Review,* reflecting the view of many
Whig leaders, suggested a financial arrangement between
the British Government and the Catholic Church as the
solution to the Irish Question. O'Connell had built the
Repeal agitation around the influence of the Catholic
hierarchy and clergy over the Catholic masses. The bishops
and priests were forced to support Irish nationalism in
order to guarantee financial contributions to their church.
If the Government would pay the salaries of the Catholic
clergy and sign a concordat with the Vatican which would
restrict the political activities of the clergy, the priests
would be freed from economic dependence on the laity
and O'Connell could no longer employ them as recruiting
agents and drill sergeants for his Repeal army.[29]

The leading Whig newspaper, the *Morning Chronicle,*
repudiated Repeal and O'Connell, but indicted the Conservative Government for encouraging Repeal by its blind

27 *Blackwood's,* 53:14.
28 *Edinburgh Review,* 78:538-49, 79:220-21.
29 *Ibid.,* 79:189-266.

indifference to Irish grievances. Peel was advised to meet the Repeal challenge in the same way that previous Whig Prime Ministers responded to Irish agitation. He should put down the Repeal movement but at the same time remove the roots of discontent nourishing the agitation. The *Chronicle* pointed to the Established Church and the property settlement in Ireland as the grievances fostering Repeal and recommended that Parliament pass legislation to satisfy Catholic complaints against the Establishment and to answer the appeal of Irish farmers for secure tenures at reasonable rents.[30]

The *Westminster Review,* a respectable and brilliant champion of Radical views, shared the general British hostility to Repeal as an answer to the Irish Question but took a more charitable position in regard to O'Connell and Repeal sentiment in Ireland. It reminded British readers that Ireland was the victim of centuries of misgovernment, oppression, and neglect. Over the ages British governments had demonstrated their contempt for Ireland, her people, religion, language, and institutions. With this historical experience as a guide to political conduct, how could O'Connell be blamed for placing his faith in agitation rather than in the parliamentary process? So long as evils like the established church, Protestant ascendancy, property rights without consideration of its duties, and a partisan administration of the law blighted the Irish landscape; "so long as Ireland is mocked with nominal union and insulted with actual inferiority, there will be, and ought to be, agitation."[31]

However, the *Westminster Review* told O'Connell that he was wrong in his claim that the English people hated the Irish people. Apathy, not hate, best described the British attitude toward Ireland and the Irish. Unfortu-

[30] The author determined the *Chronicle's* position from reading its editorials reprinted in the *Nation.*
[31] *Westminster Review,* 40:50-75.

nately Englishmen were too willing to forget the past
neglect of Ireland and too quick to forgive politicians
responsible for that neglect. They must be made to understand the suffering of the Irish people under British rule
and to realize the obligations they had to their Irish
partners in the Union. Once the British people understood the Irish situation they would force their parliamentary representatives to redress Irish grievances and to
bring the full benefits of the constitution to the Irish
people. According to the *Westminster Review* the only
answer to the Irish Question and the only satisfactory
response to the Repeal challenge was complete justice to
Ireland and her people.[32]

The Illustrated London News, the popular predecessor
of contemporary pictorial weeklies, condemned the Repeal
agitation and the demagogue who led it. It repeated the
argument that Repeal was detrimental to the economic
development of Ireland because it discouraged capital investment in Irish agriculture and industry. But the *News*
expressed great admiration for the Irish people and praised
their virtues of patience, generosity, gaiety, and wit. What
an asset these people would be to the Empire if only the
British Government could win their allegiance! The
editor insisted that their loyalty could be earned by
legislation treating the economic wounds that were bleed-
ing Ireland. He was vehement in his denunciation of the
poor law, which spread rather than diminished Irish
poverty, and of the absentee landlords who enjoyed a life
of luxury abroad from the rents they extorted from the
starving Irish peasantry. *The Illustrated London News*
joined forces with the Radicals in demanding a new
property settlement in Ireland and asked Parliament to
take action that would provide public works in Ireland
"to improve the mercantile aspects of that beautiful country, and to encourage enterprise, promote trade, check the

32 *Ibid.,* 40:72,73.

mischief of absenteeism, and induce the confidence of capitalists."[33]

Peel hoped to avoid prolonged discussions of Irish issues during the parliamentary session of 1843 and prepared only one major piece of Irish legislation, an arms bill, for presentation to Parliament. The success of the Repeal agitation in capturing the enthusiasm of the Irish masses and the attention of the British public frustrated the Prime Minister's plans and made the Irish Question the major topic of discussion in both houses of Parliament.

On April 27 Lane Fox, a religious fanatic who believed he had a divine mission to eliminate Popery from the face of the earth, gave notice of a motion calling on the Government to suppress the Repeal agitation and if necessary to ask Parliament for the legislative implements to achieve this purpose. After a private meeting with Peel, Fox decided to withdraw his motion, but the Earl of Roden in the House of Lords and Viscount Jocelyn, his son, in the House of Commons decided to carry on with the Protestant crusade. On May 9 these two champions of Irish Unionism asked the Government leaders in both Houses of Parliament what they intended doing about the public excitement engulfing Ireland. They dwelt on the large Monster Meetings where thousands listened to O'Connell poison the Irish mind with hatred of Britain, the Union, and Protestant institutions. They said that O'Connell and the priests were using the Monster Meetings as instruments of intimidation to frighten Irish Unionists into supporting a great popular agitation and the Government into surrendering sovereignty over Ireland.[34]

Wellington in the Lords and Peel in the Commons

---

[33] *Illustrated London News*, May 20, 1843, p. 331 (For other interesting articles concerning Ireland and illustrations of Irish life and episodes from the Repeal agitation see the *Illustrated London News*, June 24, July 15, August 5, 12, 19, 26, October 7, November 25, 1843).

[34] *Hansard* 68:1001, 68:1274-75, 69:1-7, 23.

replied to the heroes of the Orange and Blue. They labeled Repeal as a threat to the Empire and defended the Union as necessary to the peace, prosperity, and happiness of both Britain and Ireland. The Prime Minister and the Duke committed the Government to the maintenance of the Union, and they promised to employ the armed might of the Empire to achieve this objective. Peel said that a civil war was a horrible thing to contemplate, but it was preferable to the dismemberment of the Empire. At this time Peel and Wellington both pledged the Government to a consideration of the legitimate grievances of the Irish people.[35]

On May 29 Lord Eliot moved the second reading of the arms bill in the House of Commons. This bill was the Government's response to the request of the Irish Executive for laws to facilitate the effort to reduce crimes of violence in Ireland and was drawn up before the session without any regard to the Repeal agitation. The arms bill provided for the registration and branding of arms, the licensing of all owners, importers, distributors, and sellers of arms and ammunition. Constables were to be given the authority to interrogate and detain all those suspected of possessing illegal arms, justices of the peace were to have the right to issue warrants for entrance and search of domiciles, and the Lord Lieutenant was to be empowered to issue warrants of search applicable to entire cities, districts, and counties. Men caught with unregistered and unlicensed arms were subject to stiff fines. Those who concealed pikes, spears, or instruments that could be used as pikes or spears could be imprisoned for three years or transported to a penal colony for seven years. In violation of traditional Anglo-Saxon judicial procedure defendants had to prove that any illegal arms found on their persons or in their domiciles were not their own or were placed there without their knowledge.

35 *Ibid.*, 69:7-10, 23-25.

The Chief Secretary defended the arms bill on the grounds that all British Governments since the Union, including the Whig administrations of the 1830's, had resorted to such measures when they thought them necessary to preserve the peace in Ireland, and he asked the House of Commons to treat this measure as a nonpartisan issue. Eliot argued that the high incidence of crimes of violence in Ireland necessitated action to keep arms out of the hands of irresponsible persons in that country. He said that without the branding and licensing of arms it would be extremely difficult for Irish peace officers to track down and apprehend murderers in homicides involving firearms.[36]

Sharman Crawford, M.P., champion of Irish tenant right, Richard Lalor Sheil, M.P., O'Connell's former colleague in the struggle for Catholic emancipation, and William Smith O'Brien, M.P., led the Irish Liberal opposition to the arms bill. They insisted that Ireland needed reform legislation more than she needed an arms bill and described the Government's approach to the Irish Question as a policy of treating symptoms to the neglect of causes. The three Irish M.P.'s argued that the Peel administration could secure peace in Ireland through legislation eliminating the abuses of the Established Church, providing for secure tenures for Irish tenant farmers, and repealing the poor law. They said that the arms bill would violate constitutional liberties. The officials who would control the branding and licensing of arms and the administration of the law represented, for the most part, one class and one religion. The new laws of entry and search could be used to satisfy the sexual lusts of bestial policemen, and the alien legal notion that the burden of proof rested on the accused would lead to flagrant violations of British concepts of justice.[37]

---

[36] *Ibid.*, 69:996ff.
[37] *Ibid.*, 69:1010ff. (Crawford), 1038ff. (Sheil), 1118ff. (O'Brien).

The leader of the Opposition, Lord John Russell, refused to accept Eliot's argument that the Peel administration was following trails marked out by the Whigs. He reminded the House that when the Whigs came to power in the 1830's Ireland was in revolt against years of Tory tyranny. The Whigs had to take measures to prevent this revolt from assuming a violent form, but they had also tempered the harshness of a coercion bill with a positive program of Irish reform. Russell and other Liberals claimed that the clauses in the arms bill most offensive to the Irish were innovations of the Peel cabinet and were not based on Whig precedents. Russell said that Eliot had good intentions toward Ireland, but he insisted that Conservatives could never wean the Irish masses from Repeal as long as they continued to support and encourage a Protestant monopoly of power in Dublin Castle. He agreed with Peel that Repeal was a menace to the Empire and volunteered to support military intervention in Ireland if such an extreme measure was necessary to preserve the Union, but he upheld the right of O'Connell to agitate for an Irish parliament as long as he remained within the boundaries of constitutional methods.[38]

John Roebuck, the articulate leader of the Radicals in the House of Commons, argued that both the Whigs and the Tories possessed a coercive mentality toward Ireland. Ireland, he said, needed reform, not coercion, and the best place to start reform was with the disestablishment of the Protestant Church and the distribution of her wealth and resources for the general benefit of the entire Irish population. Roebuck claimed that only the Catholic Church, the church of the Irish masses, had any claim on Government generosity. He rejected O'Connell's claim that Repeal was the solution to all of Ireland's problems, but he did argue that the success of the Repeal agitation

38 *Ibid.*, 69:1057ff.

established the fact that Irish grievances needed parliamentary attention. Like Russell, Roebuck insisted that the Government had no right to interfere with Repeal as long as O'Connell conducted the agitation in a constitutional manner.[39]

The Irish Tories, led by Frederick Shaw, M.P., Dublin University, used the arms bill debate to acquaint the House of Commons with the extent of Repeal enthusiasm in Ireland. He insisted that Repeal disguised the real goal of O'Connell and the priests: the destruction of the Protestant Church, the confiscation of Protestant property, and the annihilation of the Protestant population. Shaw then attacked the Whig-Liberal view that the Conservative Government should abandon its Protestant allies in Ireland. He argued that the administration of Irish affairs must be conducted within the framework of the party system and that Irish Protestants constituted the only party in Ireland loyal to the British connection. Shaw not only endorsed the arms bill, he also demanded that the Government go farther and crush the Loyal National Repeal Association.[40]

Sir Robert Peel, Sir James Graham, and T. B. C. Smith, Attorney General for Ireland, were the leading Government speakers supporting the Chief Secretary. They conceded that the right to bear arms was essential but argued that the emergency situation existing in Ireland justified a local restriction of that right. These important Cabinet officials described the Whig and Liberal opposition to the arms bill as hypocrisy since not so many years before these same M.P.'s introduced and voted for similar measures. They insisted that they were making every effort to conduct the affairs of Ireland in an impartial manner, but they tried to distinguish between an impartial administra-

39 *Ibid.*, 69:1189ff.
40 *Ibid.*, 69:1136ff. Shaw attempted to illustrate the dangerous character of Repeal by quoting from poems published in the *Nation*. He also praised the "loyal" Orangemen.

tion of the law and appeasement of Irish nationalism. Graham, in replying to the Whig suggestion that the Government temper coercion with reform, reminded the leaders of the Opposition that all of their concessions to O'Connell's demands had failed to still the voice of Repeal. Smith told the House of Commons that the demands of Repealers for manhood suffrage by secret ballot, disestablishment of the Protestant Church, and tenant right were symptoms of a dangerous democratic movement threatening every political, economic, religious, and social institution in Britain and Ireland and that they should never be encouraged by a British Government.[41]

Whigs, Radicals, and Irish Liberals fought the arms bill in committee, winning some amendments and seriously delaying the Government's legislative time table. Privately, Peel admitted that the Government's arguments in defense of the arms bill were weak, and he regretted the introduction of such a controversial measure during a time of crisis in Irish affairs.[42] The Prime Minister realized that the Conservative Government's pro-Protestant Irish administration deserved criticism and that it added weight to O'Connell's anti-Union position. But eventually the Government's substantial parliamentary majority prevailed, and on August 22 the Queen signed the arms bill.

During the debate on the arms bill the news of the dismissal of the Repeal magistrates reached Westminster, and the right of the Government to dismiss the magistrates became a controversial issue, particularly in the House of Lords. Lord Clanricarde led the attack on the

41 *Ibid.*, 69:1208ff. (Peel), 1067ff. (Graham), 1051ff. (Smith).

42 On July 11 Peel wrote DeGrey that the arms bill had involved the Government in a great deal of difficulty. He admitted that the defenders of the bill could not present evidence to justify its passage, but he said that the Government could not abandon the bill without losing face. The Prime Minister told the Lord Lieutenant that many M.P.'s considered the arms bill impossible to enforce and a "gratuitous insult" to Ireland which would only encourage anti-British feeling in that country (Add. MSS 40478, B.M.).

Government, and he was ably supported by the Earls of Clancarty and Glengall, the Marquess of Lansdowne, and Lords Campbell, Cottenham, and Fortescue. Not every member of this group thought that the Repeal meetings were legal, but they all agreed that the Government violated constitutional rights by dismissing magistrates on the basis of anti-Repeal declarations by Ministers in Parliament. They argued that the statements made by Peel and Wellington on May 9, indicating the Government's intention to maintain the Union, did not have the force of law. Since technically it was illegal to report the proceedings of Parliament in the press, the Irish Lord Chancellor had no valid legal evidence to prove that the Repeal magistrates were even aware of the statements made by Peel and Wellington. In objecting to the dismissal of the magistrates a number of peers also indicated concern over the use of the Queen's name in Sugden's letter to Lord Ffrench. They emphasized that since there had been no official contact between the Queen and Parliament on Repeal it was presumptious of the Lord Chancellor to state so emphatically Victoria's views on the question.[43]

The contents of the letter to Lord Ffrench caught Peel by surprise and embarrassed the Prime Minister and other members of the cabinet. Peel recognized the basic weaknesses of the Sugden case against the magistrates, particularly when the legality of the Repeal Association and the Monster Meetings were conceded, and he deplored the irresponsible use of the Queen's authority, but he could not afford to let an important member of his administration go undefended.[44] Wellington in supporting Sugden in the House of Lords said that since the Government had made it clear that it would never Repeal the

43 *Hansard* 69:1064-68, 1094, 1289, 70:1099, 1187 (Clanricarde), 70:1121ff. (Clancarty), 70:1134ff. (Glengall), 69:1089ff., 70:1156ff. (Lansdowne), 69:1074-78, 1081-82 (Campbell), 69-1084-89, 70:1184-87 (Cottenham), 69:1293-94, 70:1130-33 (Fortescue).
44 Peel to Sugden, June 1, 4, 1843, Add. MSS 40529, B.M.

Union, those who continued to attend the Monster Meetings did so for only one reason—they expected to obtain their objectives through terror and intimidation. Wellington argued that O'Connell's speeches, with their constant emphasis on military discipline and the willingness of Repealers to die for Irish freedom, indicated nationalists would not hesitate to employ physical force when the terror induced by the Monster Meetings failed to intimidate the Government. Since the Irish administration would have to rely on the loyalty and the support of the magistrates in case of revolution, it would be unwise to retain the services of men sympathetic to Repeal. The Duke quickly dismissed the complaint that the Government could not prove that the magistrates were aware of the Government's position on Repeal with the argument that every person in Ireland was interested in and excited about Repeal and that no responsible person in that country could be ignorant of an expressed ministerial opinion on the subject.[45]

The House of Lords discussion on the dismissal of the magistrates touched on the entire Repeal question. A majority of the speakers, even those who opposed the Government's action in regard to the magistrates, criticized the Peel administration for not taking measures to put O'Connell in his place. Lord Lorton advised the Government to mobilize and arm the Protestant yeomanry against the Repealers.[46] Lord Campbell, however, insisted on the right of any portion of the British community to petition for a repeal of any law passed by the British Parliament, including the act of Union.[47] Lord Fortescue strongly urged the Government to conciliate Irish nationalist opinion with a reform of the Established Church, a tenant right bill, and a program to finance the emigration

[45] *Hansard* 69:1072ff., 70:1113ff.
[46] *Ibid.*, 69:1224ff. Lorton described Repeal as a "Jesuit conspiracy which was spreading over the entire Empire."
[47] *Hansard* 69:1074-78, 1081-82 (Campbell).

of impoverished Irish peasants to underdeveloped but potentially productive parts of the Empire.[48] Wellington, the official spokesman of the Government in the House of Lords, repeated the administration's determination never to concede Repeal, and he said that O'Connell's agitations and the money invested in them by the masses delayed the normal development of the Irish economy.[49]

On July 4 William Smith O'Brien, who had taken command of the forces of Irish Liberalism in the House of Commons, moved that "this House will resolve itself into a Committee, for the purpose of taking into consideration the causes of discontent prevailing in Ireland, with a view to the redress of grievances, and to the establishment of a system of just and impartial government in that part of the United Kingdom."[50] O'Brien, a Protestant landlord in County Clare, had little taste for political life. He resented the time spent at Westminster because it interfered with his family concerns and took him away from Clare. But he was a patriotic Irishman who believed that he had a duty to see his country well served in the British Parliament. When he entered the House of Commons in 1828 O'Brien was a strong friend of the Union because he believed that the association with rich and powerful Britain would promote peace, security, and prosperity in Ireland. For a long time he retained his faith in the potential benefits to be derived from the British connection, but by 1843 his doubts concerning the advantages of the Union were beginning to overcome his Protestant and aristocratic hostility to Irish nationalism. His experience in the House of Commons convinced him that the majority of British politicians, Whig and Tory, did not realize the unique character of Irish problems, cared little for the welfare of the Irish people, and ex-

---

48 *Hansard* 69:1293-94, 70:1130-33 (Fortescue).
49 *Hansard* 1072ff., 70:1113ff.
50 *Hansard* 70:630-31.

ploited the Irish Question for domestic political purposes.

Early in the 1843 parliamentary session O'Brien notified his family that he was giving the Union just one more opportunity to serve Ireland. He said that he would bring the poverty and discontent of the Irish people to the attention of Parliament and British public opinion and that he would suggest legislation to remedy Irish grievances and reconcile Irish nationalists to the Union. O'Brien promised his wife that if the British Parliament refused to consider his case he would join O'Connell in opposition to the Union.[51] His conservative and ultra-Protestant wife and mother were unrestrained in their loyalty to the Union and in their contempt for O'Connell and the Catholic peasant rabble supporting him. They begged O'Brien not to betray his class or to associate the family name with sedition.[52] He replied that not even his great love for his

---

[51] William Smith O'Brien to Lucy O'Brien, February 21, March 21, May 21, 31, June 2, 1843, MS. 8654, National Library of Ireland. William Smith O'Brien to Lucy O'Brien, May 22, 1843, MS. 432, N.L.I.

[52] When O'Brien finally did join the Loyal National Repeal Association in October 1843 his mother wrote him as follows: "I have long seen and felt the evil of the Repeal agitation to *my poor countrymen* and even a child must know that nothing but misery and wretchedness and increased want of employment could follow a separation between Great Britain and Ireland even supposing it to be effected without bloodshed, anarchy, and confusion. But the Queen's Speech and the late proceedings have put beyond all doubt the light in which to bring it about is to be regarded, and it is most selfish and reckless and heartless towards your wife and children to say nothing of your mother and brothers and sisters to proclaim yourself a rebel and a supporter of rebels when up to the present you were known not to be a Repealer. This act of yours my dear William if it be accomplished (which God forbid it is) places all your friends, and especially your affectionately attached mother in a most painful situation and there is no saying what the consequences of it may be to yourself and your family—I will not however anticipate evil but simply give this warning that I never will either directly or indirectly pay a shilling towards the defense of a State prosecution and must defer signing the settlement I was going to make for your children until a sufficient length of time has passed to give me full assurance that there is no danger your property may be confiscated. Farewell—if you pursue the course announced in the papers you will bring down my grey head with sorrow to the grave but however sorrowing I shall never cease to love you." (Emma O'Brien to William Smith O'Brien, October 24, 1843, MS. 433, N.L.I.)

family could divert him from his duty to Ireland and her people.[53]

O'Brien's speech supporting his motion for a parliamentary committee to examine the Irish Question, praised by Peel as "able and not intemperate,"[54] commenced a debate on Ireland which lasted for five days. O'Brien described the Repeal agitation as the expression of Irish indignation against forty-three years of oppression and misgovernment and not the creation of one man's campaign for power. He said that in 1800 the proponents of the Union promised much to Ireland and that those promises had proved false. Since 1800 taxes in Ireland increased while industries declined and the landed gentry fled the country. O'Brien told the House of Commons that if he were a Catholic second class citizenship in a Protestant dominated country would force him to become a Repealer. To Irish Catholics the Union was a symbol of Protestant ascendancy; it meant the burden of supporting a church which brought the solace of religion to only one-tenth of the population, the dependence of their own clergy on the voluntary contributions of an impoverished peasantry, the anti-Catholic abuse of no-Popery bigots in the British press and Parliament whenever matters dealing with the Catholic Church came up for discussion in Parliament, and under-representation in the House of Commons.

O'Brien turned to Peel and reminded him that he had now been in office for two years and had never introduced one measure dealing with the legitimate complaints of the

53 On June 2, 1843, in a letter to his wife Lucy, O'Brien commented on her complaint that in his effort to secure justice for Ireland he seemed to ignore the interests of his wife and children. He said that he was probably attending his last session of Parliament and that while he was at Westminster he had "an obligation to make a constitutional effort" for his country. He continued: "If I fail I shall at least have the satisfaction of thinking that I have *exhausted* every hope of good government before I fling myself into the ranks of them who seek for what every day's experience more and more teaches me to believe is the only effectual remedy for misgovernment." (MS. 8653, N.L.I.)

54 Peel to Queen Victoria, July 5, 1843, Add. MSS 40436, B.M.

Irish people. He promised Peel that the Government could win the approval of Irish Catholics for the Union if his administration indicated a determination to rule Ireland in a just and impartial manner. A successful Irish policy, according to O'Brien, must include legislation on the following subjects: the Church (he recommended endowing both Catholic and Protestant churches), landlord-tenant relations, education, parliamentary representation and the suffrage, municipal reform, the poor law, loans for railway construction, and public works.

O'Brien accused Peel of talking too casually about the possibility of civil war in Ireland. He warned the Prime Minister that though Irishmen lacked the resources to fight the British army in a conventional manner, they had the organization and the determination to wage a successful campaign of passive resistance to British rule in Ireland. And a population of over seven million united in opposition to British authority would find allies from among the large number of Irish emigrants living in the industrial cities of Britain. But, said O'Brien, Ireland offered Britain peace, not war. A peace based upon an equal partnership in the Union and justice to all people living in Ireland. He advised the House of Commons to treat Ireland and her problems in the same manner that it considered Britain and her problems. This would guarantee the loyalty of the Irish masses. And a loyal Ireland would improve the military security of Britain and strengthen the hand of the Foreign Office in delicate negotiations with potentially hostile powers.[55]

Moore O'Ferrall, Morgan John O'Connell (the Liberator's nephew), and Sharman Crawford, three of O'Brien's Irish colleagues, ably and eloquently supported his motion.

---

[55] *Hansard* 70:630ff. In the debate on O'Brien's motion Irish Liberals received unexpected support from two Conservative M.P.'s, a Mr. Rous and a Captain Smythe. These two nonconformist Tories insisted that Ireland was an underprivileged member of the Union and attributed her inferior status to the no-Popery bigotry of Irish and British Protestantism.

In their speeches they emphasized the need for tenant right legislation, a just solution to the religious question, and the urgency of public works projects as a solution to the unemployment problem. They asked British politicians to try to penetrate the peculiar nature of the Irish Question.[56]

The Whig comments on the O'Brien motion indicated that the leaders of the party realized that Repeal presented them with political opportunities and that they had the desire to exploit these opportunities by constructing an Irish policy attractive to the Irish electorate. Russell and Palmerston agreed that equality between Catholic and Protestant churches in Ireland should be the main plank in their Irish platform. But both of these experienced politicians realized the difficulties confronting a policy of complete religious equality; it meant that the Government should recognize the titles of the Catholic hierarchy, pay the salaries of the priests, and, logically, place Catholic bishops in the House of Lords. But if the Government gave the Catholic hierarchy the same financial, social, and political status enjoyed by the Protestant hierarchy and clergy, would it enjoy the same control over the former that it had over the latter? If the Government bore the costs of a Catholic establishment it should enjoy the privilege of appointing bishops sympathetic to the Union. Such a condition, however, would be bitterly opposed by O'Connell and others in Irish Catholic circles and might not receive the sanction of the Vatican.

While privately admitting the difficulties of a Catholic establishment, Russell and Palmerston decided that politicians out of office were under no obligation to spell out the details of a policy that they were as yet in no position to implement.[57] So in the debate on O'Brien's motion

56 *Hansard* 70:780ff. (O'Ferrall), 910ff. (O'Connell), 943ff. (Crawford).

57 Palmerston to Russell, June 22, 1843, Russell papers, Public Record Office, London.

they recommended equal treatment of the Catholic and Protestant churches as an effective conciliatory gesture to Irish discontent.[58] But another Whig leader, Viscount Howick (Charles Grey), in a powerful speech, rejected the notion that religious equality alone was enough to satisfy Irish Repealers. He insisted that the basis of Irish nationalism was economic discontent and that the Government should introduce legislation guaranteeing the Irish worker a fair return for his labor. He said that Parliament could not interfere with the established rights of property but that it could promote the security of Irish tenant farmers by insisting that Irish landlords live up to their responsibilities as property owners. Howick brilliantly analyzed the Irish overpopulation and underemployment problems and then recommended Government loans to encourage the start of new industries, public works projects to develop the economic potential of the country and to employ the surplus population, and a Government financed program of Irish emigration.[59]

Roebuck the Radical in his speech endorsing O'Brien's motion also dwelt on the need for a Government emigration program, and he stressed the necessity of tenant right legislation. He suggested poor law reform making landlords responsible for all of the rates, thus giving the property owning class an economic interest in the welfare of their tenants. Roebuck opposed the Russell-Palmerston-Smith O'Brien suggestion for a dual establishment of Catholic and Protestant churches in Ireland. He demanded the disestablishment of the latter and the application of her resources to the needs of the former.[60]

Peel, Graham, and Eliot led the Government resistance to the Smith O'Brien motion. Eliot admitted the existence of legitimate discontent in Ireland and conceded that

[58] *Hansard* 70:1001ff. (Russell), 1064ff. (Palmerston).
[59] *Ibid.,* 70:877ff.
[60] *Ibid.,* 70:958ff.

qualified Catholics were often passed over in appointments to office. But he claimed that the former condition resulted from social circumstances outside the province of parliamentary remedy and that the latter situation was attributable to the opposition of the Catholic middle class to the Conservative Government. The Chief Secretary denied O'Brien's position that Repeal was the response of an intelligent Irish opinion to intolerable government. He described the agitation as an emotional acceptance of a fantastic program of political, economic, social, and religious reform which promised something to everybody.

Eliot refused to concede Ireland a parliamentary representation based on population because the British Constitution had never recognized this principle as essential to parliamentary government. He then attempted to refute the charge that the Peel administration was indifferent to the Irish Question by pointing out that in the last session of Parliament the Government presented twenty-three bills dealing with Irish subjects. The Chief Secretary reminded the House that with the exception of the Lord Chancellor all members of the existing Irish administration were Irishmen. He took notice of the tenant right issue with the argument that Parliament was not permitted to introduce legislation striking at the roots of property rights, and he denied that Irish Catholics had a legitimate complaint in regard to the tithe because nine-tenths of the property bearing the burden of tithe revenue belonged to Protestants. In the course of his speech Eliot spoke with sadness of the support which members of the Roman Catholic hierarchy and clergy gave to the Repeal agitation. He asked them to consider seriously their responsibilities in encouraging movements dangerous to the peace and stability of society.[61]

Graham also reprimanded Catholic bishops and priests for their contribution to Irish nationalism, and he ex-

61 *Ibid.*, 70:697ff.

pressed the Government's intention to do justice to the needs of the Roman Catholic population of Ireland. But, he said, with a crisis in Ireland threatening to explode into violence, the Government did not think it wise to encourage agitation by discussing reforms that might be interpreted as surrender to intimidation. When Ireland was at peace, then the Government would consider reform legislation. Graham closed his remarks by censuring the Whigs for their role in obstructing passage of the arms bill, a measure he considered necessary to restore tranquility to a troubled land.[62]

Peel closed the Government portion of the debate with one of his logical masterpieces. He freely dipped into the bag of traditional Tory arguments in defense of the Union but indicated a more conciliatory attitude in regard to Irish reform than Graham. His words suggested that the Repeal crisis was forcing him to reevaluate traditional Conservative approaches to the Irish Question. However, he did make it clear that he would do nothing to lessen the influence or the financial position of the Irish Church because such action would violate his concept of the Constitution and the pledge made by the British Government to Irish Protestants in 1800.

The Prime Minister also said that as leader of the Conservative party, the party committed to the maintenance and strengthening of Protestantism, he could not make any financial offer to the Catholic Church. And he expressed the conviction that a financial arrangement between the British Government and the Catholic Church might create more problems than it solved. But Peel did outline the direction in which his Government was willing to proceed in regard to Irish legislation. He said that he was not willing to interfere with basic property rights but that he would welcome a parliamentary inquiry into the state of landlord-tenant relations in Ireland. And if the inquiry supported such legislation, he would consider introducing a bill designed to compensate tenants for improvements they made to their farms if they were evicted. Peel also said that he was not opposed to Irish franchise reform. He promised to deal with the menace of Repeal within the framework of existing laws, and he appealed to Irish Catholics to abandon an agitation threatening the peace and prosperity of their country. He urged them to place their confidence in a Conservative Government which had every intention of administering Irish affairs in an impartial manner.[63]

Early on the morning of July 13 Smith O'Brien's motion came to a vote. It received considerable Whig, Liberal, and Radical support but was defeated by seventy-nine votes.[64]

On August 8 Lord Roden presented to the House of Lords a petition signed by five thousand Unionists in County Down calling on the Government to suppress the rebellious spirit existing in Ireland. The petitioners also requested either a repeal of the procession act, which outlawed Protestant demonstrations on the first and twelfth of July, or the application of the act to the activities of the Repeal Association and the temperance societies. Speaking for the petitioners, Roden emphasized the military character of the Repeal agitation, the size and discipline of the audiences attending Monster Meetings, and O'Connell's many references to his Repeal army. Roden also claimed that Repealers were drilling in the hills. He insisted that O'Connell was threatening Britain with war and therefore the Government had an obligation to take military measures to preserve the Union and protect Protestant lives and property. Instead of permitting O'Connell to continue his seditious agitation, the Government should crush the Repeal Association and arm the

---

[63] *Ibid.*, 70:970ff.
[64] "Ayes 164; Noes 243: Majority 79." *Ibid.*, 70:1088ff.

Protestant yeomen of Ulster. Roden warned Englishmen that their country was not immune to the Repeal threat. The spirit of rebellion, once it triumphed in Ireland, would not be contained by the Irish Sea.[65]

Wellington assured Roden that the Government was fully informed of the activities of the Repeal Association and that it was anxious concerning the support foreigners extended O'Connell. But he said the procession act could not be applied to the Repealers. The act was designed to prevent religious demonstrations by either Catholics or Protestants which tended to promote violence. Repeal meetings might encourage tension between religious groups in Ireland and temperance bands might be exploited for nationalist purposes, but neither Repeal nor temperance were technically sectarian movements. The Duke insisted that within the framework of existing law the Government was doing everything possible to maintain the Union and to preserve the peace in Ireland. He said that they preferred to pursue a cautious and deliberate policy in regard to Repeal rather than initiate actions which might lead to civil war. Wellington expressed confidence that the Government's firm but calm response to the Repeal crisis would demoralize the agitators. But he promised that Peel, if he found it necessary, would ask Parliament for emergency powers to meet any extraordinary crisis in the Repeal situation.[66]

The Earl of Wicklow praised the Government's prudence in dealing with O'Connell and expressed confidence that Peel's coolness in the face of the Repeal fire would eventually destroy the Irish demagogue and his seditious movement. He did, however, endorse the petition requesting a repeal of the procession act, and he recommended that the Government should make an effort to separate the Catholic hierarchy and clergy from the Repeal movement.

[65] *Ibid.,* 71:360ff.
[66] *Ibid.,* 71:371ff.

He suggested that the grant to the Roman Catholic seminary at Maynooth should be increased and provision for the clergy following ordination should be considered. Wicklow argued that a well educated and financially independent hierarchy and clergy would no longer have to serve as the pawns of agitators.[67]

The Marquis of Clanricarde also approved of the Government's reluctance to check the Repeal agitation with force, but he sharply criticized the general character of Peel's Irish policy. He said that an arms bill and a feeble attempt to amend the poor law were inadequate responses to Irish demands for justice. It would be much better, he argued, if the Government took steps to stimulate the growth of the Irish economy and to provide employment for the rapidly increasing labor force.[68]

Lord Brougham, in reply to Clanricarde, predicted that the Irish economy would continue to decline as long as political agitation was permitted to frighten away potential investors of capital. He then launched into a bitter attack on O'Connell. He refused to accept the claim that the Repeal agitation was a constitutional effort to revive the Irish Parliament. Brougham described the agitation as a weapon of intimidation designed to coerce the Government into concessions and Irish Unionists into silence. He supported the Government's position that coercion would only instill new vitality into the Repeal agitation and that calculated indifference to O'Connell's threats would demoralize Irish nationalism. He called Roden's suggestion that the Protestant yeoman of Ulster be mobilized an invitation to religious war. Brougham counseled Wellington to ignore those foreigners encouraging Repeal. They were men without influence in their own countries —impotent Radicals in France and ignorant Irish immigrants in the United States. But Brougham did agree

67 *Ibid.*, 71:377ff.
68 *Ibid.*, 71:378ff.

with Roden that Repeal had serious implications for Britain. Of course there was little danger that Englishmen would become Irish nationalists, but they could be attracted by the radical political, social, and economic philosophy contained in the Repeal platform.[69]

William Smith O'Brien and his Irish Liberal colleagues in the House of Commons were deeply disappointed with the results of their efforts in the session of Parliament now drawing to a close. O'Brien's motion for an inquiry into the state of Ireland had been rejected by the House of Commons, and the Government had responded to Ireland's anguished cry for justice, represented by the Repeal movement, with an insulting and degrading arms bill and a totally inadequate reform of the poor law.[70] In desperation, O'Brien decided to present his case for Irish reform to British public opinion.

In mid-August British newspapers published an "Address by the Irish Members of Parliament to the English People." This address was signed by O'Brien and twenty-eight other Irish M.P.'s. The Irish Liberal M.P.'s reminded the British public that under the Constitution they possessed the ultimate power in Britain and therefore had an obligation to insist that their parliamentary representatives enact legislation to right the wrongs inflicted on Ireland through her association with Britain. The British people owed the Irish people a historic debt that

[69] *Ibid.*, 71:381ff.

[70] The main features of the Government's poor law amendment bill indicated that it was meant to conciliate the Irish gentry and to increase the Government's control over the operation of the poor law in Ireland. Eliot's bill did not meet the principal Irish objections to the poor law: the powers of the Central Board remained unlimited, there was no mendicancy clause, no concessions were made to the public works advocates, clergymen continued to be denied places on local boards of guardians, no residency requirement was included, and the clause in the original bill which punished landlords if they charged excessive rents was repealed. In the amendment bill the Government actually reduced the power of local opinion in administering the poor law by increasing the number of magistrates acting as ex-officio guardians to one half the total number (*Hansard* 69:1318ff.).

must be paid. In their address the M.P.'s listed Irish grievances needing legislative attention: the insecurity of tenant farmers, the financial drain of absentee landowning and excessive taxation, the depressed condition of industry, the burden of the established church, inadequate parliamentary and municipal franchises, under-representation in the House of Commons, Protestant ascendancy, anti-Catholic attitudes and policies of British Governments, and the absence of any local control over uniquely Irish situations. O'Brien and his friends then suggested remedies for these grievances: legislation to stimulate the economy and to lift the burden of poverty from the Irish masses, a policy of perfect equality in regard to educational and ecclesiastical matters for all religious groups in Ireland, a franchise adequate to express Irish opinion in the municipal corporations and in the House of Commons, representation in Parliament proportionate to the size of the Irish population, a larger share of Government appropriations, equality of Catholics as candidates for appointed political office, and more of a voice for Ireland in the administration of the Empire. They also recommended that the Government find a method to give Irishmen some measure of control over problems peculiar to their own country.

The Irish Liberal M.P.'s could not guarantee the British people that an immediate display of Irish gratitude and friendship would follow reform legislation. Centuries of British oppression and misgovernment had created and fostered hatreds and suspicions which would not vanish with the first attempt to conciliate Irish opinion. But they promised that in time British efforts to rule Ireland in a just manner would cement the bonds of Union and affection between the Irish and British peoples. However, they insisted, there was not a moment to spare in this effort to solve the Irish Question. Every delay strengthened the arguments of those who insisted that Ireland could only obtain justice in an Irish parliament. O'Brien and his associates closed their address with this sober statement: "Should this warning be neglected, upon you, not upon us, be the responsibility of future events."[71]

On August 24 Victoria closed the session with an address to both houses of Parliament. In her speech she expressed concern over the effort to stir up "discontent and disaffection" among her subjects in Ireland and with the attempt to repeal the Union. She pledged her Government to a policy of justice to Ireland and to the introduction of future legislation designed to promote the peace and prosperity of that country. The Queen insisted that the Union between Ireland and Britain must and would be preserved. Irish and British solidarity was vital to the best interests of both countries and absolutely necessary to the maintenance of the Empire. She expressed her confidence in the wisdom of Peel's Irish policy and in the "good sense and patriotism" of her people and servants in Ireland. She depended on them to reject and discourage "a system of pernicious agitation" which disturbed the economic life of their country, hindered its progress, and excited "feelings of mutual distrust and animosity between different classes of my people."[72]

71 *Pilot,* August 28, 1843.
72 *Hansard* 71:1007ff.

4

Peel Reconsiders the Irish Question

SIR ROBERT PEEL was an unusual British Prime Minister; he knew something about Ireland. He had served there as Chief Secretary from 1812 to 1818. As Chief Secretary, Peel had strong anti-Catholic attitudes and opposed emancipation. He insisted that Ireland needed resolute government rather than reforms involving large expenditures of money. But in his efforts to reform the inefficient Irish administration he was frustrated by the venality and nepotism of the Protestant ascendancy. He left Ireland with the conviction that the interests of that country suffered from the selfish ambitions of both the ascendancy and Catholic nationalist factions.[1]

While in Ireland Peel had the opportunity to watch O'Connell operate at close range. He appreciated his opponent's intelligence and eloquence, but the Tory, Oxford-influenced Englishman had nothing but contempt for the Irishman's vulgarity and demagogic political methods. These two men had incompatible personalities. O'Connell was quick to label the Chief Secretary "Orange Peel," and in 1815 the Irish leader's fiery and insolent tongue provoked Peel to challenge him to a duel. The two were scheduled to meet at Ostend in Flanders, but O'Connell was detained by the authorities before he could cross the Channel.[2] Bloodshed was prevented, but personal animosity existed between Peel and O'Connell until the latter's death in 1847.

Peel was the greatest of nineteenth-century British leaders until Gladstone became Prime Minister in 1868, and Gladstone had been a protegé of Peel's and reflected many of his mentor's attitudes concerning the responsibilities of public office. But at the beginning of his political career Peel was a cautious man. Events in France had made him fear a revolution that might destroy British institutions. In the 1820's and early 1830's, as his party's leader in the House of Commons, he was a conscientious Tory defending old ideas and institutions against liberal-inspired innovations. He conceded Catholic emancipation out of fear that the Catholic Question might lead to political instability that could wreck the equilibrium of the British system. But Peel's change of mind on emancipation indicated flexibility and the ability to act even when action meant personal risk. His surrender to the Catholic forces in 1829 made Peel a target for no-Popery prejudice. He was called a traitor to his class and his religion, and never again was he completely trusted by the right wing of his party. But Tories could not reject him because he was the only man capable of leading the Conservatives against the talented Whig-Radical-Irish nationalist coalition.

Catholic emancipation and the 1832 reform bill freed Peel from the political obligation to defend ridiculous

1 Peel's career as Chief Secretary is described in detail in Norman Gash, *Mr. Secretary Peel* (London, 1961).

2 Gash, 162-67, discusses the issues that led to the challenge and subsequent events. Peel emerges from the incident with more honor than O'Connell.

causes. He could turn his talents to more significant challenges. He became a national rather than a party leader. He represented the rare political example of the man who acts on the principle that the interests of the nation always supersede party needs or personal ambitions. As leader of his party he continued to defend and preserve conservative institutions—the House of Lords, the prestige of the monarchy, the Established Church, and the rights of property —because he believed they were bulwarks against the chaos and anarchy of democratic extremism. But Peel rejected the notion that the interests of the nation were inseparable from the concerns and ambitions of the landed aristocracy. He saw the nation as an organic whole, and he was prepared to accept changes that benefited society in general. Like Edmund Burke, he could accept evolution as an alternative to revolution.

In many ways Peel was defending lost causes. The House of Lords and unrestricted property rights were doomed to destruction, the Established Church could not survive in Catholic Ireland, and the monarchy would lose most of its power and a great deal of its influence. And Peel's great strengths as a national leader were his weaknesses as a practicing politician. His intellectualism prevented an appreciation for the selfish and irrational forces that influenced political conduct. While he remained above the battle, ignoring the passions of the moment, guarding the national interest, taking, he thought, the long range point of view, party politics, economic greed, no-Popery bigotry, democracy, and Irish nationalism were molding the future of British history.[3]

Although the Irish Unionist press at times was almost hysterical in its reaction to the Repeal agitation, until late

[3] G. Kitson Clark's *Peel* (London, 1936), is a brief but excellent portrait of Peel's character and political career. Peel was not a defender of unrestricted property rights, but he had doubts that Parliament could force landlords to honor the moral obligations of owning property.

April no one of importance in Dublin Castle or at Whitehall seemed aware of a mounting nationalist enthusiasm in
Ireland.[4] But on April 20 Sir Robert Peel in a letter to
Sir James Graham expressed concern over the militant tone
of the Repeal press.[5] On May 4 Graham told Peel that
many M.P.'s had indicated to him that they were anxious
to give the Government emergency powers to deal with the
Repeal crisis. The Home Secretary reported that Richard
Lalor Sheil had revealed to a reliable source that Ireland
was on the "eve of a convulsion" due to the feebleness of
the Chief Secretary, Lord Eliot, and the burdens of the
tithe rent charge and the poor rate which were driving the
"small, half-ruined Protestant properietors into the ranks
of the disaffected." Sheil advised the Government to
strengthen its military force in Ireland in preparation for
a possible insurrection. Despite the anxiety of British
M.P.'s and Sheil's gloomy assessment of the Irish situation,
Graham recommended that Peel not ask for emergency
powers to put down Repeal "until the rebellious spirit
shall have been evinced by some overt act." But he assured
the Prime Minister that he was taking the proper military
precautions. Two regiments of cavalry had already been
sent to Dublin and two regiments of infantry would soon
be on their way to join them.[6]

On May 6 Earl DeGrey, the Lord Lieutenant, sent Peel
an urgent message from Dublin. He said that within a few
months the Repeal agitation had evolved from a minor
irritation into a major menace, and he attributed this increase in Repeal strength to the support which the Catholic
hierarchy and clergy and the temperance societies gave to
O'Connell. The Lord Lieutenant went on to describe how

[4] At the time Peel seemed to think that the anti-poor law campaign
deserved the most Government attention (Peel to Graham, April 14, 1843,
Add. MSS 40448, B.M.).

[5] Add. MSS 40448, B.M.

[6] *Ibid.*

Repeal wardens organized the country behind O'Connell; the way the Irish at home, in Britain, Canada, and the United States contributed their pounds and dollars to the Loyal National Repeal Association; and how magistrates attended Monster Meetings and pledged their loyalty to the Repeal cause. He reported O'Connell's intentions to build Conciliation Hall and use it as the Irish House of Commons and to circumvent the convention act by assembling a Council of Three Hundred in Dublin. DeGrey was also upset about the way the nationalist press openly preached sedition but said that he was convinced that much of the Repeal enthusiasm was artificial. He claimed that Catholics were forced into the agitation through clerical intimidation and that many middle and upper class Irishmen supported O'Connell because they thought that nationalism might pay off in cash dividends. He also reported a rumor circulating in Dublin that O'Connell feared the Repeal monster that he had created but dared not resist the tide of Irish opinion.

DeGrey also expressed concern over the future dependability of Protestant Unionists. He said that many Irish Protestants suspected that Peel was antagonistic to Protestant ascendancy and as a result were "lukewarm" in their support of the Government. Until the present agitation fear of the Catholic masses had kept Protestants committed to the Union, but DeGrey warned Peel not to take their loyalty for granted. The Lord Lieutenant was himself a strong advocate of Protestant ascendancy and he advised Peel to court the friendship of those whose religious beliefs, traditional loyalties, and political and economic interests made them the natural defenders of the British connection. He also recommended that the Prime Minister tell Parliament that the Government would preserve the Union even if it had to employ military force. DeGrey optimistically predicted that an Irish coercion bill designed to crush the Repeal Association would enjoy the same Whig support that the attack on the Catholic Association received in 1829.[7]

On May 7 DeGrey wrote Peel that the Government, after declaring in Parliament its determination to maintain the Union, should demonstrate its firmness by dismissing Repeal magistrates. Since the declaration would make it clear to all interested parties that Repeal could only be achieved through revolution the Ministry should hardly permit the responsibility of preserving the peace to remain in the hands of men sympathetic to the anti-Union position.[8]

The next day Peel received an interesting note from Prince Albert on the Repeal question. Albert described a recent conversation with two Whig leaders, Lords Melbourne and Morpeth. They suggested that the Government should intimidate O'Connell by exploiting his alleged terror of imprisonment. Morpeth and Melbourne claimed that O'Connell was a coward with a morbid fear of jail and that a threat of prosecution would make him abandon the Repeal agitation. They argued that with O'Connell out of the way Irish nationalism would collapse because no one else could assume his leadership over the Irish masses.[9]

Francis Blackburne, Master of Rolls in Ireland, and John Doherty, Lord Chief Justice of Common Pleas and a Privy Councillor, two of Peel's chief advisors on Irish policy, and the Duke of Wellington endorsed DeGrey's recommendation that the Government ask Parliament for the authority to stamp out Repeal.[10] Peel was inclined to accept the advice of DeGrey, Blackburne, Doherty, and Wellington, so he called a cabinet meeting for May 8 to discuss the prospects for an anti-Repeal coercion bill. Just

[7] Add. MSS 40478, B.M.
[8] Add. MSS 40478, B.M.
[9] Add. MSS 40436, B.M.
[10] Graham to Peel, May 7, 1843, Add. MSS 40448, B.M.

before he entered the cabinet room the Prime Minister received a note from Lord Stanley, the Colonial Secretary. Stanley said that an attack of the gout prevented his attendance at the meeting but he wanted to warn Peel against a hasty decision to solve the Repeal problem through coercion. He reminded the Prime Minister that the existing situation was quite different from the Catholic emancipation crisis of 1829. Then the Government could outlaw the Catholic Association because it had mollified the Irish masses with the emancipation act. But in 1843 it would be impossible to temper coercion with any significant concession to Irish nationalist demands. Therefore, a harsh policy would stimulate rather than calm Irish passions. Stanley also expressed the doubt that the Repeal movement had reached the stage where the Government could present a strong legal case for its suppression. And he cautioned Peel against a ready acceptance of advice from Blackburne and Doherty because they were Irish Protestants who so hated O'Connell that they lost all perspective in evaluating any Irish activity connected with him.[11]

After Peel read Stanley's letter to the cabinet, the Ministers decided to postpone a final decision on the coercion question.[12] But following the cabinet meeting the Prime Minister instructed T. B. C. Smith, the Irish Attorney General, to consider appropriate legislation for the Government to employ against the Repealers in case it became necessary to ask Parliament for extraordinary powers.[13]

Now Peel had the difficult task of explaining to DeGrey why the cabinet had decided to take a long look at the Irish situation before employing coercion. He told the Lord Lieutenant that the cabinet was divided on the question of suppressing the Repeal Association and that even those who favored harsh legislation could not agree on the con-

11 Add. MSS 40468, B.M.
12 Peel to Stanley, May 8, 1843, Add. MSS 40468, B.M.
13 Peel to Prince Albert, May 8, 1843, Add. MSS 40436, B.M.

tents of a coercion bill. Under these conditions it was impossible to construct legislation acceptable to all the members of the Government. But Peel assured DeGrey that the Government had not abandoned the possibility of a coercion bill, and he told him about his instructions to the Irish Attorney General. He said that a coercion bill must be so carefully constructed that even the legal genius of O'Connell would not succeed in evading its consequences. In closing his letter to the Lord Lieutenant Peel suggested that officials in Dublin Castle take legal steps to muzzle the nationalist press. He said that he realized the difficulty of obtaining convictions in sedition cases brought before Dublin juries but gave the opinion that failure to secure convictions would have a less harmful effect on the public mind than the continued neglect of treason.[14]

In his next letter to DeGrey, Peel again discussed a coercion bill. He said that he shared the Lord Lieutenant's opinion that the Government should obtain power from Parliament to deal with the Repeal crisis before the session closed. But he emphasized that legislation that could easily be circumvented was worse than no legislation at all. The Prime Minister revealed that DeGrey's colleagues in the Irish administration, Eliot and Sugden, were opposed to coercion and that their opposition was a strong argument against its immediate application.[15]

On May 9 Wellington in the House of Lords and Peel in the House of Commons declared the Government's determination to preserve the Union even at the horrible cost of civil war. Peel was pleased with the response to the Government's declaration; Whig and Tory leaders pledged support to any emergency action the Government might have to take to fulfill its pledge, and DeGrey reported that O'Connell's "very angry, and vulgar, and abusive" reply to

14 Peel to DeGrey, May 8, 1843, Add. MSS 40476, B.M.
15 Peel to DeGrey, May 9, 1843, Add. MSS 40476, B.M.

Peel's statement and a drop in the Repeal rent indicated that nationalist morale was shaken. The Lord Lieutenant said that he would follow up the ministerial pledge with a warning to all Irish magistrates that future attendance at Repeal meetings would cost them their commissions of the peace. He planned to circulate this warning through the Lord Lieutenants of the various counties.

In this letter to Peel DeGrey argued that the Government could not defeat the Repeal movement without using coercion unless it was prepared to apply the provisions of the procession act to Repeal and temperance demonstrations. He said that the temperance movement had been captured by O'Connell and converted into an instrument of agitation to further the cause of Repeal. He described how the temperance bands formed an important part of all Repeal demonstrations and how their military dress and music contributed to the dangerous public excitement sweeping Ireland. DeGrey predicted that if the temperance bands with their flags and banners were not prevented from marching, they would in time provoke clashes between Orangemen and Repealers.[17]

Peel's confidence in the good effects of his statement to Parliament was quickly shattered by the consequences of Sugden's dismissal of Lord Ffrench and the other Repeal magistrates. Peel knew from DeGrey that the Irish administration intended to discipline Irish magistrates participating in the Repeal agitation, but he was surprised and disappointed over the case Sugden presented justifying the dismissals. Of course Peel had no choice but to defend the Lord Chancellor in Parliament, but in private he and Graham censured Sugden for his lack of judgment in conceding the legality of the Repeal meetings, for implying that statements made by Ministers in Parliament had the

---

16 May 11, 1843, Add. MSS 40478, B.M.
17 *Ibid.*

force of law, and for an irresponsible use of the Queen's name and authority.[18]

Through the months of May and June those who supported a hard line toward Repeal continued to press Peel for coercive legislation. Reports flowed in from Ireland claiming that French agents had infested the country and were working closely with the Repealers;[19] that O'Connell was undermining the loyalty of British troops in Ireland;[20] that Repealers were meeting secretly and conducting military drill in the hills;[21] that O'Connell was losing his influence over the Irish masses to extremists; and that he was prepared to either lead a rebellion or to start a no-rent campaign to regain his position.[22]

Most of the letters and reports from Ireland supported DeGrey's thesis that Ireland was on the verge of civil war. Orangemen were restless and spoiling for a fight. Protestants living in predominantly Catholic communities feared for their lives.[23] Charles Butler Stevenson, Rector of Cal-

[18] Peel to Sugden, June 1, 1843, Add. MSS 40529, B.M.; Graham to Sugden, June 3, 1843, Graham Papers (microfilm), National Library of Ireland. Sugden defended the contents of his letter to Ffrench on the following grounds: the agitation was technically legal but it did threaten the Union, and since the Government had declared its intention not to concede Repeal the objectives of the agitation could only be achieved through violence. In case of a rebellion the Government could not rely on the loyalty of Repeal magistrates. He considered the attempt to distinguish between a statement by a Prime Minister in the House of Commons and a public proclamation useless quibbling since all Ireland was waiting to hear from Peel on the Repeal question and Irish newspapers published the parliamentary declarations. He excused his use of the Queen's name by arguing that Peel also referred to the Monarch in making his statement (Sugden to Peel, June 4, 1843, Add. MSS 40529, B.M., Sugden to Graham, June 1, 1843, Graham Papers).

[19] J. Gardner to Peel, June 4, 1843, Add. MSS 40530; Lord Westmeath to Peel, May 26, 1843, Add. MSS 40528, B.M.

[20] Gardner to Peel, June 4, 1843, Add. MSS 40530, B.M. This charge was often made in the *Evening Mail* and other anti-Repeal newspapers.

[21] Lord Roden to Peel, May 31, 1843, Add. MSS 40528, B.M.

[22] Graham to Peel (containing a letter from W. Strange to Lord Eliot, May 1, 1843) June 5, 1843, Add. MSS 40448, B.M.

[23] "They (the Ministers) have sent over troops to Ireland and have cooped them up in such places as Dublin, Cork, and Fermoy, while in more isolated parts of the country, *Protestants attached to British*

lan, pleaded with Peel to crush the Repeal movement before Protestants and Catholics were at each others throats.
He said that the Repeal agitation stimulated anti-Protes-
tant fanaticism among Catholics and made Protestants
believe that Catholics were preparing to annihilate them.
Stevenson reported that his Protestant parishioners were
ready to arm themselves in defense of their homes because
they believed that it was more noble to die in battle than to
accept slaughter in their beds.[24] Lord Farnham wrote Graham that conflict between Catholics and Protestants in
Ulster was sure to take place before June 13, and he asked
the Home Secretary to order all the Irish county lord
lieutenants, deputy lieutenants, and justices of the peace
in England to return and face their local responsibilities.[25]
Orange fanatics endorsed DeGrey's demand that the processions act be applied to Repeal demonstrations and
Roden's plea that the Government arm the Protestant
yeomanry of Ulster.[26] No-Popery opinion, the major ingredient in nineteenth-century British nativism, insisted
that O'Connell and the Irish Catholic hierarchy were using
Repeal as a screen to hide their real objective, the triumph
of Catholicism in the British Isles. These anti-Catholic
zealots insisted that Peel destroy Repeal to protect Protestant institutions and liberties.[27]

With skill and patience Peel and Graham parried the
thrusts of those demanding tough tactics in Ireland. They

---

connexion are left to the tender mercies of infuriated masses that are not
only clamouring for repeal, but are eagerly panting for the well known
signal, that is intended to divert them to bloody onslaught . . . deeds of
blood will be commited if the army is not scattered through the country."
(John W. Lindsay, Mitchelstown, to Lord Eliot, May 24, 1843, Chief-
Secretary's correspondence, State Paper Office, Dublin).

[24] Stevenson to Peel, June 3, 1843, Add. MSS 40529, B.M.

[25] Graham to Peel, June 4, 1843, Add. MSS 40448, B.M. Graham sent
Farnham to Ireland to counteract the influence of Lord Roden on the
Orange lodges.

[26] Roden to Peel, May 31, 1843, Add. MSS 40529; Graham to Peel,
June 18, 1843, Add. MSS 40448, B.M.

[27] Rev. R. J. McGhee to Peel, May 8, 14, 1843, Add. MSS 40528, B.M.

ignored the no-Popery zealots, ordered investigations of all reports of French spies and Repeal efforts to undermine the loyalty of the army,[28] demanded proof for the charge that Repealers were engaged in military activities,[29] and explained to Orangemen that the processions act could be applied only to those demonstrations which were obviously sectarian in character.[30] Both Peel and Graham opposed the suggestion of arming the Protestant yeomen of Ulster. They believed that any such decision would convince Irish Catholics that the Government was determined on war and might provoke them into initiating a defensive conflict.[31]

Peel returned to the subject of coercion at the cabinet meetings of June 7 and 11. After careful analysis of the Irish situation the cabinet decided that legislation to outlaw the Loyal National Repeal Association, to prohibit Repeal meetings, or to prevent the collection of Repeal rent would prove futile. O'Connell would probably find a way of evading the bill, and any successful effort to sabotage coercive legislation would enhance his reputation with the Irish masses and encourage the growth of the Repeal agitation. The cabinet also discussed the possibility of giving the Lord Lieutenant discretionary powers to prohibit any public meeting in Ireland which he considered dangerous to the public peace or to the maintenance of British rule. Similar authority had been given to the Lord Lieutenant in 1829 in a successful effort to destroy the Catholic Association. However, the cabinet decided to reject this extreme measure because it also could be cir-

28 The log of the Military Secretary in Ireland (Kilmainham Papers, National Library of Ireland) records the investigations of Repeal sympathy among British soldiers stationed in Ireland. Most accusations were without foundation, and when it was established that a soldier did make a pro-Repeal or pro-O'Connell statement there were usually indications that he was under the influence of alcohol. Army officers were ordered to keep their men away from the influence of Catholic priests who were Repealers.

29 Peel to Roden, June 3, 1843, Add. MSS 40530, B.M.
30 Graham to DeGrey, July 9, 1843, Graham Papers.
31 Graham to Peel, June 18, 1843, Add. MSS 40448, B.M.

cumvented by the Repealers. For example, the Catholic clergy could hold simultaneous meetings all over Ireland in their chapels and churches on Sundays. These meetings, called for a publicly announced religious purpose, could be converted into Repeal rallies. And the Government could do little to prevent the discussion of Repeal in the reformed corporations, the poor law boards, and other local government bodies.[32]

Peel explained to DeGrey that the cabinet resisted the arguments for coercion because it feared that harsh measures in Ireland would encourage rather than discourage nationalism. He endorsed Stanley's position that there was little similarity between the Repeal and Catholic emancipation crises. In 1843 the Government could not make a significant concession to Irish public opinion to soften the blow of coercion. The Prime Minister used the arms bill debate to illustrate how little support the Government would get from the Whigs if it decided to press for anti-Repeal legislation in the House of Commons.

In his letter to DeGrey Peel also discussed a serious problem confronting the Cabinet in relation to the Repeal Association. The Anti-Corn Law League was modeled on O'Connell's recipe for popular agitation, and any legislation designed to destroy the Repeal movement would automatically embrace the free traders as well. Therefore any attack on the Repeal Association would force Whigs, Chartists, Radicals, free traders, and all those "who are in favor of democracy or of mischief and confusion" to rally around O'Connell. This alliance in protest against coercion for Ireland would blur the distinction existing between those who supported Repeal and those who opposed it but at the same time defended the right to peti-

32 Peel to DeGrey, June 12, 1843, Add. MSS 40478, B.M. Eliot suggested giving the Lord Lieutenant these broad powers as he did extending the processions act to cover Repeal demonstrations. However, he opposed outlawing the Repeal Association (Eliot to Graham, June 10, 1843, Graham Papers).

tion for a Repeal of the Act of Union. With this distinction between Repealers and Liberals obscured in a common effort to protect civil rights, Irish nationalism would become respectable in Britain, and the Government would find it doubly difficult to deal with discontent, dissatisfaction, and radicalism in both islands.

Peel closed his letter to the Lord Lieutenant with a statement of the objective the Government expected to achieve by remaining firm in its intention to preserve the Union without resorting to repressive legislation against the Repealers. He expressed the hope that when Irish nationalists realized the Government would not bow to intimidation they would abandon O'Connell, and Repeal would then wither away. Peel predicted that O'Connell might then try to regain his standing with nationalist opinion by transferring attention away from his failure to obtain an Irish parliament to a new agitation directed against the payment of rents. He told DeGrey that he personally would welcome this change in tactics because an attack on property rights would antagonize the moderate and intelligent element in the Repeal movement and reveal to British opinion the dangerous economic and social implications of Repeal.[33]

It is clear from Peel's letter to DeGrey that the cabinet discussions of Repeal on June 7 and 11 finally convinced the Prime Minister that coercive legislation would be an unsatisfactory and even risky response to O'Connell's challenge. Instead, he decided to confront the Repealers with an appearance of indifference to the pressure of Irish opinion, military preparations to resist an agitation that

[33] Peel to DeGrey, June 12, 1843, Add. MSS 40478, B.M. DeGrey was unhappy with the decision not to employ coercive legislation to put down Repeal. He wrote Peel that Protestants in Ulster were convinced that the Government had deserted them and reported that the *Evening Mail* was bitter in its attacks on the Administration. DeGrey described the Repeal question as a contest between Catholic and Protestant and insisted that the Government should support its old friends the Protestants (DeGrey to Peel, June 15, 1843, Add. MSS 40448, B.M.; DeGrey to Graham, June 16, 1843, Graham Papers).

might become a revolution, legal action against Repeal leaders and journalists when they transgressed the borders of sedition, and the construction of an Irish policy which would eventually destroy the foundations of Irish nationalism.

Peel believed that if he treated O'Connell as a minor irritation he would create doubts as to the effectiveness of their leader in the minds of the Irish masses. O'Connell had based his agitation on the promise that Irish public opinion acting in a constitutional manner could force the British Government to grant Ireland her own parliament. If the Government made it clear that Irish public opinion had no influence on cabinet decisions or conduct, the followers of O'Connell might reject the author of a false proposition.

Peel's cabinet colleagues accepted his thesis that the Government's refusal to acknowledge the significance of the Repeal Association or the merit of its program would in time demoralize the nationalist rank and file, but they disagreed as to what would follow the collapse of the agitation. Sir James Graham feared that O'Connell, frustrated in his effort to achieve either Repeal or reform legislation for Ireland through constitutional methods of agitation, would be forced by his compulsion to dominate the Irish scene to place himself at the head of a revolutionary movement. He believed that O'Connell would wait until the close of the parliamentary session, when the Government would find it difficult to obtain adequate powers to deal with an Irish emergency, before openly revealing the revised character of the national movement.[34]

34 Graham to Peel, June 17, 25, 1843, Add. MSS 40448, B.M. DeGrey agreed with Graham that O'Connell would wait until Parliament adjourned before altering the course of Repeal, and he rejected Peel's thesis that Repeal would wither away. He said that too many nationalist leaders had a vested interest in Repeal to let it die a natural death. He argued that O'Connell needed the Repeal rent and the Catholic Church wanted to use Repeal to destroy the Established Church (DeGrey to Peel, June 15, 17, 1843, Add. MSS 40478, B.M.).

Eliot and DeGrey seldom shared a point of view on any Irish issue, but they did agree that O'Connell would never command a movement to destroy the Union through the use of force. The Lord Lieutenant doubted his Irish opponent's courage for combat, while the Chief Secretary was convinced that O'Connell had too much common sense to permit the slaughter of his people in a hopeless cause. Eliot expected O'Connell to respond to the defeat of Repeal in a manner more consistent with his personality —he would initiate another popular agitation, one probably directed against the payment of rent.[35]

While the cabinet was in doubt as to the consequence of a Government victory over the forces of Irish constitutional nationalism, Peel and Graham could not afford to ignore the possibility of civil war. They feared that even if O'Connell refused to lead a revolutionary movement some of the hotheads in the Repeal movement might convince a considerable number of Irish nationalists that their only hope for freedom lay in a military effort against the British Government. In June, to meet the threat of insurrection, the Government strengthened the military forces in Ireland with regiments sent from Canada, India, and Gibraltar. At the same time the naval and marine forces in the vicinity of Cork were reinforced with additional men and equipment. In July Graham ordered the military commander in Ireland, Sir Edward Blakeney, to prepare all the military barracks and stations in Ireland for siege. Extra supplies of biscuits, salt meats, rum, cannon, and ammunition, along with ordnance and supply experts, were dispatched to Ireland.[36] Five high ranking army officers were sent to various parts of the country with letters of introduction

[35] DeGrey to Peel, June 17, 1843, Add. MSS 40478, B.M.; DeGrey to Graham, June 19, 1843, Eliot to Graham, June 20, 1843, Graham Papers.

[36] Information concerning the Government's military preparations in Ireland can be found in the correspondence between Graham and DeGrey, Graham Papers; Peel and DeGrey, Peel Papers; and the Kilmainham Papers.

to leading members of the gentry and constabulary officials requesting their cooperation with the military.[37] No doubt these officers had instructions to report on the progress of Repeal, the potential military strength of Irish nationalists, the possibilities of an insurrection, and the readiness of local militia groups to aid the regular army in suppressing a rebellion.[38]

Although Peel and Graham disagreed with Irish Unionist suggestions that the Government arm the Protestant yeoman units, the Duke of Wellington supported this Protestant request and demanded that the Government act on it.[39] Peel was reluctant to antagonize the Duke by flatly rejecting an idea on which he was so insistent. Therefore, Graham instructed DeGrey to conduct an investigation into the strength and combat readiness of the Ulster yeomen and to store arms and ammunition for their use in case the Government was forced to call on their services. He insisted that the investigation be carried out with maximum security so that Irish Catholics would have no suspicions that the Government was contemplating the use of the yeomen. If they believed that Irish Protestants were to be mobilized for action against the Repealers they might initiate defensive action, and the onus of instigating a religious conflict would be placed on the Conservative Government. Graham suggested to De-Grey that perhaps the army was in the best position to conduct a secret inquiry into the affairs of the yeomen. He insisted that DeGrey take no action in regard to calling out the Irish Protestants without first consulting the Home Office.[40] When the Lord Lieutenant replied

37 Kilmainham Papers, June 3, July 12, 15, 1843.

38 The Kilmainham Papers reveal how the British Government in 1843 made extensive use of the army to report on Repeal strength in Ireland. The army collected information on the size of Repeal meetings, Repeal sentiments in various parts of the country, and the activities of anti-Union ballad singers.

39 Graham to Peel, June 18, 1843, Add. MSS 40448, B.M.

40 Graham to DeGrey, June 21, 22, 24, 1843, Graham Papers; Graham to Peel, June 21, 1843, Add. MSS 40448, B.M.

that it would be impossible to obtain the information Graham wanted without tipping off the Repealers, the Government abandoned the inquiry but instructed De-Grey to store arms and ammunition for Protestant use in case of an emergency.[41]

In addition to his plans to frustrate and demoralize Repealers by a show of indifference to their agitation and his military preparations to deal with a possible rebellion, Peel began to lay legal snares to entrap Irish nationalist leaders. He ordered the Irish law officers to prosecute the authors of all seditious articles, ballads, and speeches and those who tampered with the loyalty of British troops stationed in Ireland.[42] However, the law officers demonstrated little enthusiasm in carrying out the instructions of the Home Office. Graham was so discouraged by the apathy and timidity of the people in Dublin Castle that he wrote Peel of his lack of confidence in the Irish executive: "it does not only sleep, but it is dead."[43]

O'Connell, of course, was the main target of the Government's legal strategy. Peel and Graham expected O'Connell to become bolder in his public statements the longer the Government continued to ignore him. And in his effort to retain the confidence of the Irish masses in the face of the apparent Government indifference to Repeal he might say or do something to provide the Peel administration with grounds to prosecute him for sedition. In August the Government began to prepare a brief against O'Connell. Reporters were assigned to all the meetings where he

41 DeGrey to Graham, June 26, 1843, Graham to DeGrey, June 28, 1843, Graham Papers.

42 Graham to Sugden, June 29, 1843, Graham to DeGrey, June 13, 1843, Graham to Eliot, September 7, 1843, Graham Papers; Peel to DeGrey, August 19, 1843, Add. MSS 40478, B.M. Graham was very worried about the influence of ballad singers in creating an anti-British opinion in Ireland (Graham to DeGrey, June 29, 1843, Graham Papers), and he considered the national songs published in the *Nation* "very mischievious and exciting" (Graham to Peel, June 25, 1843, Add. MSS 40448, B.M.).

43 September 5, 1843, Add. MSS 40449, B.M.

was scheduled to appear, and they were instructed to take down every word he said. DeGrey was requested to collect all the evidence which might support charges that O'Connell was preparing to lead a rebellion, subverting the loyalty of Her Majesty's soldiers, violating the convention act by his decision to summon the Preservative Society to Dublin, and discouraging the payment of rents, tithes, and poor rates.[44]

In 1843 O'Connell won a major victory unknown to himself or to anyone else outside the inner circles of Government. He had forced Peel and his cabinet to take a long hard look at Ireland and to reevaluate traditional British responses to the Irish Question. While the Prime Minister maintained an indifferent pose to the Repeal fury raging in Ireland and continued to reply to demands that he do something about Irish nationalism with calm assurances that the Government would preserve the Union, in private he conceded the failure of the Union to achieve its primary objective—the complete assimilation of Ireland into the British system. He admitted that forty-three years after the Act of Union Ireland was neither a willing partner nor an intrinsic part of Britain. He accepted O'Connell's success in mobilizing millions of people in support of Repeal as convincing proof that the Irish masses despised the British connection and viewed themselves as conquered people held in bondage by a British army of occupation. In his effort to understand why the Union had failed to achieve a harmony of interests and goals between the populations of Ireland and Britain, Peel was forced to conclude that much of the responsibility for this failure rested with the British Government. In their administration of Irish affairs British politicians ignored the reli-

[44] Reference to the Government's legal strategy against O'Connell can be found in the following correspondence: Graham to DeGrey, June 13, 1843, Graham to Sugden, July 4, 1843, Graham to DeGrey, August 3, 12, 1843, Brewster to Lucas, August 26, 1843, Graham to Eliot, September 12, 1843, Graham Papers. The Government's plan to indict O'Connell for sedition will be discussed in some detail in the next chapter.

gious, economic, social, and political traditions which distinguished industrial and Protestant Britain from agrarian and Catholic Ireland. Instead of making an effort to bridge the gaps isolating religions and classes within Ireland and developing mutual interests beween Englishmen and Irishmen, the leaders of British political parties perpetuated and encouraged the tensions dividing Orange and Green, Saxon and Celt, and exploited them for political purposes.

Peel decided in the summer of 1843 to construct an Irish policy which in time would make the Act of Union a spiritual as well as a legal bond between the two islands. His years of experience as Irish Chief Secretary left him with no illusions as to the difficulty of his task. He knew the hatreds and suspicions that separated Irish Protestants from their Catholic neighbors and Irishmen of all persuasions from the people on the other side of the Irish Sea. These animosities had deep historical roots and long traditions, but every year the effort to assimilate Ireland into the British system was delayed the more likely was the permanent failure of the Union and the continuation of Ireland as a malignant tumor within the Empire.

In order to win the approval of Irish opinion for the British connection Peel decided that he must alter the anti-Catholic direction of Conservative party policy. He entertained little affection for the Church of Rome or her Irish clerical servants, but Catholicism was the religion of the Irish masses and they would never demonstrate friendship to a Government or a party antagonistic to their faith. To convince Irish Catholics that the Union offered to them and their country prosperity and a more comfortable existence the Government must prove Britain's intention to administer Irish affairs in a just and impartial manner. This meant carrying out all of the implications of the emancipation act. Any Irish Catholic presenting himself as a candidate for Government office must receive a fair consideration of his qualifications, and the Government must be as sensitive to the appeals of the Catholic majority as it had always been to the claims of the Protestant minority. Graham shared Peel's enthusiasm for a policy which would cement the bonds of Union by conceding justice to Irish Catholics. Together the two men began to plan for the achievement of Irish-British unity.

Before they could enlist Irish Catholic support for the Union Peel and Graham had to find a method of weakening the hold Irish nationalism had on mass opinion. Peel, a man who usually approached political problems with a maximum degree of rationality, had difficulty understanding an ideology like nationalism which made an appeal to the emotional and mystical as well as the material needs of human nature. He considered Irish nationalism a fragile edifice resting on an artificial alliance between demagogue, priest, shopkeeper, and peasant. He believed that such an unnatural partnership encompassing conflicting class interests was held together only by a common allegiance to an underprivileged church. The Catholic Church was the spiritual home of the Irish masses, but it lacked the financial resources to fulfill adequately its religious mission. In contrast, the Church of Ireland, serving a handful, enjoyed a monopoly of Government concern and a substantial income from tithes paid directly by property owners but indirectly through rents collected from Catholic tenant farmers.

But Peel and Graham knew that the Catholic Question was complicated by social, political, and economic overtones. Members of the Catholic middle class naturally resented a denial of educational opportunities and their second class status when it came to appointments in the Irish administration. Catholic tenant farmers paid exorbitant rents to Protestant landlords or their representatives and were in constant danger of eviction at the whim of the landowner. Underpaid, poorly housed, politically unrepresented agricultural and urban laborers and impoverished parish priests and their curates were Catholics, while rack renting and sometimes absentee landlords, prosperous merchants, and comfortable parsons were, for the most part, Protestants. This meant that an issue which was on the surface religious in character had deep economic, social, and political roots. Catholicism and Protestantism had become the badges distinguishing classes as well as religions. While most of the emotional content of the Irish Question centered on theological issues, the essence of the question was the attempt of a besieged minority, bolstered by an alien legislature, police force, and army, to maintain religious, political, economic, and social ascendancy over an underprivileged and resentful majority increasingly aware of the power of organized and disciplined numbers.[45] In Ireland, religious differences symbolized all the interests dividing the parasitical aristocracy from the ambitious and aggressive peasant democracy.

Because Irish Catholics were second class citizens in the United Kingdom and because British opinion and the British Parliament considered the Catholic Church a vehicle of religious error as well as a menace to British institutions, Catholic bishops and priests were forced by their own economic needs and the bitterness of their flocks to lend their considerable influence to the anti-Union cause. Ireland indeed presented a unique situation in the Age of Metternich—a revolutionary Catholic hierarchy and clergy encouraging agitations threatening existing political institutions and traditional property rights.

If temperaments created by British Protestant upper class backgrounds made it difficult for Peel and Graham to understand the emotional dynamism and historical rationale of Irish nationalism, their English experiences made

---

[45] Even though the Irish police force was recruited in Ireland and included a number of Catholics, and the British army in Ireland had many Catholic Irishmen serving with it, both the army and the police force were under the control of the British Government and it is correct to describe them as alien.

them appreciate, and perhaps overestimate, the influence of class interest as a factor in shaping political attitudes and conduct. They believed that the British Government could settle the Irish Question by dividing the Irish nationalist coalition into its component parts, giving to each interests and objectives transcending their allegiance to Repeal. First the Catholic hierarchy and clergy should be led out of the nationalist fold by some concessions to the financial needs of their church; then the Catholic middle class should be lured from O'Connell's influence by the prospects of educational and professional opportunities provided by a friendly British Government; and, finally, Irish tenant farmers should be insured some security in their holdings. If the British Parliament would pass legislation consistent with this outline, Peel and Graham were convinced that Britain would be rewarded with the collapse of Irish nationalism and with an Ireland wedded to Britain through the firm ties of mutual economic and class interests. The Catholic gentry, clergy, middle class, tenant farmers, and proletariat in Ireland would find that they had much more in common with their counterparts in England, Scotland, and Wales than they had with each other. Irishmen, like Englishmen, would be far too busy pursuing the concrete economic goals appropriate to their classes to waste their time and energies pondering unrealistic abstractions like Repeal.

The key plank in Peel's Irish platform was financial relief for the Catholic Church, but it posed serious political difficulties. Concessions to the material needs of the Catholic Church, if not handled in a subtle manner, would jar the sensitive no-Popery nerves of British nativism and provide O'Connell with another weapon to undermine British influence in Ireland. Peel well remembered the hysterical opposition of British public opinion to Catholic emancipation and how O'Connell used previous advances made by British politicians to the Catholic hierarchy and

and to Rome to stimulate anti-British sentiment in Ireland and to tighten his hold over the Catholic bishops and priests.

Peel considered many suggestions in his effort to solve the Catholic Question in Ireland. Lord Eliot recommended a direct endowment to the Catholic Church, the money to be raised by taxing Irish property.[46] Articles published in Radical and Whig journals and speeches by Whig and Radical politicians indicated that many Whigs and Radicals in the House of Commons were prepared to endorse endowment of the Catholic Church.[47] Eventually Peel and Graham came to accept the principle of endowment, coupled with an agreement with the Papacy concerning the political activities of the Irish hierarchy and clergy, as the logical solution to the Catholic Question, but in the summer of 1843 their Conservative attitude in regard to the primacy of the Protestant Church and their fear of the political hazards connected with any negotiations with the Catholic hierarchy and with Rome made them shrink from direct financing of the Catholic Church.[48] Instead, they were inclined to settle for legislation removing one of the last remnants of the penal laws—the restrictions on the inheritance of property by the Catholic Church—and for an increase in the Maynooth grant which would raise the standard of living for seminarians and provide a higher level of education for those studying for the priesthood.

In the seventeenth and eighteenth centuries anti-Catholic penal laws prevented the education of Irish priests in Ireland. Candidates for the priesthood were forced to go to the Continent for seminary training. The French Revolution made it difficult for young Irishmen to travel abroad, and the Irish Parliament and British politicians feared that

---

46 Eliot to Graham, September 20, 1843, Graham Papers.

47 Whig views on the Catholic Question were presented in the previous chapter.

48 Graham to DeGrey, June 29, 1843, Graham Papers; Graham to Peel, June 18, 1843, Add. MSS 40448, B.M.

those who were educated in continental seminaries would be influenced by the ideology of the Revolution and return to Ireland as potential revolutionaries. To avoid the contamination of French radicalism the Irish Parliament in 1795 decided to endow a Roman Catholic seminary at Maynooth, County Kildare. After the Act of Union the British Parliament honored the commitment of the Irish Parliament with an annual grant to Maynooth. But every year when the grant came before Parliament it provoked a no-Popery outburst from M.P.'s who objected to endowing Romanism and treason.

The Government's decision to encourage Catholics to bequeath property to their church and to increase the Maynooth endowment resulted from Peel's acceptance of a thesis concerning the relationship between Irish nationalism and Catholicism then fashionable in some British intellectual circles. According to this thesis the Catholic hierarchy and clergy embraced nationalism because they were dependent on the generosity of the anti-British laity. Priests were not leaders of Irish nationalist opinion but paupers forced to encourage the prejudices of the peasant masses so that pennies would continue to drop into the collection plates on Sunday morning.[49]

Proponents of this thesis also emphasized the connection

[49] This thesis was presented in a pamphlet, *The State of Ireland Considered, and Measures Proposed for Restoring Tranquility to that Country*, by Lord Alvanley (London, 1841), and later in an article in the January, 1844 (79:189-266) issue of the *Edinburgh Review* by Nassau Senior. Alvanley recommended an increased grant to Maynooth and financial aid to other seminaries and grants by the Board of Works to build Catholic chapels. Senior advocated direct financial aid to the bishops and priests to supplement inadequate personal incomes, an increase in the Maynooth grant, and a charitable bequests act permitting the Catholic Church to inherit property. Senior's views are significant because they represented the opinions of the Whig hierarchy and indicated that Peel could rely on the support of Russell and Palmerston in any effort to improve the financial condition of the Catholic Church in Ireland. The contents of a letter from Graham to Peel, September 6, 1843 (Add. MSS 40449, B.M.), make it clear that the two men were interested in Alvanley's ideas, and the character of Peel's Irish legislation in 1844 and 1845 demonstrates the influence of Alvanley and Nassau Senior on his Irish policy.

between the quality of the priesthood, the economic difficulties encountered by the Catholic Church, and the nationalist role of the clergy. They claimed that young Catholic seminarians were trained in an environment totally lacking the basic necessities for civilized living and in an intellectual atmosphere consistent with the narrow limits of the Counter-Reformation mentality. They were denied the experiences which produced cultivated, cosmopolitan, and sophisticated scholars and gentlemen. When the newly ordained priest left the uncomfortable and narrow confines of Maynooth he was sent out to minister to the spiritual needs of illiterate wretches. In order to maintain his influence over this rabble he had to accept all of the assumptions and values of his parishioners. This mendicant career could have little attraction for the sons of the gentry and middle class, so the Catholic Church was forced to recruit her clergy from the ranks of the peasantry. Naturally this peasant hierarchy and clergy shared all of the prejudices of their class. They harbored resentment against a Government and a people they held responsible for the poverty of their families and the miserable status of their church. This resentment was nourished and intensified by experience in a seminary strangled by the niggardly endowment of a British Government.[50]

Peel expected the charitable bequests act which he planned to present to the House of Commons in the 1844

[50] A letter from Graham to Peel, September 24, 1843 (Add. MSS 40449, B.M.), reveals that the Home Secretary believed that the impoverished condition of the Catholic Church determined the quality of clergy she recruited. But a writer in the *Dublin Review* (12:265-78), in reviewing the Alvanley pamphlet, argued that promises of economic security would not necessarily attract young men from the more prosperous classes into the priesthood because the spiritual life was a vocation rather than a profession. He also insisted that the Catholic Church in Ireland did attract a representative number of young men from the middle class and the gentry into its seminaries. He agreed, however, that a better seminary education would improve the quality of the clergy, and he endorsed the recommendation that the Government increase the Maynooth grant.

session to begin the process of emancipating the Catholic clergy from their dependence on the laity, and he believed that an increased grant to Maynooth, also to be presented to Parliament the following year, would elevate and broaden the quality of education in the seminary and encourage young men from respectable backgrounds to select careers in the Catholic Church. Peel looked to the day when Ireland would have a cosmopolitan Catholic hierarchy and clergy, independent in mind, spirit, and interest from nationalist opinion, and attached through gratitude and sound reason to the British connection.

Since the charitable bequest and Maynooth bills were pieces of legislation demanding careful planning which would delay their presentation until the session of 1844, Peel and Graham decided to take immediate steps to demonstrate the Government's friendly intentions toward Irish Catholics and their church. Peel, Graham, and Eliot were in complete agreement that a "new departure" was needed in the management of Irish affairs—one that would "direct the stream of patronage in a new direction"—and they were convinced that it was time for the Government to disregard the favorite slogan of Dublin Castle: "You cannot conciliate your enemies, therefore give everything to the most zealous of your friends."[51]

On June 22 Graham wrote DeGrey that the Repeal crisis demanded more from the Government than strengthening the military garrison in Ireland. He said that the Government had an obligation to eliminate the causes of agitation. Every effort should be made to gain the support of Irish Catholics for the Union. This support might be given if the Catholic middle class was given its "fair share of the patronage of the Crown." Graham expressed his belief that a considerable portion of the Catholic middle class was hostile to the anti-British agitation of O'Connell

[51] Graham to Peel, June 18, July 15, 17, 1843, Add. MSS 40448; Peel to Graham, June 16, 1843, Add. MSS 40448, B.M.

and the priests. These people might become outspoken in their criticism of Repeal if they could expect their pro-Unionist sentiments to reward them with economic, social, and professional advancement. But if the Government continued to ignore the Catholic middle class in its patronage, these potential allies would be forced to suppress their anti-nationalistic feelings and to jump on the Repeal bandwagon to protect their own interests. Graham pleaded with DeGrey not to continue a policy of exclusive Protestant appointments to Irish office at such a critical period of Anglo-Irish relations.[52]

DeGrey was not inclined to accept the Home Secretary's advice or opinions on the Catholic Question. He was a competent, dependable, and hard working public servant, but he entertained no affection for damp, cold Ireland or her Catholic population. The Lord Lieutenant accepted the Protestant ascendancy, no-Popery views of his Under-Secretary, Edward Lucas, and treated with contempt the advice of his colleague, Lord Eliot, who was committed to winning Irish Catholic approval of the British connection.[53] The growing bitterness between the Chief Secretary and the Lord Lieutenant and the incompatibility of their views on the Catholic Question made it difficult for the

52 Graham Papers.
53 Peel and Graham blamed Lucas' influence for DeGrey's hostility toward Irish Catholics and his support for Protestant ascendancy (Graham to DeGrey, June 22, 1843, Graham Papers; Graham to Peel, July 9, 1843, Add. MSS 40448, B.M.). In June it appeared that Lucas would step out of the Irish picture. He resigned his office because he resented the presence of Tighe Hamilton as Chief Clerk. He considered Hamilton a Whig. Graham and Peel would have been happy to accept Lucas' resignation, but since DeGrey insisted that he was indispensable they agreed to find Hamilton another position, and Lucas withdrew his resignation. Later Graham attempted to reduce the influence of Lucas on DeGrey by persuading Lady DeGrey that Lucas' advice on Irish policy was not always sound. However, the Lord Lieutenant's wife indicated that she was as much captivated by Lucas as her husband and insisted that the only time his advice swayed DeGrey was when it was supported by the facts of the Irish situation. It was quite clear that the DeGreys considered Lucas the most competent Irish expert in the Administration (Lady DeGrey to Graham, October 9, 1843, Graham to Lady DeGrey, October 14, 1843, Graham Papers).

Government to counter the influence of Repeal with a dynamic program of Irish reform. DeGrey continued to insist that the Government's primary obligation in Ireland was the maintenance of Protestant ascendancy. He considered Protestants the only reliable Unionists in Ireland and Catholics inherent traitors. He demanded that Protestant loyalty be rewarded and encouraged by a guaranteed monopoly of political power and that Catholics be excluded from all offices which might provide them with opportunities to wreck the Union. DeGrey refused to consult with Eliot when it came to appointments to Irish office and personally carried out a policy of Protestant monopoly and Catholic exclusion.[54]

Graham was so disgusted with DeGrey's refusal to consider an alternative to Protestant ascendancy that he advised Peel to abolish the office of Lord Lieutenant and to rule Ireland directly from Whitehall. Peel shared this impatience with DeGrey's obstinacy; he strongly endorsed Eliot's view that since the Chief Secretary must defend Irish policy in the House of Commons, he should have a voice in appointments to Irish office; and he was sympathetic to suggestions that there should be a complete overhaul of the Irish administration.[55] However, he dared not

54 DeGrey's attitude toward attempts to conciliate Catholic opinion can be found in his letter to Peel, August 18, 1843 (Add. MSS 40478, B.M.). Eliot was particularly upset when he arrived in Dublin in August and discovered that Catholics had been discriminated against in promotions to high positions in the Royal Irish Constabulary (Eliot to Graham, August 26, 1843, Graham to DeGrey, September 3, Graham Papers). DeGrey replied to Eliot's charge with the argument that he made his Constabulary appointments on the recommendations of the Inspector General of the Irish Constabulary, Colonel Duncan McGregor. He said that he was unaware of the religious affiliation of the men he promoted but conceded that McGregor was more kindly disposed to the Protestant members of the Constabulary than the Catholics in the force. DeGrey admitted that most of the Catholic R.I.C. men were loyal and dependable but expressed his opinion that a few had been tampered with by Repealers (DeGrey to Graham, September 5, 1843, Graham Papers).

55 Graham to Peel, July 16, 17, 1843, Add. MSS 40448, B.M. Peel and Graham frequently discussed the Irish Administration in their correspondence of early September (Add. MSS 40448, B.M.).

remove DeGrey or make radical alterations in the Irish Government in the midst of a crisis threatening the very existence of the United Kingdom. In spite of his obvious limitations DeGrey's military record, his courage under fire, his determination to maintain the Union, and his high standing in Irish Protestant circles would prove positive attributes in case the Repeal agitation produced a rebellion. If DeGrey was removed while the agitation was in full bloom, O'Connell and other Irish agitators might reach the erroneous and dangerous conclusion that the Government was yielding to the intimidation of mobilized Irish nationalist opinion.[56]

In August Peel and DeGrey had a frank exchange of views on the Catholic Question. During July the Government promoted Richard Keatinge from third sergeant to the Irish Prerogative Bench. Peel then recommended that John Howley, a Roman Catholic who had performed well as assistant barrister for Tipperary, be appointed Keatinge's successor as third sergeant. He wanted to use Howley's advancement in office to illustrate that the Catholic middle class could profit by loyalty to the Union.[57] DeGrey was most reluctant to promote Howley. The Lord Lieutenant admitted that Howley had done a

---

[56] While Peel and Graham shared most of Eliot's views on Ireland, they thought that the Chief Secretary lacked the courage of his convictions in dealing with the ascendancy. They particularly resented the appointment of a Pennyfather to replace Tighe Hamilton as Chief Clerk. They thought the Pennyfathers controlled far too many Irish offices and they objected to the continuation of this nepotism. Eliot had made the appointment because he was in Dublin in August and September while DeGrey was on holiday (Graham to Peel, September 18, 1843, Add. MSS 40449, B.M.). The Government's confidence in DeGrey as a man competent to meet the challenge of rebellion is revealed in Graham's letter to Lady DeGrey, October 14, 1843 (Graham Papers). However, the Peel-Graham correspondence in the months of August, September, and October 1843 (Add. MSS 40448, 40449, B.M.) makes it clear that after the Repeal crisis was over, the Government would be happy to accept the Lord Lieutenant's resignation. The two ministers knew that the Irish climate had taken a serious toll on his health and would finally force him to resign.

[57] Peel to DeGrey, July 24, 1843, Add. MSS 40478, B.M.

good job in his Tipperary post and that he had won the respect of Protestants in the legal profession, but argued that he lacked all of the qualifications for third sergeant and that important legal positions should not be offered as bait to capture Catholic loyalty.[58] DeGrey insisted that it was foolish to make friendly overtures to Irish Catholics. Most of the talented Catholic members of the Irish middle class had already associated themselves with the Repeal agitation, and if the Government offered positions to anti-Repeal Catholics it would have to scrape the bottom of the barrel. DeGrey said that he had no inclination to co-operate in any attempt to conciliate Irish Popery by appointing unqualified personnel to posts in the Irish Government.[59]

In a long letter to DeGrey on August 22 Peel strongly censured the Lord Lieutenant for obstructing the Government's new Catholic policy. He rejected as both unrealistic and unreasonable the thesis that it was hopeless to compete with Repeal for the loyalty of Irish Catholics. Peel insisted that continued British rule in Ireland within the framework of the Constitution would be impossible if Irish Catholics maintained a solid front in opposition to the British connection. He conceded DeGrey's position that most Irish Catholic candidates for Government favor could not match their Protestant rivals in educational background or in a long record of loyalty to Britain. But he

58 DeGrey argued that Howley lacked the legal background for the post of third sergeant and the independent income for the position and that the promotion might lead him to expect a future promotion to the bench, an honor certainly beyond his talents. DeGrey insisted that there were no Catholics in Ireland worthy of holding more than an assistant barrister position (DeGrey to Peel, July 30, 1843, Add. MSS 40478, B.M.). Sugden also feared that Howley's advancement might establish a bad precedent but agreed with Peel that it might win some Catholics over to a pro-Unionist position (Sugden to Graham, September 5, 1843, Graham Papers). Sugden's reservations concerning the Howley appointment contradict the *Evening Mail's* contention that he promoted it (September 13, 1843).

59 DeGrey to Peel, August 18, 1843, Add. MSS 40478, B.M.

argued that "considerations of policy and also of justice" demanded a "liberal and indulgent" evaluation of their qualifications. He said that if Roman Catholics were permanently excluded from the benefits of partnership with affluent Britain they would have no choice but to agitate for Repeal as the only road to financial, social, and political success.

The Prime Minister refused to accept the Protestant myth that Irish Catholics lacked qualification for Government office because they were innately inferior to Protestants. He reminded DeGrey that Irish Protestants had long enjoyed opportunities for higher education denied to Catholics. It was this educational advantage, plus a monopoly of Government patronage, rather than any racial superiority over the Catholic Irish that gave them their position. According to Peel the time was long overdue for the Government to provide opportunities and incentives to Irish Catholics. If the Government continued to foster Protestant ascendancy it would encourage the educational, social, and economic disparity that made Ireland two nations. But if the Government abandoned its alliance with Irish Protestants, carried out the full implications of the emancipation act, and provided Catholics with the educational opportunities to advance in Government service and in the professions there was no reason why the Catholic population in time would not produce a crop of talented young men eager to serve the interests of the Empire.

Peel then went on to warn against the inevitable consequences of a continued Government sponsored Protestant ascendancy in Ireland. In retaliation Irish Catholics would return a large block of M.P.'s dedicated to subverting British rule in Ireland and to obstructing the process of parliamentary government for the United Kingdom. The Irish Question would always remain a cancer eating away at Imperial unity, an obstacle frustrating the

integration of Ireland into the British constitutional system, an example of the failure of the British Constitution
to harmonize various points of view, and a chink in the
military defenses of Britain.

In conclusion Peel insisted that Britain had no other
reasonable choice but to base its Irish policy on the as-
sumption that a large portion of the Catholic population
could be persuaded by justice to abandon Repeal. And
the only way the Government could demonstrate its intention to concede justice to the claims of Irish Catholics
was by appointing some of them to positions in the Irish
administration. In the existing Irish situation the appointment of a man solely on his qualification for office was not
necessarily the best policy. If the Government could make
a dent in O'Connell's control over the Catholic population
it would be worth the risk of appointing a few Catholics
with weak credentials.[60]

In late August Howley accepted the position of third
sergeant and his promotion did, as Peel expected, create
a considerable stir in Ireland.[61] Leading Catholics, including O'Connell, praised the Government for honoring
one of their coreligionists, but ascendancy leaders interpreted Howley's advancement as another indication of
Peel's readiness to appease Repealers at the expense of
Protestant interests.[62] The Prime Minister expected such
a reaction from Irish Tories and ignored it. He preferred
to take satisfaction in the favorable impression the Howley
promotion made on the Catholic middle class.

60 Add. MSS 40478, B.M. Peel's letter to DeGrey on Catholic policy
received the warm endorsement of Graham (Graham to Peel, August 24,
1843, Add. MSS 40478, B.M.).

61 Howley was permitted to retain his Tipperary assignment, assuring
him an income, and it was made clear to him that he must not expect
a promotion to the bench.

62 On September 2, 1843, Eliot sent Graham a report on the reaction
of Irish opinion to the Howley appointment (Graham Papers). The
Evening Mail (September 4, 6, 13), attacked the promotion of Howley
as an insult to Irish Protestants and to the legal profession.

While he was considering measures to limit the influence of Repeal on the Catholic clergy and middle class, Peel did not neglect the agrarian issue. Prompted by Lord Eliot, some enlightened Irish landlords, and Liberal and Radical opinion in the House of Commons, he decided to include the need of Irish tenant farmers for security of tenure as a plank in his Irish platform. On a number of occasions he indicated his interest in the plight of the tenant farmer class. In a speech to the Lichfield Agricultural Association he reminded landlords that property had duties as well as rights and the prime duty was to protect the welfare of those who tilled the soil.[63] In July Peel revealed to a number of people how impressed he was with a letter he received from James Fintan Lalor, the future patron saint of Irish agrarian radicalism. Lalor suggested that the Government could separate the Irish peasant masses from Repeal by legislation guaranteeing secure tenures at fair rents. During the debate on Smith O'Brien's motion Stanley expressed the Government's concern with land reform when he said that he would not oppose a motion to set up a parliamentary commission to inquire into the conditions of landholding and tenant-landlord relations in Ireland.[64]

The Lalor-Peel correspondence presents an intriguing mystery. The Peel papers in the British museum contain a letter from Lalor sent in early July. In this letter Lalor described himself as one who had once been "more than a Repealer" but who had become a Conservative in "point of feeling . . . and in point of principle" out of disgust with O'Connell and other agitators and as a result of "reflection and experience." He said that now he looked to a Conservative Government and to the Irish landlords for the peace

---

[63] This mild censure of the landed gentry provoked the *Evening Mail* to accuse Peel of placating O'Connell by selling out the interests of Protestant property (October 2, 1843).
[64] *Hansard* 70:1084-85.

and prosperity of the Irish people. Lalor told Peel that
political agitation must cease if the Irish people were to
prosper, and he volunteered his help to the Government's
effort to defeat Repeal. He questioned, however, the
sources and the validity of the Government's Irish intelligence and offered to provide the kind of information
which only a man intimate with Repeal could possess.
Lalor promised that this information would be of "a
general nature and not in reference to individuals." He
asked Peel to write him in care of Miss Butler, Mary-
borough, Queens County, so that his Repeal family and
friends would not know that he was in communication
with the Government.[65]

On July 5 and 8 Peel wrote the future prophet of Irish
agrarian radicalism and invited him to send the information he had volunteered.[66] Lalor immediately replied, but
his letter is not among the Peel papers. It is obvious, however, that Peel was impressed with what Lalor had to say.
He wrote DeGrey that Lalor expressed "views" much more
dispassionate and comprehensive than Irish letters gener-
ally contain," and he asked the Lord Lieutenant to investigate their author.[67] Peel sent Lalor's letter to Graham, and
the Home Secretary's comments indicated that Lalor argued that the British Government could frustrate Repeal
and solve the Irish Question by reconciling the conflicts
dividing the landlord and tenant farmer classes, and that
he promised to forward a comprehensive plan to achieve
this goal. Graham had some doubts that Lalor was really
the author of the letter because he felt the style reflected a
clerical mind.[68]

On July 26 Peel sent the letter to Prince Albert with the
following comment: "This letter is from a Roman Catholic
—the son of a great agitator—scarcely of the rank of gentle-

65 Add. MSS 40530, B.M.
66 Add. MSS 40531, B.M.
67 Peel to DeGrey, July 21, 1843, Add. MSS 40478, B.M.
68 Graham to Peel, July 18, 1843, Add. MSS 40448, B.M.

man," but a writer with "more enlarged and comprehensive views on the past of Ireland than is usually found
in such communications." Three days later Albert returned the letter with the comment that the handwriting
made it impossible for him to read the entire contents.[69]
On August 24 DeGrey sent Peel a report on Lalor not
really adding any information that Lalor didn't reveal
himself. The Lord Lieutenant described him as bright
but poorly educated with a surly attitude toward life.[70]

Peel soon heard from another Irish authority on the
land question. On September 1 the Earl of Devon, a
benevolent landlord and a stanch supporter of Peel's Irish
policy, wrote the Prime Minister a long letter from Ireland
reporting on the character of the Repeal agitation and the
forces sustaining it. Devon was convinced that most Repealers followed O'Connell out of a sense of blind loyalty
and seldom bothered to evaluate the objective of the agitation. He believed that the few Repealers who were concerned with goals wanted to improve the material position
of the Catholic Church, secure equality of opportunity for
Catholics, and to obtain legislation providing economic
security for tenant farmers. Devon argued that the strength
of Repeal rested upon O'Connell's intelligent decision to
organize his agitation around legitimate demands for
justice and that the only way the Government could
destroy his influence over the Irish Catholic population
was by making some concessions to these demands. He
told Peel that if tenant farmers were secure in their holdings and on friendly terms with their landlords they would
not risk this economic and emotional security by engaging
in anti-Union agitations.

[69] Add. MSS 40437, B.M.; Prince Albert to Peel, July 29, 1843, *ibid.*
[70] Add. MSS 40478, B.M. I am indebted to Thomas P. O'Neill of the
National Library, Ireland, who first discovered that Lalor contacted Peel.
His information was of importance when I was using the Peel papers in
London.

While Devon recommended legislation to provide security of tenure, he did not believe that this was the best
solution to the agrarian problem. He insisted that Ireland
would know peace only when landlords voluntarily and
in good spirit fulfilled their moral obligations to the tillers
of the soil. Devon suggested that perhaps the Government could make landlords realize their economic and
social obligations by initiating an inquiry into landlord-
tenant relations. Such an inquiry, he predicted, would
establish facts which would help the Government construct a land reform program, but even more important,
it would create a public opinion in Britain and Ireland
which would pressure the landlords to accept the duties
connected with the ownership of property.[71]

Devon's letter convinced Peel that the Government
should take the initiative in establishing a parliamentary
commission of inquiry into the Irish agrarian question
rather than wait for the suggestion to come from the Opposition benches. He obtained the consent of his cabinet
for such a commission, and he invited Devon to serve as
its chairman. On September 20 Lord Devon accepted the
Government's invitation, and through the remainder of
the year he worked with Peel and Graham in selecting
other members of the commission and in planning the
procedures of the inquiry.[72]

By late August signs indicated that Peel's June decision
to defeat Repeal by a pose of calculated indifference to
the progress of the agitation had produced the desired
results. Police officials reported that tenant farmers in all
sections of Ireland were so busy bringing in an abundant
harvest that they had little time or inclination to think
about politics. Lords Devon and Clare wrote Peel and
Eliot that the tenants on their Irish estates had lost interest

71 Add. MSS 40533, B.M.
72 *Ibid.*

in Repeal and had no intention of continuing their contributions to the Loyal National Repeal Association.[73]

The decline of Repeal enthusiasm in Ireland and O'Connell's apparent indecision as how to combat this apathy increased the confidence of Peel and his colleagues and made them eager to seize the initiative in Irish affairs. But they realized that before they could implement a new Irish policy they must completely destroy O'Connell's control over Catholic opinion. If they could convict him on a sedition charge and put him in prison perhaps they could shatter the myth of his invincibility. Then the Government would have the favorable climate it needed to destroy the nationalist coalition and to convert Irish anti-Unionist sentiment into mass affection for the British connection.

[73] Clare to Peel, August 25, 1843, Add. MSS 40532, B.M.; Eliot to Graham, September 2, 1843, Clare to Eliot, September 9, 1843, Devon to Eliot, September 8, 1843, Graham Papers.

5

Peel Confronts O'Connell

THE QUEEN'S SPEECH closing the session of Parliament proved a serious obstacle to O'Connell's efforts to retain the confidence of the Catholic masses. Throughout the spring and summer of 1843 he assured his followers that if the Government and the British Parliament rejected their demand for Repeal of the Union, they could still depend upon the Queen's sense of justice and her love for her Irish subjects to restore the Irish Parliament. But now Victoria had made it clear that while she would encourage and support her Prime Minister's efforts to enact Irish reform, she would also stand behind him in his determination to preserve the United Kingdom.

O'Connell first replied to the Queen's speech at a Loyal National Repeal Association meeting in the Corn Exchange on Tuesday, August 29. He described the Queen's statement as the "excess of stupidity and impudence" but denied that it was a true indication of her views on the Irish Question. He insisted that she was merely echoing the opinions of her ministers, and he promised to liberate their "lovable Queen" from those "miscreants" and Ireland from tyranny. O'Connell asked the Association to appoint a committee to help him draft an address to their fellow British subjects all over the world detailing the case for Repeal. He said that this address and their loyalty to Repeal would be the Irish nation's reply to the Peel inspired Queen's speech.[1]

A week later in the Corn Exchange rooms O'Connell repeated the charge that the Queen's speech in reality was a pronouncement by Peel and that Victoria had become a captive of Tory politicians. He accused the Prime Minister and his cabinet colleagues of treason in their effort to undermine the loyalty and the love that the Irish people entertained for the monarch. He went on to suggest that he might adopt a policy of passive resistance to any British effort to destroy Repeal. He said that there were many ways he could create chaos in the ranks of Ireland's enemy. For example, the Irish people could subsist on potatoes and leave the harvest rotting in the fields and they could refuse to consume excisable commodities. But O'Connell did not commit himself to passive resistance; he merely said that he would consider it: "He would not shrink from anything that the laws of God and man would approve for the restoration of their country's rights."[2]

On Wednesday, September 13, O'Connell presented the completed *Address to the Inhabitants of the Countries Subject to the British Crown* to the Repeal Association. The address included the usual list of Irish grievances: Protestant ascendancy, unequal representation in Parliament, inadequate municipal and parliamentary franchises, landlord absenteeism, overtaxation, exploitation of tenant farmers by landlords, and discrimination against Catholics in appointments to Government office. It argued that the

[1] *Freeman's Journal*, August 30, 1843.
[2] *Ibid.*, September 5, 1843.

refusal of either Whig or Tory administrations to govern Ireland with impartial justice demonstrated that Ireland could achieve peace and prosperity only through the guidance of a native parliament. O'Connell requested the support of world opinion for Ireland's constitutional struggle for legislative independence, and he promised to continue the effort to repeal the Union. In the address the Repeal leader again insisted that the ministers forced the Queen to condemn Repeal against her will and better judgement.[3]

At the Monster Meetings O'Connell, in even more emotional language than that used at the Corn Exchange, made every effort, despite the Queen's expressed views on Repeal, to preserve the fiction that Victoria had a deep devotion for the Irish peasant masses and that she would acknowledge the plea of Irish national opinion for political liberty. He assured the hundreds of thousands who came great distances to hear and see him that the Queen did not mean what she said on August 24. Like Ireland, she was the prisoner of Peel and his henchmen—"a selfish degraded administration who having got into power to serve an unworthy party, seek to continue their authority by exciting the anti-Irish passions of the English people against this oppressed nation."[4] These traitors to the best interests of monarchy might attempt to turn the Irish people from their loyalty to the Queen by placing anti-Repeal statements in her mouth, but the Irish people from bitter experience knew the character of their adversaries and they would not desert their beloved sovereign.

In addition to his attempt to preserve admiration for Victoria among the Irish masses, O'Connell told rain

---

[3] "Lastly, to crown all, they (the Ministers) conclude the session with a speech—which they cause the Queen to pronounce, of course the Minister's speech—full of sound and fury—giving us for all relief and redress—for all conciliation and kindness, the absurdity of ministerial assertion, and the insolence of half-whipt ministerial anger." (*Nation*, September 16, 1843.)

[4] *Freeman's Journal*, September 12, 1843.

drenched Connacht audiences at Loughrea and Clifden
that he would not wage war against the British unless they
initiated violence. He said that if he was forced to fight
he was confident that the men of Connemara who despised
"Saxon tyranny" would stand behind him. At the banquet following the Loughrea outdoor meeting, O'Connell
warned the foes of Repeal that if they crushed the agitation
they might reap a bloody harvest. He said that he designed
the Repeal Association as a safety valve to frustrate more
violent expressions of nationalist sentiment.[5]

After a few weeks of belligerent attacks on the Government and veiled threats of active and passive resistance to
legislation constructed to destroy the Repeal Association,
O'Connell decided that the tactics used at Mallow in June
to sustain public confidence in himself and Repeal could
be most dangerous in September. The decline in Repeal
rent was only one sign that the Irish masses were impatient
with the progress of constitutional agitation. It was now
apparent to all that 1843 would not be the Repeal Year
and that Peel was not prepared to make any major concessions to the demands of organized Irish national opinion. But the discipline, the enthusiasm, the patience, and
the confidence of the Repeal rank and file must have their
reward or frustration might transform these virtues of the
agitation into a desperate, wild, and futile effort to achieve
by force of primitive arms what constitutional agitation
had failed to win by reason, petition, and moral intimidation. The ugly, melancholy Irish winter was setting in.
For the peasantry, making pikes and plotting rebellion
would serve as an escape from the monotony and misery
of short, rainy days and the long, cold, damp nights.
Several incidents, small in themselves but omens of a
bloody future, convinced O'Connell that he must pacify
rather than excite his followers.

5 *Ibid.; Pilot,* September 20, 1843.

The Repeal leader was obviously disturbed with the effect his response to the Queen's speech had on some of the Repealers. On September 11, during a Repeal Association meeting at the Corn Exchange, E. W. O'Mahony received a great round of applause when he said that the "Repealers of Ireland now defied the whole Saxon oligarchy to murder any of them" and went on to describe the Prime Minister as "silly, ridiculous, do-nothing Peel." Again he heard shouts of approval when he said that at O'Connell's command millions of Repealers would rush into battle "with a wild shout of joy, which would make the heavens ring." They would either die in battle or win a parliament for Ireland.[6] This desire to die for "old Ireland" appeared contagious and the clergy seemed most susceptible to the virus. The Rev. Dr. Kirwan told the Clifden Monster Meeting banquet audience that the Catholic clergy of Ireland lived with and for their people and "with the people and for the people every good priest is ever prepared to die."[7]

Militant speeches at the Corn Exchange, on public platforms, or in public houses could indicate a drift away from constitutional toward physical force nationalism, or they could be merely gusts of hot air produced by the excitement of the Repeal agitation, but the proposal of William Conner of Inch was a truly dangerous threat to O'Connell's style of agitation because it outlined an alternative course of action. On Monday, September 18, while O'Connell was still in the West, Conner, a kinsman of Fergus O'Connor, the Chartist leader, and a man who had proved his devotion to the tenant right cause by serving a prison sentence for its advocacy, gave notice of the following motion which he intended to introduce at the next Monday meeting of the Association: "That until our

[6] *Freeman's Journal,* September 12, 1843.
[7] *Pilot,* September 20, 1843.

national right of self-legislation comes into the possession of our own parliament and of a valuation and perpetuity of the farm to the tenant, we, Repealers, shall pay no rent, court cess, rent-charge, tithe, poor rate, or any charge out of land."

Conner defended his proposal with the argument that since nothing had been accomplished for Ireland by the traditional tactics of constitutional nationalism it was time for the Repeal Association to adopt a new departure. He said that "a starving people have been too long paying away pounds, shillings, and pence while their just rights are withheld from them," and that they must not be permitted to starve "while their crops are taken from them to pay rents and taxes." Conner realized that the members of the Repeal Association might refuse to accept his motion so he asked the journalists in attendance to carry his message to the Irish people through the newspapers they represented.

With his father in the country, John O'Connell took charge of the anti-Conner forces. He praised Conner's dedication to the tenant right cause but asked him to withdraw from a position which might encourage the Irish masses to abandon constitutional nationalism and to come into direct conflict with the police and the military. The "Young Liberator" said Conner's tactics, if adopted by the Association, would tarnish the Repeal cause and drive men of influence and character from its ranks. He threatened to move Conner's expulsion from the Association unless he withdrew his motion by the next day. O'Connell then submitted a series of resolutions condemning Conner's strategy as "grossly illegal and tending directly to create and encourage criminal outrage and violence throughout the country," refusing to place the notice on the Association records, and labeling all those who put forward such suggestions as "madmen or traitors to the glorious cause of Repeal, to the noble people who support the cause, and to 'Old Ireland.' " These resolutions received the enthusiastic and unanimous endorsement of those present in the Corn Exchange rooms.[8]

Conner in reply to John O'Connell said that he would rather surrender his life than withdraw the notice of motion, and he announced his resignation from the Loyal National Repeal Association. On Thursday, September 21, John O'Connell moved the acceptance of the resignation, and everyone seemed happy to see and hear the last of William Conner in the Corn Exchange. In seconding young O'Connell's motion William J. O'Neill Daunt described the no-rent proposal as an "anti-social doctrine" and insisted that the Repeal Association was as anxious to defend the rights of landlords as it was to insist that they honor their duties as property owners.[9]

When Daniel O'Connell returned to Repeal headquarters on September 27 he censured members of the Repeal Association for handling Conner with kid gloves. He said that this enemy of property rights should have been tossed out on the street as soon as he expressed his subversive ideas. He described Conner as a mischief maker attempting to make an impression and a coward who waited until the President of the Repeal Association was out of town before attempting to commit Irish nationalism to an anti-property position. O'Connell called Conner a traitor to Repeal, insisted that his name be erased from the books

8 *Ibid.; Nation,* September 23, 1843. Conner was arraigned at the 1842 spring assizes for a speech he made at Wolf Hill, December 26, 1841. In that speech he claimed that landlords were responsible for the evils of Ireland—tenant insecurity and the outrage and murder resulting from that insecurity. They squeezed the tenant farmer in an economic vise of rent, tithes, taxes, and poor rates. He argued that the laws of the land were constructed to benefit the class interests of the gentry. For this speech Conner was found guilty of sedition on six counts and sentenced to prison for six months (*Evening Mail,* September 29, 1843). In 1848 James Fintan Lalor became a national figure and won permanent fame for suggesting a program similar to the one recommended by Conner in 1843. The *Nation* and the rest of the Repeal press endorsed O'Connell's condemnation of Conner.

9 *Nation,* September 23, 1843.

of the Association and, like Daunt, associated Repeal with the legitimate rights of property.[10]

The *Evening Mail* used Conner's motion as evidence that O'Connell was preparing a no-rent campaign to distract the attention of the Irish masses from his failure to obtain Repeal and that the Repeal movement was implicated in a no-rent agitation then underway in Carlow.[11] When the Repeal Association repudiated Conner and defended property rights and when John O'Connell pointed out that Carlow was one of the few counties where Repeal had little influence, the *Mail* still refused to accept the pro-property commitment of the Repeal leaders as sincere. The editor claimed that O'Connell's and Daunt's attacks on Conner were pious masks to hide the agrarian radicalism at the heart of the Repeal agitation. He said that O'Connell shrewdly tried to camouflage his real intentions and that Conner was punished because he had stupidly let the cat out of the bag.[12]

The apparent restlessness in Repeal ranks, the no-rent campaign in Carlow, Conner's attempt to commit the Association to agrarian radicalism, and a decline in the Repeal rent to the lowest point since mid-May—all helped convince O'Connell that he must use his great powers of persuasion to curb the impatience of his followers and to prepare them for a long struggle for Irish reform.[13] At the Clifden banquet he told his audience that he might be forced to slow down the Repeal agitation and that neither the scoffs of his enemies nor the misguided advice of his friends would force him into precipitate action. Prudence and circumstances would determine his future conduct. The people might have to stand by him longer than

10 *Freeman's Journal*, September 28, 1843.
11 *Evening Mail*, September 20, 1843.
12 *Ibid.*
13 On September 25 the Loyal National Repeal Association announced its weekly rent collection as £ 689, 11s, 6d, the smallest weekly return since May 8.

originally anticipated. He would have to postpone assembling the Preservative Society until early 1844. Again O'Connell mentioned the possibility that Repealers might resort to techniques of passive resistance if the Government resorted to coercion. They could "checkmate the Government of England" by letting crops rot in the fields. Britain's foreign relations were in too delicate a condition for her to push the Irish people to the wall. O'Connell promised the people at Clifden that he would accept nothing short of Repeal as the price of disbanding his forces and that by the last scheduled Monster Meeting at Clontarf, in early October, the discipline of the Repealers would be complete and nine-tenths of Ulster would be committed to the cause of self government.[14]

On Sunday, September 24, O'Connell was at Lismore in County Waterford. While there he warned Repealers that the Government might attempt to bribe them with something less than an Irish parliament, but he assured them that he would never consent to dishonorable terms. However, he said, the "stage coach of the constitution was going down hill too rapidly" and he found it necessary to act as "a drag upon the wheels." They should not listen to those who advised them to go faster than their leader recommended. Their safety was in his hands "and he would consent to the shedding of no man's blood, save his own." He would take them safely and successfully through the current crisis if they left the management of the agitation to his direction. They would have Repeal—not at once but in degrees.[15]

At the Lismore banquet O'Connell again cautioned prudence and warned against unrestrained enthusiasm— an obvious rebuke to those members of the Repeal clergy who harped on war and martyrdom. Once more he compared the Repeal agitation to a stage coach needing a

14 *Pilot*, September 22, 1843.
15 *Ibid.*, September 27, 1843.

brake on its wheels to reach the bottom of the hill in safety. He said that his duty was now to restrain when formerly it had been to excite. O'Connell concluded his remarks with an appeal for public confidence in his leadership while he continued to plan and negotiate future steps in the Repeal march to victory, and he challenged the Government to test in the courts the legality of the nationalist agitation.[16]

At Mullaghmast in County Kildare on October 1 O'Connell asked the Repealers of the Midlands to continue their support for constitutional nationalism. He promised them that he would achieve an Irish parliament without the hardships and the human sacrifices of war. "Ireland," he said, "is worth dying for but also worth disciplining yourself for." He conceded that the time might come when it would be necessary for them to risk their lives for Irish independence, but he insisted that they should never depart from constitutional principles by initiating an armed conflict with the British. They must retain the right on their side.

O'Connell's remarks at Mullaghmast indicated that he had abandoned any hope of pressuring Peel into making concessions to organized Irish opinion. He seemed to be preparing his forces for a long struggle and an eventual renewal of the Whig alliance once Russell and Palmerston were in office. He promised that when Conciliation Hall was completed and when the Tories no longer held office he would submit his plan for an Irish House of Commons to the Queen. He insisted that they could accomplish nothing for Ireland as long as unprincipled men like Peel, phony heroes like Wellington, and "turncoat Whigs" like Graham and Stanley controlled the British Government. O'Connell concluded his speech with a typical example of his mob oratory designed to tranquilize and flatter a public opinion dangerously close to anarchy: "Yes, among the

16 *Ibid.*

nations of the earth, Ireland stands numbered one in the physical strength of her sons, and in the beauty and purity of her daughters. Ireland, land of my forefathers, how my mind expands and my spirit walks abroad in something of majesty when I contemplate the high qualities, inestimable virtues, the true purity of your green fields and productive mountains! Oh! what a scene surrounds us—it is not only the countless thousands of brave, and active, and peaceable, and religious men that are assembled, but nature has written her character with the finest beauty in the verdant plains that surround us. Let any man run around the horizon with his eye and tell me if creative nature ever produced anything so green and so lovely, so undulating, so teeming with production. The richest harvests that any land can produce are those reaped in Ireland; and then, hers are the sweetest meadows, the greenest fields, the loftiest mountains, the purest streams, the noblest rivers, the most capacious harbors—and her water power is equal to turn the machinery of the whole world. Oh, my friends, it is a country worth fighting for; but above all, it is a country worth being tranquil, determined, submissive, and docile for, disciplined as you are, in obedience to those who are breaking the way and trampling down the barriers between you and your constitutional liberty."[17]

The Government, the editor of the *Evening Mail*, con stabulary officials, and intelligent, interested, and experienced observers of the Irish scene interpreted the decline in Repeal rent, increasing peasant interest in the normal pursuits of agriculture at the expense of agitation, and O'Connell's decision not to assemble his Council of Three Hundred before the end of the year as indications that Repeal and its leader were in full retreat.[18] Naturally Peel and his colleagues were pleased that their method of han-

17 *Ibid.*, October 2, 1843.
18 Earl of Devon to Lord Eliot, September 8, 1843, Lord Clare to Eliot, September 9, 1843, Graham Papers; Graham to Peel, September 22, 23, 1843, Add. MSS 40440, B.M.; *Evening Mail*, September 29, 1843.

dling the Irish crisis resulted in a victory without the use of coercion, but they had no intention of permitting the Repeal leaders to escape the consequences of insulting and defying the Government. The Irish legal authorities, with prompting from the Home Office in London, continued to prepare sedition cases against nationalist newspaper editors and Repeal leaders. Wellington was particularly insistent that journalists and Repeal orators be prosecuted for articles and speeches directed against the loyalty of British troops stationed in Ireland.

Wellington and Irish legal authorities claimed that articles published in the Galway *Vindicator,* the *Nation,* and the *Pilot* encouraged Irishmen serving in the British army to refuse to fight against an Irish nationalist or popular cause. They also argued that these articles attempted to intimidate the Government by emphasizing that the British army had a large proportion of enlisted men who might join forces with Irish nationalism in a crisis.

On September 25 the *Pilot* had printed an editorial, "The Army, the People, and the Government," which insisted that the army was the servant of the taxpayers. The editorial also emphasized that since enlisted personnel came from the lower classes they should not be used to serve the class interests of their aristocratic officers. In the same issue of the *Pilot* there was an article about three soldiers who cheered for Repeal at the Loughrea Monster Meeting. This article described the army as a two edged sword, which could be used against the Government which wielded it, and stressed the class conflict dividing officers and enlisted men. This same issue of the *Pilot* also contained an editorial devoted to General Andrew Jackson. The former American President was described as a "fiery eyed" Celt and "an Irishman" who was wounded on the cheek at twelve by a "British brute." Jackson was portrayed as a lawyer by vocation and a soldier by circumstance who had not "served his apprenticeship as a hireling to the committing of murder like Wellington." In October 1843, because of the articles and editorials in this issue of the *Pilot*, the editor, Richard Barrett, was indicted for sedition and alienating the loyalty of British soldiers.

The Government also investigated some letters on the "Duty of a Soldier" published in the *Nation* and John Cornelius O'Callaghan's pamphlet, *The Irish in the English Army and Navy and the Irish Arms Bill*, which sold around forty thousand copies. O'Callaghan claimed that there were forty-two thousand "Paddies" in the British army and that this large Irish element would be a source of weakness to a British Government which attempted to suppress Irish nationalism through military methods. He also argued that British soldiers were responsible, decent men who would not shoot down patriots engaged in a legitimate struggle for national independence. The Irish law officers decided that the *Nation* and O'Callaghan were technically innocent of sedition. Government officials also ordered an investigation of the ballad singers who entertained the people with songs praising O'Connell and Repeal and ridiculing Peel, Wellington, and the British Government.[19]

In the effort to collect evidence against O'Connell the Government used the services of a journalist named Ross who was assigned by the *Standard* (London) to cover Repeal activities in Ireland. Early in September the Home Office sent a member of the London metropolitan police, a man by the name of Hughes, to Dublin to pose as a journalist to assist Ross in collecting evidence against O'Connell and the rest of the Repeal hierarchy.[20] O'Connell quickly discovered Hughes's true identity and pur-

[19] The Peel-Graham correspondence in early September 1843 (Add. MSS 40449, B.M.) and the Eliot-Graham correspondence in early and mid-September (Graham Papers) reveal the Government's anxiety concerning the nationalist press.

[20] Graham to Eliot, September 4, 11, 18, 1843, Graham Papers.

pose, and for some time the Government spy feared for his life. But his anxieties vanished when O'Connell insisted that Repealers extend him every courtesy, make him comfortable at meetings, and furnish him with all of the information he requested.[21]

While Peel and Eliot seemed content with developments in Ireland, Graham and Wellington still feared an insurrection.[22] The Duke was particularly nervous and requested leave to go over to Ireland and deal with the situation, but he was persuaded by Peel to remain in London. Peel and Graham believed that Wellington's presence in Ireland would disturb rather than pacify the elements of discontent.[23] Graham suspected that the Loyal National Repeal Association was a constitutional front hiding a revolutionary conspiracy. These suspicions seemed to be confirmed when a Repeal Warden in County Meath named MacLoughlin was captured by the police with papers on his person indicating that he was a member of a secret revolutionary society which used O'Connell's name

[21] In a report submitted to Eliot by John Dopping, R.M., it was stated that at the Mullaghmast Monster Meeting, October 1, O'Connell recognized and exposed Hughes as a Government spy and that when Hughes admitted his official position, the Repeal leader directed his followers to show him every courtesy. But it was also noted that O'Connell kept the speakers at the meeting in line (Graham Papers). On October 3 Eliot reported to Graham that Hughes was so well treated at the Corn Exchange he no longer considered himself in danger of being assaulted (Graham Papers).

[22] Wellington was also convinced by his Orange friends in Ireland that O'Connell would lead a no-rent campaign to distract attention from his failure to obtain Repeal (Eliot to Graham, September 25, Graham to Eliot, September 21, 1843, Graham Papers). Graham did not dismiss the possibility of a no-rent campaign but he was more concerned about O'Connell leading a revolt: "he has arrived at a point when not to advance is dangerous; and he will either be pushed forward by the crowd, which follows him, or his spell will be broken." (Graham to Peel, September 23, 1843, Add. MSS 40449, B.M.)

[23] On September 16, 1843, Graham wrote Peel that Wellington wanted to go to Ireland "and believes that the winds and waves will obey him and that in his presence there will be a great calm. I entertain an opposite opinion. If there were a rebellion, his iron hand would crush it. I doubt much whether his preventive measures would be of a soothing or tranquilizing character." (Add. MSS 40449, B.M.)

and other Repeal symbols and slogans as part of its system of signs and passwords. Graham was confident that if MacLoughlin could be made to talk he would implicate the Repeal leadership in a conspiracy to destroy the Union by violence. The Home Office instructed Eliot to do everything possible to induce MacLoughlin to become a Government informer.[24]

Eliot, who was in full charge of the Dublin situation while DeGrey was on sick leave, refused to take the Mac-Loughlin incident seriously. He told Graham that it was clear that the Meath Repeal Warden was a Ribbonman and that all Ribbonmen endorsed Repeal to attract members into their lodges, but that this did not mean that all Repealers were Ribbonmen.[25] Eliot accepted O'Connell's sincerity in condemning secret societies. He knew the Repeal leader was much too clever to become involved with physical force nationalists: "They are dangerous to him and useless. He now wields the power of the masses; he has at his command the priesthood and peasants of Ireland. What good would a parcel of Ribbon lodges with their oaths and signs and passwords do him? Is he a man to trust his neck to a parcel of low uneducated persons?"[26]

Major E. Priestly, a constabulary official, in describing

24 Graham to Peel, September 16, 1843, Add. MSS 40449, B.M.; Graham to Eliot, September 19, 1843, Graham Papers. In his letter to Eliot Graham admitted that Peel thought there was little chance to connect MacLoughlin with O'Connell.

25 Eliot to Graham, September 20, 1843, Graham Papers. Ribbon lodges were secret societies organized in the eighteenth century to protect the economic interests of tenant farmers and agricultural laborers. Sometimes they were linked with proletarian movements in the cities. Ribbonmen fought the tithe, excessive fees by the Catholic clergy, exorbitant rents, and evictions with strong methods. They burned hay ricks, maimed cattle, and occasionally shot a landlord or his agent or a farmer that occupied the land of a man recently evicted. The term Ribbonmen came from the fact that members of the lodges wore a green badge. The movement probably was a response to the formation of the Protestant Orange Order. For more information on Ribbonmen and other proletarian protest movements see R. B. McDowell, *Public Opinion and Government Policy in Ireland, 1801-1846* (London, 1952), 59-65.

26 Eliot to Graham, September 22, 1843, Graham Papers.

Repeal activity in Tipperary and Limerick, also dismissed the probability of an insurrection. He said that the endorsement Repeal received from French and American republicans alienated many conservative Catholics and that O'Connell's abolitionist sentiments antagonized many Irish-Americans, particularly those residing in the Southern and border states. Priestly reported that many tenant farmers in Munster were complaining about excessive rents and indicating their impatience with the slow march of Repeal, but he insisted that most Irish peasants in the fall of 1843 were too occupied with an abundant harvest and with preparing their turf for winter to join revolutionary conspiracies or combinations against the payment of rent. He credited the temperance and Repeal movements with pacifying and disciplining the Irish masses to the point where there was little danger of violence in rural Ireland.[27]

September 23 was an important date in the 1843 Repeal chronicle. On that day Eliot informed Graham that the Irish Attorney General, T. B. C. Smith, and his staff had decided that the portion of O'Connell's *Address to the Inhabitants of the Countries Subject to the British Crown* dealing with the monarch constituted seditious libel, and that if the newspaper versions of the address corresponded to the actual words used by the Repeal leader in the Corn Exchange, the Government would have excellent grounds to prosecute.[28]

In this letter and in one sent on September 29 Eliot discussed the many difficulties involved in prosecuting O'Connell. There was the risk that the Government in bringing O'Connell to trial might rescue him from the consequences of his own words and actions. Since he could not redeem his pledge to deliver Repeal before the end of the year and he would never lead a revolutionary movement,

[27] Priestly to Eliot, September 4, 30, 1843, Graham Papers.
[28] Graham Papers.

he was about to be exposed as a windy old fraud. But once he was arrested and brought to trial he would become a martyr and the Irish masses would rally to his cause. And of course there was always the possibility that a Dublin jury would acquit O'Connell, and in Ireland this would be interpreted as a Government defeat and the flame of Repeal would burn brighter. However, in weighing the potential benefits to be derived from a prosecution against the potential dangers, the Chief Secretary decided that it would be better to arrest O'Connell and bring him to trial than to ignore his defiance of the Government. He reasoned that legal action against its leader would force the Repeal Association either to submit to this humiliation, thereby admitting all the threats of the summer were idle boasts, or to resist the arrest, abandon the mask of constitutionality, reveal the seditious character of the agitation, and give the Government the necessary evidence and opportunity to smash it. And of course there was a good chance that an impartial jury could be found to vote for a conviction. Once O'Connell was behind prison walls the myth of his invincibility would be destroyed along with his hold over the Irish masses. Even if the Government failed in its efforts to convict O'Connell, it would have demonstrated its determination to deal sternly with treason and its intention to preserve the Union.[29]

As soon as Graham received word from Dublin that the Irish law officers thought that they had the makings of a good case of seditious libel against O'Connell, he contacted DeGrey and Sugden and asked them to meet with him in London so they could all discuss the ramifications of a prosecution with Peel, the British Attorney General, Sir Jonathan Pollack, and the Solicitor General, Sir William Follette.[30] But while Graham and Peel were planning their London conference with the Irish administration,

29 Graham Papers.
30 Graham to DeGrey, September 25, 1843, Graham to Sugden, October 2, 1843, Graham Papers.

Eliot discovered that there was a serious flaw in the Government's case against O'Connell.

Because of legal technicalities the case against O'Connell would lose much of its strength if the Government could not establish that the words used by the Repeal leader in the Corn Exchange on September 13 were exactly the same as the contents of the address published in the newspapers. For this evidence the Government had to rely on the testimony of Ross. However, when the Irish Attorney General interviewed the journalist from the *Standard* he learned that Ross stopped taking notes shortly after O'Connell began to speak and that he obtained his copy of the address from T. M. Ray, Secretary of the Repeal Association, after the meeting was over. Ross failed to initial the copy he received from Ray before he sent it off to the editor of the *Standard,* he could not remember who was at the meeting, except for O'Connell, and he could not recall if the address was unanimously adopted by the Repeal Association (these last two points were important because the Irish legal authorities considered making charges against all those present in the Corn Exchange rooms on September 13).[31] The unsatisfactory testimony of its chief witness forced the Government to seek the services of more reliable journalists. Irish legal experts decided to use Jackson of the *Morning Herald* since his report of the Repeal meeting was more extensive than the one submitted by Ross, and he was present when Ray handed the *Standard* correspondent an official copy of the address.[32]

[31] Eliot to Graham, September 29, 1843, report from T. B. C. Smith to Eliot, October 3, 1843, Graham Papers.

[32] Eliot to Graham, September 29, 1843, Smith to Graham, October 5, 1843, Graham Papers. Smith thought that they would use the Arbitration Courts against O'Connell as evidence of sedition. He said that they were not technically illegal but they were an attempt "to bring the Constitution of the country and the administration of justice into contempt." Eliot did not want to use the *Times* Irish correspondent because he was Catholic and his paper was hostile to the Government (Eliot to Graham, October 6, 1843, Graham Papers).

When Peel, Graham, DeGrey, Sugden, Follette, and Pollack met at Lord Lyndhurst's house in George Street, Hanover Square, on Tuesday, October 3, to discuss the prudence of prosecuting O'Connell, they were confronted with a new development in Dublin. On October 2 Eliot sent Graham a copy of the following notice which was issued by the Loyal National Repeal Association, published in the nationalist press, and posted throughout the city of Dublin.

REPEAL CAVALRY
CLONTARF MEETING

The Committee for this great National Demonstration, being apprised of the intention of many Repealers to appear mounted at "Conquer Hill!!!" Clontarf, recommend the following rules to be observed for the regulation of the Cavalcade at this first

MUSTER AND MARCH OF THE MOUNTED
REPEAL VOLUNTEERS!!!

1st—All mounted Repealers of the City, or from the South and West side of the County, to muster on the open ground, Harcourt-street fields, on Sunday the 8th of October, at 12 o'clock at noon, and form into troops, each troop to consist of twenty-five horsemen, to be led by one officer in front, followed by six ranks, four abreast, half distance, each bearing a wand and cockade, distinguishing the number of his respective troop.

2nd—That regulation wands and cockades will be furnished by the Committee to such gentlemen of the City or County as shall apply, and be approved of, to lead each troop.

3rd—That no person shall be permitted to join the Cavalcade without a cockade and wand; and that until one Troop is complete no second Troop shall be formed.

N.B.—The Committee will make the necessary arrangements, to prevent delay or confusion, at the Turnpike Gates.

4th—Each Horseman to take and keep the place assigned to him on joining his Troops, and remain in rank until dismissal of the parade in the meeting field.

5th—That such Troops as shall have formed by half-past 12 o'clock to proceed in their order at slow time by the following route—Harcourt-street, Stephen's green, West; Grafton-street, Westmorland-street, Sackville-street, Britain-street, Summer-hill, Ballybough-bridge, Clontarf-road.

6th—The mounted Repealers from the Northern parts of the County to muster and form, as above prescribed, at the Southern extremity of the Howth-road, and bring up the rear of the Dublin Cavalcade to the meeting-field, Conquer Hill.

7th—That the Chairman and members of the Committee, bearing wands and cockades, do form the mounted staff in advance; and that the muster, march, and parade, at the meeting-field, shall be under their sole order and direction until dismissed after the proceedings of the meeting have commenced.

8th—That the Horsemen on the meeting ground shall keep a proper distance from the platform, so as not to incommode those attending on foot; and it is earnestly requested on the other hand, that no obstruction or interruption will be offered to the Cavalcade by those on foot or in vehicles, so that the order and regularity of the march may be preserved.

GOD SAVE THE QUEEN!
MOUNT FOR REPEAL!—MARCH FOR CLONTARF!

The Committee will meet at the Corn-Exchange each day during the ensuing week, from Four to Five o'clock. Corn-Exchange, 30th September, 1843.[33]

[33] *Nation*, September 30, 1843.

After reading the announcement of the Clontarf meeting Eliot was convinced that the use of military terms like march, muster, troops, cavalry, and cockades provided the Government with sufficient grounds to outlaw the cavalcade and perhaps the meeting itself.[34] Many Protestant leaders urged him to ban the parade to Clontarf because the proposed route would interfere with Sunday religious services. However, the Irish law officers could not agree on the wisdom of outlawing the Clontarf cavalcade and meeting. The Attorney General wanted Eliot to let the meeting take place because it might produce further evidence that could be used against O'Connell in the court room. Smith was supported by one of his assistants, but the other defended Eliot's view that the Government could not maintain its dignity or prestige by permitting a Repeal demonstration of such an obviously military nature.[35]

The notice of the Clontarf meeting was written and issued by a committee of the Loyal National Repeal Association while O'Connell was in Kildare in connection with the Mullaghmast Monster Meeting. As soon as he returned to Dublin he reprimanded the committee for posting and publishing a notice which could lead to legal reprisals. He then had a new notice sent out which omitted all of the military terms included in the original publicity, and he promised to change the parade route so that it would not interfere with any Protestant religious services.[36] On October 3 Eliot wrote Graham that the new

34 Eliot to Graham, October 2, 1843, Graham Papers.

35 Eliot included the comments of Smith's assistants, Greene and Brewster, as well as the opinion of the Attorney General in his letter to Graham.

36 *Pilot*, October 4, 1843. In the revised Clontarf notice "Repeal Cavalry" was changed to "Repealers on Horseback," "Conquer Hill" disappeared from the first paragraph, "at this first muster and march of the mounted repeal volunteers" was eliminated, "troops" were changed to "groups," "cockades" were no longer referred to, and words like "muster," "march," and "parade" were eliminated (*Freeman's Journal*, October 3, 1843). T. B. C. Smith commented that the revised notice

notice and O'Connell's willingness to satisfy Protestant religious sensibilities convinced him that the Clontarf meeting and procession, like previous Repeal demonstrations, was completely within the framework of the law and that the members of the Irish administration were in unanimous agreement that it should not be banned.[37]

Before the Chief Secretary's altered view on the Clontarf meeting reached the Home Office, Peel, Graham, Sugden, DeGrey, and the British law officers had already reached a decision on the Irish situation. The Prime Minister and his Home Secretary ordered DeGrey and Sugden back to Dublin with instructions to prevent the Clontarf meeting and to complete arrangements for the prosecution of O'Connell.[38] Graham realized that the Government's decision to crack down on Repeal would mean a critical two weeks in Ireland. Since Clontarf was to be the site of the last Repeal demonstration of the year many thousands of people from all sections of Ireland, and nearly a thousand Repealers from Liverpool and Manchester, planned to be in Dublin for the occasion. Would hundreds of thousands of Irish nationalists in a high state of excitement permit

must have been authored by a lawyer with the obvious intention of avoiding the processions act (Eliot to Graham, October 3, 1843, Graham Papers). Since Protestant leaders did protest to the Lord Mayor that the route of the Clontarf procession would disturb their religious services, Eliot could have used this as sufficient grounds to ban the cavalcade if O'Connell had not agreed to change its route (DeGrey to Graham, October 7, 1843, Graham Papers; *Evening Mail*, October 6, 1843).

37 Graham Papers.

38 There can be no doubt that DeGrey had some discretionary powers to deal with the situation, but it is also clear that he had orders to use the Clontarf meeting notice as the issue to justify a crackdown on the Repeal Association. In a letter marked confidential and dated October 6, 1843, Peel declined an invitation to spend a weekend with the Duke of Buccleuch because of the "continued agitation in Ireland." He told the Duke that "we have thought it expedient to require Lord DeGrey and Sir Edward Sugden to return to Ireland—and, if the law will permit, to adopt some measures for bringing the present state of things to an issue. . . . The notice of a cavalry Repeal meeting near Dublin for Sunday next appears to afford a favourable opportunity for action." (Add. MSS 40533, B.M.)

the authorities to ruin their combination holiday and patriotic demonstration, and would they stomach the final humiliation, the arrest of their leader? An insurrection could start in Ireland on the day the Government announced its intention to prevent the Clontarf meeting, the day the meeting was to be held, or any period shortly after the arrest of O'Connell. So in order to support the Irish authorities in their dangerous mission, Graham ordered two naval vessels, one designed for river navigation, to Cork and a large number of soldiers to Kingstown to await DeGrey's orders.[39]

When the Lord Lieutenant arrived in Dublin on Friday morning, October 6, rumors immediately spread through the city that he had returned to suppress the Repeal movement.[40] Even O'Connell was convinced that DeGrey would ban the Clontarf meeting.[41] But Lord Eliot, thinking that the Clontarf issue had been settled, was sure that DeGrey's sole purpose in coming to Dublin was to be present when O'Connell was arrested.[42] So the Lord Lieutenant had to reverse the Chief Secretary's decision and initiate the legal process which would result in a ban on the Clontarf demonstration. At one o'clock Friday afternoon he met with Eliot, Sugden, Smith, and the other Irish law officers and said that he wanted a proclamation outlawing the Clontarf meeting ready for a session of the Irish Privy Council which would be called for ten o'clock the next morning. DeGrey then arranged for 2,500 soldiers, 500 Dublin

[39] Graham to DeGrey, October 6, 1843, Graham Papers.
[40] On October 6 the *Evening Mail* reported that the Government would issue a proclamation "cautioning her Majesty's subjects from attending meetings convened under the pretext of petitioning for the Repeal of the Legislative Union—such merely being calculated to excite alarm, and lead to a breach of the peace. . . ."
[41] In his letter to Graham on October 7 (Graham Papers) DeGrey reported that O'Connell told Hughes, the Government reporter, that very morning that he knew the Government would issue a proclamation banning the Clontarf meeting. DeGrey also said rumors of a proclamation were all over the city of Dublin.
[42] Eliot to Graham, October 5, 1843, Graham Papers.

policemen, and 400 constables to maintain order at Clontarf and in the city from the time the Government
proclamation was posted until it was obvious that there
was no danger to the peace.[43]

When the Privy Council met at ten on Saturday morning there were some objections to the phrasing of the
proclamation submitted by the law officers, and they were
asked to rewrite it. This revision delayed the posting of
the proclamation until three in the afternoon.[44] In the
proclamation the Lord Lieutenant, with the advice and
consent of the Privy Council, banned the Clontarf meeting because it had the character of a military display and
because men experienced in language of a seditious and
inflamatory nature planned to put in an appearance on
Conquer Hill. DeGrey said that the Repeal leaders did
not call the Clontarf meeting to exercise their constitutional right of petition. He insisted that their real motives were to encourage hate and contempt for the Government and the Constitution and to intimidate Her
Majesty's ministers by a display of military force. Since
the objectives of the meeting were so obviously seditious,
he argued that he had no choice but to outlaw the Clontarf demonstration and to threaten all those who planned
to defy the proclamation with the certainty of legal prosecution. DeGrey asked all of the Irish magistrates to help
the Government suppress the Clontarf meeting, keep people away from the meeting site, and prosecute those defying the orders of the Irish Administration.[45]

Since the Repeal leaders expected a Government ban

43 DeGrey to Graham, October 6, 1843, Graham Papers. DeGrey, once
he arrived in Dublin, had to decide whether the revised Clontarf notice
destroyed the Government's case for a ban on the meeting. After he talked
to the Irish law officers he ruled that the new notice was just a correction
and supplement and not a cancellation of the original advertisement
(DeGrey to Graham, October 7, 1843, Graham Papers).

44 DeGrey to Graham, October 11, 1843, Graham Papers.

45 *Pilot,* October 9, 1843.

on Clontarf ever since DeGrey arrived in Dublin on Friday morning, they were only surprised by the last minute posting of the proclamation. But as soon as O'Connell knew the contents of the Government order he assembled the Repeal hierarchy in the Corn Exchange rooms to consider a reply. Many of the Young Irelanders welcomed the proclamation as an opportunity to cross swords with the Government. Now that the Government had issued a challenge, they hoped that O'Connell would redeem his pledge at Mallow to fight and, if necessary, to die for Ireland.[46] But O'Connell knew the vast chasm that separates words from deeds. If Irishmen fought for Ireland they most certainly would die because they would oppose well trained and equipped British soldiers. Despite the Mallow pledge and other boasts, O'Connell was too responsible a leader to send pike-armed followers to slaughter. Ignoring the hotheaded young men, he ordered compliance with the Government proclamation even though he considered it technically illegal. O'Connell bitterly denounced DeGrey for waiting to post the proclamation until it would be almost impossible for the Repeal Association to turn back the thousands of people on their way to Clontarf. But the Association quickly sent out notices that the Clontarf meeting had been canceled to those assembling at Tara, Kells, and Navan, and messages were also sent to Catholic priests living in the area near the meeting site asking them to turn back people on the way to Clontarf. Then O'Connell drew up a notice to be posted in all sections of Dublin calling off the Clontarf meeting, asking the people to remain calm and to stay in their homes on Sunday, and attacking the Government for its tardy publication of the proclamation. A large number of priests and lay Repealers volunteered to go out on the roads early Sunday morning to keep people coming to the meeting away from Dublin,

46 Charles Gavan Duffy, *Young Ireland*, 1:175-91.

and Tom Steele hurried to Tara to halt the procession which was to march from there to Clontarf.[47]

Late Saturday afternoon the Dublin streets were crowded with people reading the Government proclamation which was posted on bridges, pillars, and post offices and the notice from the Repeal Association hanging next to it. Policemen were stationed in all sections of the city to prevent the defacing and destruction of the proclamation. Just before evening set in workmen began the job of tearing down the speaker's platform and the refreshment tents at the Clontarf meeting site.[48]

On Sunday Dublin was quiet—a testimony to O'Connell's control over the Irish masses and the efficiency of the Repeal Association. No one questioned, at least openly, the orders from their leader. During the early morning hours a large number of troops with four cannon took command of Conquer Hill in Clontarf and the road leading to it. Many members of the constabulary were assigned to Clontarf to augment the military force while policemen patroled the streets of Dublin. During the day three hundred Repealers and a substantial number of soldiers arrived in Dublin from Liverpool. Most of the residents of Dublin took O'Connell's advice and stayed at home, but a few curiosity seekers wearing Repeal caps (shaped like a Chinese mandarin headdress—grey on top, turned up with a white border, ornamented with a single row of shamrocks) wandered the roads near the Clontarf meeting grounds. At three in the afternoon Lieutenant General Blakeney, K.C.B., Commander of Her Majesty's forces in Ireland, accompanied by other important army officers and Colonel McGregor, Inspector General of the Irish constabulary, appeared on Conquer Hill and stayed about an hour. At five the soldiers were ordered from

---

[47] *Pilot,* October 9, 1843.
[48] *Ibid.*

their duty posts. So ended a quiet but tense day in Dublin.[49]

As the events of October 6, 7, and 8 clearly indicate, O'Connell deserves the credit for the preservation of peace in a potentially explosive situation. Many members of Parliament agreed with him that DeGrey deserved a reprimand for posting the Government proclamation so late Saturday afternoon, and there were many in Ireland who suggested that the last minute ban on the Clontarf meeting was part of Government strategy to deliberately provoke a revolution so that it would be justified in crushing Irish nationalism by military force.[50] But we know that the delay in posting the proclamation was the result of inefficiency or stupidity rather than a sinister plot to massacre the Irish masses.[51] No matter what the explanation or justification for DeGrey's tardy ban on the Clontarf meeting, it was O'Connell's reluctance to use physical force, his good sense, and his control over the Irish people that prevented slaughter in Dublin on October 8.

On the other hand, it could be argued with merit that the Government's delay in revealing its intent concerning the Monster Meeting had a beneficial effect. If DeGrey had notified O'Connell on October 6 that he was going to ban the Clontarf demonstration it might have produced

49 *Evening Mail*, October 9, 1843.

50 Graham, in defending the Government's conduct in regard to the proclamation, described to the House of Commons the military character of the original notice of the Clontarf meeting. He said that the revised notice was not satisfactory. Graham claimed that DeGrey and Sugden were given final authority to deal with the Clontarf issue during a meeting they had with him in London. He said the proclamation was not published until late Saturday afternoon because it took that long for it to be printed and receive the Great Seal of Ireland (*Hansard* 72:774ff.). We know that the Home Secretary's statement to Parliament was not quite accurate. DeGrey and Sugden were called to London to discuss a prosecution of O'Connell and not Clontarf, it was pretty definitely decided before they left London that they would issue a proclamation banning the Clontarf meeting, and the lateness in the publication of the proclamation resulted from a controversy concerning its wording.

51 DeGrey to Graham, October 11, 1843, Graham Papers.

a lengthy deliberation in the Corn Exchange and throughout the country on what the Repealers should do in reply to the Lord Lieutenant. The extra time might have given extremists in the national movement time to mobilize and defy O'Connell's order to obey the proclamation. But since the Repeal leaders had only minutes to reach a decision, O'Connell was able to dictate the nationalist response to the Government challenge.

The Monday, October 9, meeting of the Loyal National Repeal Association was moved from the Corn Exchange to Calvert's Theatre Royal in Abbey Street to accommodate all those who wished to attend. Hours before meeting time the streets leading to the theatre were jammed with Repealers. When the meeting opened the crowd inside the theatre was so large that people had difficulty breathing. A tremendous cheer greeted O'Connell when he entered the building. The meeting began with one of the Manchester Repealers presenting an address to O'Connell which emphasized that Ireland would fight if the Government used force to defeat Repeal. Although the address reflected a point of view O'Connell often expressed, the Repeal leader cautioned the Manchester man against using strong language. He said that "the period is now come when caution and coolness are the virtues of patriots and steady men—when to excite will be in itself entirely wrong, for it would be counteracting the policy of mine to keep the country tranquil, to keep yourself in the right, and not to do any violence to your enemies."

After Father Tyrrell, the parish priest of Lusk, read the resolutions and the petition for Repeal which would have been presented the previous day at Clontarf, O'Connell gave his speech. He conceded that the original notice advertising the Clontarf meeting contained imprudent language, but he said that the Government knew that the Repeal meetings posed no danger to the public peace and therefore it had no just cause to ban the Clontarf demonstration. O'Connell refused to accuse the Government of deliberately planning to slaughter the Repeal masses by posting its proclamation so late that the Repeal Association would have difficulty in turning back the thousands of people on their way to Conquer Hill. But he insisted that DeGrey's handling of the situation was a perfect way "to entrap the people into a massacre" if that had been his design. But the longer O'Connell talked the more passionate he became and the less reluctant to charge the Government with conspiracy to murder unarmed people: "Having enforced my obedience to the law, I next proclaim my thorough conviction that the conduct of the Government was calculated in the highest degree to produce the massacre of innocent people." Regardless of the shabby motives and conduct of the Government, O'Connell commanded his followers to remain calm and peaceful and to obey "everything having the form of legal authority." "I want to carry the Repeal of the Union without one drop of blood—without one crime—without disturbing the social state or the social order. I want to carry it in such a way that I can face my Redeemer at the moment of my accounting and have no sin upon me to answer for from the advice I offer in conducting the Irish people."

O'Connell then moved on to discuss plans for the future of the Repeal movement. He predicted that the Government would outlaw the Loyal National Repeal Association, and he promised that immediately following such a proclamation he would be the first to defy the authorities by entering the Corn Exchange rooms. He also announced his intention to continue and expand the work at the arbitration courts and to initiate another phase in his campaign to restore the Irish parliament. Sometime before the next session of Parliament, and when the people were calm, on two Sundays, following Mass, there would be simultaneous Repeal meetings in every parish in Ireland. At these meetings Repeal petitions and lists of Irish grievances would be presented to the people for their signatures. O'Connell also suggested action on a plan to prevent the interest payable out of Irish estates from leaving the country, but said that the details of such a plan would have to wait until the Preservative Society met in Dublin. He closed his speech with another appeal to the Irish people to remain calm and with the following resolution: "That whilst we repeat to the people of Ireland our conviction 'whoever commits a crime gives strength to the enemy': and while we pledge them and ourselves to a perfect obedience to the law, we at the same time avow before the inhabitants of the British Empire and before the people of the civilized world, that we will never desist from the legal and constitutional pursuit of the Repeal of the Union until an Irish parliament is in College Green again." The resolution obtained a unanimous vote and the meeting closed with three ringing cheers for the Queen, O'Connell, Old Ireland, and Repeal.[52]

That evening the Loyal National Repeal Association gave a banquet at the Rotunda to honor the Repealers from Britain who had come over to participate in the Clontarf demonstration. About twenty-five hundred sat down to an abundant table and they had a variety of wines to enjoy. While the meal was in progress Repeal bands from Manchester and Birmingham entertained the diners with a selection of patriotic airs. Banners with Repeal slogans decorated the walls of the room, and O'Connell sat in a large chair with harps, surmounted by imperial crowns of crimson and silver on each side of his throne. After the meal was concluded O'Connell rose, toasted the Queen, Prince Albert, and other members of the royal

[52] *Freeman's Journal,* October 10, 1843.

family, the bands played "Rory O'More," and O'Connell toasted the Irish people—"the best in the world." He then launched into an attack on the Government for provoking violence by waiting until it was almost too late to ban the Clontarf meeting, repeated his plan to summon simultaneous meetings in every Catholic parish in Ireland to sign Repeal petitions and lists of grievances, argued that Ireland did not want complete separation from Britain and that Repeal would foster a real bond between the two islands, promised that there would never be a Catholic ascendancy in a free Ireland, and toasted Repeal, the Catholic hierarchy and clergy, and the Repealers of Britain. After O'Connell sat down other Repeal leaders got up to toast many men and many things—once O'Connell had to rebuke one of the Repealers from Britain for using militant language—and the banquet came to an end with three cheers for the Queen, the Liberator, and Old Ireland.[53]

At the Wednesday, October 11, meeting of the Loyal National Repeal Association Francis Morgan, a Dublin solicitor, took full responsibility for the original notice of the Clontarf meeting and apologized to O'Connell and his comrades for the difficulty his poor choice of words had caused them. He said that the purpose of the notice was to lay down rules that would protect the foot marchers from the mounted men. O'Connell praised Morgan's manly admission of error and saved his anger for the Lord Lieutenant and the Privy Council. They had deprived the Irish people of their right to petition on the ridiculous grounds that the Repeal meetings tended to disturb the public peace. He had instituted the Repeal movement "to tranquilize the public mind" and to keep Irish nationalism true to peaceful and constitutional methods of agitation.

[53] *Ibid.*

O'Connell bluntly accused members of the Peel administration of a lust for Irish blood. He said that he had
learned that Wellington, Sugden, DeGrey, and Lyndhurst
had met in London the previous week to discuss ways and
means to destroy Repeal. He also said that he had heard
rumors that the decision of the meeting was to issue the
proclamation banning the Clontarf meeting so late that the
Irish people would not have time to make preparations to
defend themselves, giving the British soldiers a military
advantage. O'Connell concluded that the facts appeared
to support the rumors. He warned that the military mind
in both London and Dublin had assumed a dangerous influence over the Government's Irish policy. Since it was
clear that a number of prominent members of the Government were anxious to spill Irish blood and would seek
every opportunity to crush Irish nationalism with violent
methods, O'Connell said, he found it necessary to protect
the lives of his followers by demanding that they obey
the law whether it was just or not.

The Repeal leader then attempted to preserve confidence in eventual victory. He told his followers that they
must perfect their organization and remain true to the
principles of constitutional agitation. And he lectured
them on the dangers of revolution and reminded them
how the British Government used the rebellion of 1798 to
justify the Act of Union. Another futile rebellion might
reduce Ireland to an even more severe state of slavery.
The man who a few weeks before the Clontarf disaster
claimed that he had the disciplined manpower to win Repeal by military means if necessary now warned the Irish
people that a disorganized, unarmed people had no possibility of success in combat against a trained army. But he
promised that he would send out eight petitions in areas
where Monster Meetings had been held, that these petitions would collect a hundred thousand names, and that

the pressure of Irish public opinion would finally wear down the resistance of British politicians as it did in the struggle for Catholic emancipation.[54]

While O'Connell concentrated on maintaining the morale of Repealers and their confidence in his leadership and methods of agitation, the Government was preparing the next step in its campaign against Repeal—the arrest of O'Connell and his close associates. Government leaders still feared that such a direct attack on the national hero might finally drive the Irish masses to rebellion. So, after consulting with the Duke of Wellington, Graham ordered two more infantry divisions, a division of dragoons, and two companies of artillery to Ireland to supplement the already large force at DeGrey's disposal. The Duke and the Home Secretary were concerned for the safety and morale of the outnumbered Protestant Unionists of Munster in case of a rebellion. To protect this minority they sent a fleet of threedeckers to Queenstown and ordered the Admiralty to send one ship up the Shannon and to station another off Limerick.[55]

Lord Eliot was convinced that O'Connell's arrest would not disturb the peace of Dublin where the Repeal Association could and would maintain discipline, but he feared that the peasants in the country, made militant and overconfident by O'Connell's emotional speeches and guarantees of victory and led by demagogues and priests, might attempt to avenge the insult to their leader and their cause. Eliot's attitude toward a revolt seemed to support O'Connell's charge that some members of Peel's cabinet longed for an opportunity to shoot down Repealers. He

---

[54] *Pilot*, October 13, 1843. This meeting also featured another attack by O'Connell on Irish-American defenders of slavery. He called them "degenerate" Irishmen and among the worst of racial bigots. He said that he would reply to some Irish-Americans in Cincinnati who had defended slavery; he would do this to uphold the reputation of Irishmen on a great moral issue.

[55] Graham to DeGrey, October 12,, 14, 1843, Graham Papers.

appeared anxious to teach these "misguided people" a convincing lesson concerning "the difference between disciplined troops and an undisciplined rabble."[56]

On Saturday, October 14, Daniel O'Connell, John O'Connell, Thomas Steele, Charles Gavan Duffy, Richard Barrett, Thomas M. Ray, Rev. Thomas Tierney, Rev. Peter James Tyrrell, and John Gray, M. D., were arrested on charges of attempting to undermine the Constitution and to alienate the loyalty of Her Majesty's forces in Ireland.[57] O'Connell received the warrant for his arrest with great courtesy, and there was no sign of an impending insurrection in any section of the country. Within a few days the Government demonstrated its confidence that the situation in Ireland had passed the crisis stage by withdrawing some of its military force.[58]

While neither the proclamation banning the Clontarf meeting nor the arrest of O'Connell provoked a revolution, they did stimulate a temporary revival of Repeal enthusiasm. The rent for the week ending October 16 was a handsome £1,232, 13s, 6d and the next week it skyrocketed to £2,287, 19s, 6d. DeGrey's proclamation and the arrest of the Repeal leaders also encouraged a number of important people, led by William Smith O'Brien, M.P., to cast their lot with the Repeal movement.

When O'Connell appeared in the Corn Exchange on October 16, two days after he was charged with sedition, he

56 Eliot to Graham, October 12, 1843, Graham Papers.

57 Father Tyrrell died during the preliminary stages of the trial. "His death was attributed to fatigue, endured on the night before the Sunday fixed for the Clontarf meeting. When the news of the proclamation reached him he was in bed; he immediately got on horseback and spent the greater part of a bleak October night in the open air, making arrangements to prevent his parishioners from going to Clontarf. A week later he was arrested for conspiracy, and in a few weeks he was carried to his grave" (Duffy, *Young Ireland*, 2:18). DeGrey decided to include John O'Connell in the indictment because he was "clever and cunning and if left out will act for and with his father during any period of imprisonment." (DeGrey to Graham, October 10, 1843, Graham Papers.)

58 Graham to DeGrey, October 16, 1843, Graham Papers; Graham to Peel, October 17, 1843, Add. MSS 40449, B.M.

did not seem disturbed about the future. Again he asked Repealers to remain calm and promised that six months of peace would result in an Irish parliament in College Green. He also proposed a plan for buying up mortgaged absentee estates and placing them on sale for Irish tenant farmers.[59]

Under the impetus of the revived Repeal fervor Conciliation Hall was completed and the arbitration system was expanded, but within a few weeks the Irish masses came to realize that O'Connell's promises of a quick victory were only pep pills to sustain nationalist morale. A declining Repeal rent was an accurate gauge of the disillusionment and indifference sweeping through Repeal ranks. For the week ending November 27, only £636, 8d was collected, and by December 26 the rent had dropped to £473, 3s, 3d, and for the week ending January 2, 1844, the Association collected the embarrassing sum of £289, 2s, 2d.

Perhaps many Repealers lost their enthusiasm for the cause when they began to suspect that even O'Connell was no longer confident of victory. Early in 1843 he made it clear that he was prepared to accept federalism as an alternative to Repeal, but when the Repeal agitation captured the imagination and enthusiasm of the masses he rejected federalism as a possible compromise and insisted that Repeal was the only satisfactory answer to the Irish Question. After Clontarf and his arrest, however, O'Connell again hinted that he was ready to accept a federal contract from the British Government.[60] His swing back to federalism, with the implication that he never really expected to win Repeal and only used the agitation to extort concessions from British politicians, shocked many Repealers, particularly the young men at the *Nation* office.[61]

[59] *Nation,* October 21, 1843.
[60] *Ibid.*
[61] *Ibid.*

By the close of 1843 the Young Irelanders had certainly
lost confidence in O'Connell, and they doubted a Repeal
victory as long as he was at the helm of the national movement. But they were reluctant to lead a revolt in the Repeal Association since it would only create confusion at a
time when unity was essential if the organization was to
survive. As the *Nation* put it: "We needs must follow the
only general who can muster an effective army though his
plan of battle did not tally with ours."[62]

While Repeal was sliding downhill in the fall and winter
of 1843, the Government, confident that it had scored a
final victory over O'Connell and Irish nationalism, made
its plans for the future of Ireland. The Irish Attorney
General, T. B. C. Smith, was busy rounding up journalists
to testify against O'Connell and insuring that nationalist
sympathizers would be eliminated from the jury trying the
Repeal leaders.[63] Peel and Graham continued to plan legislation which would destroy Irish nationalism and line up
Irish Catholic opinion solidly behind the British connection. They decided to introduce an Irish registration
and county franchise bill, and they told Eliot that they
were prepared to consider all of his views on Irish legislation "not excluding the reconstruction of Maynooth with
an enlarged grant, and a scheme for the payment, in some
shape or other, of the Roman Catholic clergy."[64] Graham
reminded the Chief Secretary that Dissenters and Presbyterians in Britain would resent contributing to the
maintenance of a Roman Catholic establishment and insisted that he stick to his original suggestion that endow-
ments to Irish Catholicism must be supported by Irish
resources. He also warned Eliot that no commitments

[62] *Ibid.*
[63] Smith to Graham, October 11, 1843, Graham Papers. Smith said that
Hughes feared for his life and wanted to return to London until the
start of the trial. He recommended leave and said that Ross could cover
the Repeal meetings until the trial.
[64] Graham to Eliot, October 20, 1843, Graham Papers.

should be made to Irish Catholic bishops on paper or in private conversations.[65]

Some officials in the Irish administration were convinced that O'Connell would attempt to negotiate with the Government to avoid a prison sentence. Eliot said that O'Connell would try to stay out of prison because he was afraid that in his absence extremists would take charge of the Loyal National Repeal Association. The Chief Secretary was persuaded that Gavan Duffy and some of his Young Ireland friends were prepared to lead a revolutionary movement but were frustrated by O'Connell's refusal to endorse any departure from constitutional methods of agitation. But Eliot was afraid that the Repeal leader would not be able to restrain the energy or the passion of the young men, particularly if he was in prison, so he advised his superiors at Whitehall to exploit O'Connell's fear of prison and his mendacity by purchasing with money and amnesty his removal from the nationalist movement. He said that if "a bridge of gold" would facilitate O'Connell's retreat from Repeal, the Government "ought to make one for him." Without the name and prestige of O'Connell Repeal would collapse, and the Government would have little difficulty in handling any of the young extremists who might try to wear his mantle of leadership.[66]

Graham was fascinated with Eliot's suggestion that the Government negotiate with O'Connell in an effort to separate him from Repeal, but he warned that the Kerry fox was "such a rogue" that it would be "impossible to treat with him except at a fearful risk of treachery." However, he agreed that without O'Connell Irish nationalism would dwindle to a minor concern, and he said that he would be willing to come to terms with him if the Repeal leader would publicly declare that the conciliatory mea-

65 *Ibid.*
66 Eliot to Graham, October 18, 1843, Graham Papers.

sures then under cabinet consideration were entirely satisfactory to Irish needs. He added: "money has seldom pro-
curred for a nation, by the baseness of one man, such
inestimable benefits." Graham ordered Eliot not to make
any offer to O'Connell without first clearing it with
Whitehall.[67]

After discussing with Eliot the possibilities of reaching
an agreement with O'Connell, Graham wrote to DeGrey
on the subject and expressed this opinion:

"I believe that O'Connell is seriously alarmed. He is
quite capable of seeking terms and of crying for mercy;
but he is such a rogue, that he must be kept at arms length
and touched like pitch. Yet he is the life and soul of the
conspiracy; and if he were withdrawn from it, it would
soon dwindle into insignificance.

"Imprudences would be committed; the law would be
flagrantly violated: openings would be given, through
which the whole power of the State would be brought to
bear on the insurrection and we should soon be enabled to
settle the whole affair with comparative ease.

"It would by no means surprise me, if O'Connell in his
fright were to seek the means of escape from his present
position. Should he take this course it would be unwise to
drive him to desperation, although to treat with him,
except as a supplicant, is impossible."[68]

Future events indicated that the Government seriously
overestimated Gavan Duffy's rashness and underestimated
O'Connell's sincere devotion to Irish freedom and reform.
O'Connell never offered to sell his principles for either
money or mercy, and he never made any effort to avoid
trial or the consequences of a verdict of guilty. In fact,
the people in Dublin Castle and in Whitehall were completely mistaken about his frame of mind in the fall and
winter of 1843. He indicated no depression or fear con-

67 Graham to Eliot, October 20, 1843, Graham Papers.
68 Graham to DeGrey, October 20, 1843, Graham Papers.

cerning his future. In December he was at Derrynane
enjoying the hunting. He wrote P. V. FitzPatrick: "I
already feel the immense benefit of my native air and my
delightful exercise. I am regaining strength and vigour to
endure whatever my sentence may be. You will believe
that I shall endure it without shrinking or compromise,
come what may."[69]

On December 17 he again wrote FitzPatrick expressing
pleasure with his hunting holiday. He said that the only
grievance he held against T. B. C. Smith was that the
start of the trial would permit him only another fortnight
in the Kerry mountains.[70] This was not a man obsessed
with fear but a leader relieved from the burdens of a
responsibility he was too old and too tired to bear. He was
a man who could view even prison as a welcome change
from holding the reins of an agitation now so frustrated
that it might at any time explode into violence. In prison
O'Connell would be the martyr patriot deserving the respect, the sympathy, and the loyalty of his defeated followers. If he remained at Conciliation Hall, O'Connell would
be an exploded myth scorned as a fraud. In defeating
Repeal the Government had preserved the myth and the
reputation of its leader.

In February 1844 the Repeal defendants were convicted,
fined £2,000, and sentenced to a year in prison. But in
September of the same year the Law Lords, by a vote of
three to two, reversed the Dublin court's decision on the
grounds that the prosecution drew up an improper indictment, and tried its case before a packed jury. O'Connell
and his friends were released from Richmond Gaol and
received as conquering heroes by the nationalist masses.
O'Connell refused to take advantage of his victory. His

---

69 O'Connell to FitzPatrick, December 9, 1843, W. J. FitzPatrick, *Correspondence of Daniel O'Connell*, 2:310.
70 *Ibid.*, 2:311.

prison existence was comfortable, but it had changed him. Suddenly he seemed old and tired, without any zest for agitation. His decision to abandon the Clontarf meeting, followed by the failure to exploit his legal vindication by intensifying the activities of the Repeal Association, crushed the spirit of Irish constitutional nationalism. But the defeat of O'Connell and Repeal in 1843 was not the product of cowardice or faulty tactics so much as it was a misreading of the times.

Like most political leaders, O'Connell became a captive of past successes. He expected Peel and his associates to react to the Repeal movement in the same way that they had to the agitation for Catholic emancipation. In the 1820's he had convinced Tory leaders that if they did not concede emancipation the extremist element in Ireland would push him aside, take control of the Catholic movement, and then substitute physical for moral force. In 1843 he seemed to assume that if Peel was again faced with the choice of concessions to Irish grievances or the possibility of civil war he would follow the precedent of 1829 and select the former. And if Peel refused to bow his knee to expediency, O'Connell expected the Whig leaders to exploit the Irish crisis as an instrument to embarrass and perhaps topple the Conservative Government. Once in power there was a strong probability that Russell and Palmerston would attempt to quiet troubled Irish waters with a conciliation policy and a reconstruction of the Irish nationalist-Whig alliance.

O'Connell apparently failed to perceive that while the situation in Ireland during 1843 resembled the one prevailing in 1829, in Britain conditions were quite different. Throughout the 1820's there was a considerable body of enlightened parliamentary opinion favorable to Catholic emancipation. In 1829 Peel and Wellington knew that any attempt to suppress the Catholic Association without conceding emancipation would not command majority support in the House of Commons. Therefore, an Irish revolutionary movement in resistance to coercion would enjoy the sympathy of a respectable body of British opinion, and the seeds of rebellion could spread to a Britain already saturated with social, political, and economic discontent. So Catholic emancipation was a British as well as an Irish issue and the Government's responsibility to preserve peace and order throughout the United Kingdom dictated a surrender to the leading demand of Irish Catholic opinion.

But in 1843 no respectable Tory, Whig, or even Radical M.P. accepted Repeal as a satisfactory solution to the Irish Question. Both the Tory and Whig leadership argued that an independent Ireland would weaken Britain's defenses and threaten a dissolution of the Empire. Radicals insisted that the Union could create peace, prosperity, and stability in Ireland if only British politicians governed the sister island in a fair and impartial manner. During the Repeal crisis British no-Popery and Unionist parliamentary opinion were leagued in opposition to the demands of Irish nationalism for an independent legislature in Dublin. Whig and Radical spokesmen did not hesitate to exploit Irish discontent to embarrass the Government, but at the same time they assured Peel of their support in his determination to preserve the Union.

When Peel challenged Irish nationalism on the issue of the Clontarf meeting, O'Connell had no choice but to retreat. His anti-physical force convictions and his common sense would not permit him to lead the Irish masses in a futile and destructive war against disciplined British troops. But when O'Connell surrendered to the Government ultimatum he removed the most effective weapon from the arsenal of constitutional agitation—the implied threat of revolution if that was the only alternative to total defeat.

6

Epilogue: Peel's Irish Policy, 1844-1845

DURING THE TRIAL of O'Connell and the other "Traversers," Repeal activity was for all practical purposes suspended in Ireland. Peel decided to use the comparative tranquility in Ireland to prepare the parliamentary ground for a new Irish policy. In a secret memorandum distributed to members of the cabinet on February 11, 1844, the Prime Minister expressed the opinion that the conviction and the imprisonment of O'Connell would lessen his influence with the Irish masses and encourage a temporary lull in Irish agitation. "Now if ever," he said, "there is the prospect of detaching from the ranks of agitation and Repeal a considerable portion of the moderate Roman Catholics and of doing this consistently with the honour of the Government. . . ."

In this memorandum Peel recommended to his colleagues an increase in the Maynooth grant and legislation encouraging and permitting wealthy Irish Catholics and Protestants to endow Catholic priests with glebes for their permanent use. He described the existing Maynooth grant as an inadequate method of providing either first rate instruction or a respectable standard of living for the young seminarians—the future leaders of the Irish masses. The Government's niggardly endowment produced a Catholic clergy hostile to the Government, thereby subverting the original intention of the grant. In addition the seedy character of the seminary attracted students from the lowest classes of society and repelled the sons of the gentry and middle class. But if the Government endowed Maynooth in a generous spirit and improved living standards and the level of instruction, the Catholic clergy would be somewhat emancipated from dependence on the nationalist masses for financial support, and the priestly vocation would attract young men from those sections of Irish society potentially more sympathetic to the British connection than the peasantry.

Peel also suggested extending the parliamentary suffrage to "bona-fide" freeholders not able to meet the suffrage requirements of the reform bill of 1832. This concession would give a semblance of equality with England "with no practical inconvenience" because the small Irish property owner was potentially a supporter of conservative principles. Since the last municipal reform bill led to Repeal corporations in the leading Irish cities, Peel indicated little enthusiasm for significant changes in the municipal franchise.

In concluding his memorandum the Prime Minister reminded his associates that the Guizot government in France might fall at any time and that a new leftist regime might try to consolidate popular support by initiating a war against Britain. He also mentioned the tensions in Anglo-American affairs and emphasized that during any war with France or the United States, or even in a period of tension with these potential enemies, a hostile Ireland would constitute a serious weakness in Britain's defenses.

Ireland must be pacified, and to achieve this goal Catholic priests not yet completely committed to agitation must be separated from the nationalist coalition.[1]

Peel's attempt to conciliate "respectable" Irish Catholic opinion was seriously undermined by the pro-Protestant ascendancy prejudices of the Lord Lieutenant. In June Peel obtained an important break when poor health forced DeGrey to resign his post. Lord Heytesbury, the new Lord Lieutenant, was an experienced diplomat, an ideal man for this sensitive assignment because he had refrained from political activity and aroused no hostility from any section of Irish opinion.

The Prime Minister instructed the new Viceroy to act with complete impartiality in administering Irish affairs. He must of course defend the Protestant establishment, a major bulwark of British influence in Ireland, but that did not mean encouraging Protestant ascendancy. If Heytesbury could treat individuals of all faiths with impartial justice, and even encourage Catholic middle class ambitions for advancement, Peel was confident that the Government could win the friendship and even the support of wealthy and intelligent Irish Catholics and release them from the bondage of the dictation of their priests and the intimidation of mass opinion.[2]

In late August 1844 Peel received encouraging news from the Lord Lieutenant. Heytesbury had learned that a number of prominent Catholics were out of sympathy with the Repeal movement and willing to endorse the Union in exchange for the recognition of the validity of the diocesan titles of Catholic bishops, a moderate provision for the Catholic clergy, and diplomatic relations with the Vatican to gain Papal support for the concessions granted to Irish Catholicism. Peel expressed satisfaction with this possible crack in the Irish national front, advised Heytesbury to

[1] Add. MSS 40540, B.M.
[2] Peel to Heytesbury, August 1, 8, 26, 1843, Add. MSS 40479, B.M.

encourage further dissensions within Repeal ranks, but refused to commit himself to specific guarantees.[3]

Before proceeding with final efforts to conciliate the Irish Catholic gentry, middle class, and moderate clergy, Peel decided to enlist Rome in his cause. Peel instructed Graham to have Lord Aberdeen, the Foreign Secretary, prepare a brief concerning the Repeal activities of the Irish hierarchy and clergy for presentation to the Pope and Prince Metternich. He believed that the Austrian leader would be most willing to help convince the Vatican that the political activities of Irish bishops and priests were "disgraceful to religion, and dangerous to other thrones as well as to that of England." The Lord Lieutenant collected speeches made by Archbishop MacHale, Bishop Higgins, and other prelates and priests that "excited rebellion, treason, and bloodshed" for use at Rome and Vienna.[4] William Petre, a prominent English Catholic, was dispatched to Rome as unofficial ambassador to support the Government's charge against the Irish hierarchy and clergy. With the aid of the Hapsburg envoy at the Papal court, the British Government succeeded in obtaining an official censure of clerical nationalism.[5]

3 Heytesbury to Peel, August 29, 1843, Peel to Heytesbury, September 5, 1843, Add. MSS 40479, B.M.

4 The idea of employing the Vatican as an ally came from DeGrey. On October 30, 1843, Graham informed Peel of the Lord Lieutenant's suggestion (Peel Add. MSS 40449, B.M.). Peel agreed to this proposal and advised Graham to instruct Aberdeen, the Foreign Secretary, to proceed with the Vatican strategy and to seek Metternich's aid in carrying it out. Graham complied with Peel's recommendations and reported to his chief that DeGrey had prepared a collection of speeches made by MacHale, Higgins, and others "that excited rebellion, treason, and bloodshed" for use at either Rome or Vienna (Peel to Graham, November 1, 1843, Add. MSS 40449, Graham to Peel, November 2, 1843, Add. MSS 40449, B.M.). As late as October 1844 the Lord Lieutenant was collecting material for submission to Rome through the Foreign Office (Peel to Heytesbury, September 29, October 4, 1844, Add. MSS 40479, B.M.).

5 The efforts of the British Government to obtain support from the Vatican in its effort to curb the political activities of the Irish hierarchy and clergy is discussed in John F. Broderick, The Holy See and the Irish Repeal Movement, 1829-1847 (Rome, 1951), pp. 163ff. Father Broderick is charitable in his interpretation of clerical activities in Rome and Ireland.

On October 15, 1844, Cardinal Philip Fransoni, Prefect of Propaganda, sent a letter to Archbishop Crolly of Armagh, the Irish Primate. Fransoni reminded Crolly that the Vatican had previously cautioned Irish bishops and priests to avoid political activity and informed him that the authorities in Rome had learned that they were still denouncing the British Government from public platforms, in the press, and from the altar. He said that these reports had troubled the Holy Father, who wanted his clergy to avoid involvement in secular concerns. By becoming involved in politics bishops and priests lowered their dignity and invited criticism of the Church they represented. Fransoni recommended that the Irish hierarchy and clergy confine their efforts to religious affairs and "cherish among the people quiet, tranquility, and peace, which is the bond of Christianity and constantly teach by example, precept or deed, submission to the temporal power in those matters which pertain to civil affairs. . . ."[6]

Archbishop Crolly presented Fransoni's message to a meeting of the Irish hierarchy. All the prelates agreed that the Cardinal's advice was excellent, but they differed on how it applied to their individual conduct. Some of them accepted it as an order to refrain from encouraging the Repeal agitation and demonstrated their intention to cooperate with the Vatican's wishes. The majority, however, interpreted Fransoni's comments as a counsel in prudence—in other words the Vatican's message was ignored by most of the bishops.[7]

Finally, in the fall of 1844, Peel launched his Irish pro-

[6] The original Latin version of Fransoni's letter can be found in Broderick, pp. 232-33; this English translation appeared in Irish newspapers.

[7] This description of the fate of the Vatican directive when submitted to the meeting of bishops comes from a letter sent by John Cantwell, Bishop of Meath, to O'Connell and published in the Nation, January 18, 1845.

gram in the House of Commons with the introduction of a charitable bequests act designed to eliminate the legal barriers that restricted the Catholic Church from inheriting or bequeathing property. The Government's proposal created a twelve man board, with a minimum of five Catholic members, to supervise all charitable bequests in Ireland. Bequests involving the Catholic Church were to be decided exclusively by the Catholic members of the board. Although the charitable bequests act was primarily designed to improve the financial status of the Catholic Church in Ireland, Peel also intended to use the Catholic members of the board as intermediaries in future relations between the Government and the Catholic hierarchy.[8]

The charitable bequests act had a mixed reception in Ireland. Young Irelanders, those Repealers associated with the *Nation*, accepted the bill as beneficial to Irish interests.[9] But O'Connell, supported by Archbishop Mac-Hale, denounced the bequests act because it prevented religious orders and their members from inheriting property, the jurisdiction of the board interfered with the rights reserved by canon law for each bishop in his own diocese, and, most important, the Government intended to exploit the provisions of the bill to gain an influence over the hierarchy and clergy.[10] All of the members of the hierarchy condemned a provision in the act which invalidated real property bequests made for religious and charitable purposes within three months of death. This provision was viewed by the bishops as an obvious attack on the integrity of the Catholic clergy. Since members of the

---

8 In a letter to Heytesbury, November 30, 1844, Graham made clear the Government's intention of using the Catholic members of the Charitable Bequests Board as a body to consult on all questions concerning the Roman Catholic Church in Ireland (Graham Papers).

9 Denis Gwynn, *Young Ireland and 1848* (Cork, 1949), 26.

10 Letter of Archbishop MacHale published in the *Nation*, December 14, 1844. The Government did make some concessions to MacHale's objections. The Attorney General was instructed to accept the statement of the bishop in the diocese as final evidence.

Repeal Association were divided on the merits of the charitable bequests act, it was excluded as a legitimate topic for discussion at Association meetings,[11] but O'Connell continued to attack Peel's scheme from the public platform and in the columns of nationalist newspapers. From all indications, it seems clear that the objections raised by O'Connell and MacHale to the charitable bequests act were supported by a majority of the Irish hierarchy and clergy and by most of the members of the Repeal organization.[12]

Realizing that O'Connell's opposition to the charitable bequests act was carrying Irish opinion, the Government took immediate steps to counter the effects of the Irish leader's hold on the Irish clergy and masses. Archbishop Crolly, the Primate, Archbishop Murray of Dublin, and Bishop Kennedy of Killaloe, the federalist who had played a prominent role in the agitation of 1843, were persuaded to accept positions on the charitable bequests board, and the Vatican's support for the bequests act was solicited with the promise that this proposal was the first in a series leading to the endowment of the Catholic Church in Ireland.

On December 23, 1844, Graham advised Peel to ". . . instruct Mr. Petre sedulously to cultivate a good understanding with the Holy See, and as far as possible to make intelligible there the struggle which has commenced in Ireland. The Papal authority to a considerable extent is at stake in this conflict. The heads of the Roman Catholic Church in that country, acting under a rescript from the Pope inculcating peace and obedience to the constituted authorities of the realm, have determined to cooperate with the legislature in giving effect to a measure framed specially for the purpose of facilitating and securing the permanent endowment of the hierarchy and of the paro-

---

[11] *Op. cit.*, p. 27.
[12] This conclusion is based on letters, articles, and petitions published in the *Nation* during the autumn of 1844.

chial priesthood. A powerful party represented by Archbishop MacHale and O'Connell rejects the advice of the Holy Father, repudiates all cooperation with the State even for the promotion of Roman Catholic objects, and in a rebellious spirit of democratic insubordination bids defiance both to the control of the See of Rome and to the conciliatory advances of the British legislature. It is important that they should know at Rome the language in which concordats are spoken of in Dublin; a specimen is to be found in Mr. O'Connell's speech, of which a report is transmitted by Lord Heytesbury; and this is exactly the state of affairs in which an authoritative declaration from Rome in favour of the Archbishops against the recusants would tell with great effect, and in a sense conducive to the maintenance of superior ecclesiastical power, which there is a strong disposition to set at naught in Ireland."[13]

The Catholic prelates who accepted positions on the charitable bequests board were sincerely convinced of the benefits to be derived from the Government's concession. Archbishop Murray admitted that the act passed by Parliament had its blemishes but gave the Church an opportunity to obtain the financial and property resources necessary to expand its activities. It was a beginning and a foundation on which to build. The Government had made a friendly overture and it would be ridiculous to reject it in blind partisan passion. There was always the possibility that in time the Ministry would further amend the bill to meet Catholic objections.[14]

Undoubtedly the O'Connell-MacHale faction sustained a severe blow with the announcement that three members of the Irish hierarchy had consented to cooperate with the Government. The rift in Catholic circles had now widened

---

13 Add. MSS 40450, B.M.

14 Murray's letter to the clergy and laity of Dublin, *Nation*, December 28, 1844. Bishop Kennedy later changed his mind about accepting a position on the board and his place was filled by Bishop Davern.

to include the hierarchy and clergy as well as the laity. The intensity of bitterness between the two factions was well illustrated when Richard Barrett, editor of *The Pilot,* O'Connell's press mouthpiece, insinuated in the columns of his paper that Archbishop Murray was insane and not responsible for his actions.[15]

Peel and his Cabinet associates were elated with the immediate results of the charitable bequests act. They had pushed it through Parliament with no significant opposition, they had successfully used it to establish contact with influential members of the Catholic hierarchy, and through the provisions of the act they had created an effective instrument to destroy the Irish Catholic nationalist coalition. Peel was confident that the split in the coalition was permanent since intelligent Catholics now had evidence to prove that the British Government was sincere in its promises to concede justice to Ireland.[16] Lord Eliot optimistically predicted an alliance between the Government and the Irish hierarchy and the end of O'Connell's control over the Irish masses.[17] Eliot certainly exaggerated the

[15] Quoted in the *Nation,* October 11, 1844.

[16] "The issue of the Charitable Trusts Act, next best to amicable cooperation with Dr. Murray and the most moderate of the Roman Catholic prelacy will be the schism in the Roman Catholic body, produced by no low intrigues, no specious promises not likely to be realized, but by a proposal for the practical carrying out of a Trust Bill so reasonable and so conciliatory on the part of the Government that the rejection of it will show that peace is not the object, and will be indefensible in any public assembly, wherein there must be some regard for reason and justice." (Peel to Heytesbury, August 26, 1844, Add. MSS 40479, B.M.)

[17] "To bring the Roman Catholic hierarchy into connection with the State was in itself a great step towards an alliance between the Roman Catholic Church and the Government. To do this in spite of O'Connell and MacHale was to dissolve existing party bonds and to make the distinction between parties in Ireland, as in England, political and not religious. The Roman Catholic party as such has ceased to exist. O'Connell can no longer rely on the support of the Church. He has coaxed and he has menaced the most esteemed prelates of the Roman Catholic Church and his threats and his cajolements have proved equally unavailing; Drs. Crolly and Murray have withstood both.

"They will be supported in the course that they have taken by the

Government's victory over the Repeal leader and was too hopeful concerning the consequences of that victory, but O'Connell did suffer a defeat, and Peel had inserted a wedge into the nationalist coalition that threatened to separate the Liberator's most important ally, the Catholic clergy, from the Repeal movement.

However, O'Connell, still a clever fighter, did manage to salvage something from this clash with Peel by exposing the negotiations between the Government and the Vatican. A reliable Roman source had informed O'Connell that William Petre, with the aid of Metternich, had prevailed on the Pope to condemn the Repeal activities of the Irish clergy and that the British Government was discussing a concordat with the Vatican that would give the former control over the political allegiances of Irish bishops and priests.[18]

This information, presented to the Repeal Association by O'Connell, raised a storm of protest in the Association and in the nationalist press.[19] Irish Catholics insisted that they would not accept Papal interference in Irish politics and that they would not honor any agreement between the Vatican and Whitehall restricting the political conduct and opinions of their bishops and priests. The strong reaction in Ireland to the news of the Petre mission, the Vatican censure of the Repeal activities of the hierarchy

moderate section of the Roman Catholics, not an inconsiderable one in point of property as of intelligence, and encouraged by success they will dare to withdraw themselves a still greater distance from the political position in which they have hitherto stood. Such was the lines of the language held by Sergeant Howley by Mr. Corballis, and by one or two of the Roman Catholics who were at my house last night." (An undated letter from Eliot to Heytesbury included in a letter from the Lord Lieutenant to Peel, December 19, 1844, Add. MSS 40479, B.M.)

18 *Nation*, January 11, 1845. According to Charles Gavan Duffy, the Roman source might have been Dr. Paul Cullen, head of the Irish College in Rome and later Archbishop of Dublin (*Young Ireland*, 133).

19 See the report of the December 31, 1844, meeting of the Repeal Association reported in the *Nation*, January 4, 1845, and the editorials printed in the *Nation*, January 4, 18, 1845.

and clergy, and the rumors of a concordat forced Archbishop Crolly to release to the public the contents of the letter he received from Cardinal Fransoni and to declare his opposition to a Rome-Westminster alliance.[20]

Lord Heytesbury eased the tension somewhat by publicly informing Archbishop Murray "that there never existed the slightest intention of entering into any negotiations with the Papal See upon the subject of concordat."[21] The issue was finally laid to rest in February 1845 when Dr. Cullen wrote Archbishop Murray from Rome that he had the assurances of the Pope that the reports of a concordat between Britain and the Vatican were "quite unfounded."[22]

Although the rumors of a concordat were denied by responsible sources in Dublin, London, and Rome, they, along with the reality of the Petre mission and the letter of censure from Propaganda, made Irish nationalists wary of the possibility of an agreement between the Government and the Vatican—an alliance that would deprive Irish agitation of its most important agent, the Catholic priest. To a certain extent the fears of a concordat healed the breach in the national Catholic coalition, diminishing Peel's original victory over O'Connell. The Prime Minister would have to exercise caution in future attempts to lure the Catholic hierarchy and clergy into the Unionist camp.

While Irish Catholics were busy debating the merits of

[20] "With regard to the Concordat between the Pope and the British Government, which has so justly excited alarming apprehensions in the mind of the clergy and laity of Ireland, I can only state, in the most solemn manner, that I know nothing of it, directly or indirectly, except by public rumor, and that I shall join the Prelacy of Ireland by using every influence in my power to prevent any such scheme, which would be destructive of the independence and purity of our holy religion." (Crolly to O'Connell, January 13, 1843, published in the *Nation*, January 18, 1845.)

[21] Heytesbury to Murray, published in the *Nation*, January 18, 1845.

[22] *Nation*, February 15, 1845.

the charitable bequests act and denouncing the rumored concordat, Peel and Sir James Graham were putting the finishing touches on the Maynooth bill. This measure was the most important plank in the Government's Irish program. If successful it would be a major step toward the Government's objective of gaining an influence over the political inclinations of the Catholic clergy. At first all went well for the administration. Heytesbury presented an outline of the bill to the Catholic bishops, who immediately indicated approval of the Government proposal.[23] But then William Ewart Gladstone, President of the Board of Trade, resigned from the cabinet because his High Church conscience would not permit him to be associated with a scheme to endow religious error. However, subtle mental gymnastics would permit Gladstone to vote for the bill as a member of Parliament. The resignation of a cabinet member over the Maynooth question seriously wounded the Government by implying that the Prime Minister might be prepared to compromise the Protestant establishment.[24]

On April 3, 1845, Peel introduced the Maynooth bill into the House of Commons. In recommending passage of

[23] Graham to Heytesbury, November 30, 1844, Graham Papers.

[24] "Now it is my deliberate unvarying conviction that my official participation in the measure you contemplate with regards to the College of Maynooth would give to everyone the right to say of me, 'that man cannot be trusted;' and when that was said with justice, nothing would remain either to defend or abandon." (Gladstone to Peel, January 21, 1845, Add. MSS 40470, B.M.) In July 1844 Peel talked with Gladstone about his intention of opening direct negotiations with the Vatican through the British envoy in Florence about Roman Catholic questions in Britain and in particular his new Irish policy. At the time Gladstone made it clear that as a member of the Cabinet he could not support any measures leading to endowment of the Catholic Church. However, to avoid embarrassing Peel during the process of getting his Irish policy through Parliament, Gladstone offered to resign from the Cabinet immediately and to accept temporarily a foreign assignment. He even was willing to go to Florence and conduct negotiations with Rome until a competent Catholic, probably Petre, was permanently assigned the post (Gladstone to Peel, July 12, 1844, Add. MSS 40470, B.M.).

the bill he insisted that an increase in the Maynooth grant involved no betrayal of Protestant principles. With the act of Union the British Government made a pledge to continue the support of a seminary first established by an Irish Protestant Parliament in 1795. The Prime Minister said that as long as Parliament was committed to the endowment of Maynooth, it should be generous in its support so as to win the friendship and gratitude of the priests educated at the college. He told the House of Commons that it was not surprising that young men leaving Maynooth were hostile to the British connection. The buildings at the college were in serious need of repair and modernization, faculty salaries were too low to attract teachers with talent, and the trustees were not permitted to incorporate, which restricted the college from buying, inheriting, or bequeathing property.

Peel then outlined the Government's plans for Maynooth. The Maynooth trustees would be incorporated and permitted to hold property to the amount of three thousand pounds per annum; the college would be permitted to accept voluntary contributions; and the annual grant would be raised from nine thousand to twenty-six thousand pounds and changed to a permanent endowment to avoid the no-Popery hysteria that enveloped the House of Commons every time the grant was up for renewal. The increased grant would provide higher faculty salaries, more student stipends, and attractive scholarships for honor scholars. Peel also asked Parliament to appropriate thirty thousand pounds to cover the necessary repairs in college buildings. He then suggested changes in the administration of the college. Under existing regulations the Lord Lieutenant and three judges were ex-officio visitors, but in the future the Crown would appoint five visitors and the trustees of the college three. Only the visitors appointed by the Catholic trustees would exercise any authority over the teaching of religious doctrine and discipline within the college. However, the Lord Lieutenant retained the right to visit Maynooth anytime he believed such a visit necessary. Peel concluded his statement to the House of Commons by assuring British M.P.'s that the Maynooth bill would conciliate many Catholics now hostile to British rule in Ireland, provide a better educated and more sophisticated Catholic clergy, and promote pro-Unionist sentiments among the Catholic hierarchy and clergy.[25]

Most of the Whig and about half of the Conservative M.P.'s agreed with Peel that the Government should be generous in fulfilling its obligation to Maynooth and that it should do everything possible, consistent with principle, to obtain the friendship of the ministers of a religion commanding the allegiance of the Irish masses.[26] Radical M.P.'s were forced to wrestle with their consciences. Did the increased Maynooth grant violate too much their conviction concerning the separation of Church and State? John Bright said that it did and opposed the bill; Richard Cobden said that it did not and supported Peel's proposal.

The most vocal opposition to the Maynooth bill came from the Tory wing of Peel's own party. They represented the Established Church, Protestant ascendancy, landed property tradition of British conservatism. This right-wing faction still harbored resentment against Peel for conceding Catholic emancipation in 1829 and was bitter about the Prime Minister's recent leanings toward free trade. The members of this group seemed convinced that the Maynooth bill was the beginning of a process that would end in an endowed Catholic Church. They accused Peel of facilitating the spread of religious error and of undermining the Protestant foundations of the British Constitution. They described Maynooth as a breeding ground

25 *Hansard* 79:18ff.
26 *Ibid.*, 79:52ff., 67ff., 90ff.

for rebellion and denied that the Government had a permanent obligation to finance the education of agitators.[27]

Disraeli, leader of the Tory opposition to the bill, went so far as to attack the integrity of the leader of his party. He argued that party government, essential to the British system, was based on the conflict between parties on all issues presented to the House of Commons. Disraeli described Peel as a "Machiavelli with dirty hands" for destroying the party system by acting as a parliamentary middleman passing Whig bills with the support of men elected to oppose those measures.[28]

Another opponent of the Maynooth bill attacked it on liberal and nationalist grounds. He objected to the very existence of Maynooth because its sheltered education produced a bigoted and ultramontane clergy loyal to Rome rather than Britain. Wouldn't it be better, he asked, to educate Catholic priests in secular colleges where they could mingle with Protestant and Catholic laymen and thus develop a broader outlook on life? This speaker also suggested that the Government adopt German and Austrian precedents. In those countries the Catholic Church was controlled by the state and priests were forced to place loyalty to the state above any allegiance to Rome.[29]

British press and periodical comments on the Maynooth bill followed the parliamentary pattern. Whig journals and newspapers commended the Prime Minister for his good sense and statesmanship, while Tory publications reveled in a no-Popery orgy. They described the bill as a Jesuit-Ultramontane plot to subvert the Protestant British Constitution, Maynooth as a diabolical influence on Irish life, and Peel as a betrayer of Protestant and Conservative principles. *The Dublin University Magazine,* the *Blackwood's* of Irish Toryism, encouraged Irish Protestants to

27 *Hansard* 79:58ff., 512ff.
28 *Ibid.,* 79:55ff.
29 *Ibid.,* 79:501ff.

organize their own nationalist agitation since they could no longer depend on Conservative politicians in the House of Commons to defend Protestant and Unionist principles.[30]

In general, British public opinion was violently anti-Catholic and supported the opponents of Maynooth. Public meetings were held in every section of Britain to protest the Government's Irish policy, and anti-Maynooth bill petitions flooded the House of Commons. Many of the M.P.'s who supported the bill frankly confessed that they were not reflecting the views of their constituents.[31]

Although the Maynooth bill received the approval of both Houses of Parliament, it was a costly victory for Peel. The anti-Catholic prejudices expressed by opponents of the bill, in and out of Parliament, diminished its significance as a generous gesture to Irish Catholics. And in his effort to woo the Catholic hierarchy Peel severed the tenuous bonds that held together the various factions in the Conservative party. British Tories would never forgive what they considered Peel's betrayal of Protestant interests, and while they brooded they also waited for an opportunity for revenge.

Members of the Government were fully aware of the fact that the efforts to destroy Irish nationalism by concessions to Irish Catholicism would probably destroy the Conservative administration. On April 12, 1845, Lord Aberdeen wrote the following comments to Princess

30 These statements are based on articles on the Maynooth question published in the *Quarterly Review, Edinburgh Review, Frasers Magazine, Blackwood's Magazine, British Quarterly,* and the editorials of the *Times* and *The Dublin University Magazine,* 25:506-19.

31 *Hansard* 79:63, 614. The best analysis of the reaction of British no-Popery opinion to Peel's Irish policy can be found in two articles by Professor Gilbert Cahill: "Irish Catholicism and English Toryism," *Review of Politics,* 19:62-76 and "The Protestant Association and the Anti-Maynooth Agitation of 1845," *Catholic Historical Review,* 43:273-308. A good summary of British public opinion reaction to the Maynooth bill is presented in R. B. McDowell, *Public Opinion and Government Policy in Ireland, 1801-1846* (London, 1952), 219ff.

Lieven: "We are now engaged in a great measure of domestic policy, which by the footing on which we propose to place the colleges of Maynooth is little less than the endowment of the Roman Catholic Church in Ireland. You recollect the excitement against the emancipation act of 1829. The opposition to our present measure is quite as decided and as powerful. It will be carried, however, without any difficulty in Parliament, for it is not there that the strength of the opposition is to be found. There is no doubt that a great majority of all classes out of the House are strongly opposed to the measure. We carried emancipation in Parliament without much difficulty, but it left a root of bitterness amongst our friends which was the real cause of our overthrow in 1830. The same effect may perhaps be now produced, and should this be the case it would afford me no cause of regret: for defeat in maintaining a great principle of justice and liberality cannot be regarded with the same feelings as a miserable squabble about sugar or cotton. We are determined to persevere not only with this but with other measures for the advantage of Ireland."[32]

In a letter to John Wilson Croker, March 22, 1845, Graham admitted that the members of the gentry were hostile to the Government's Irish policy and that this hostility endangered the existence of the ministry. But the cabinet was prepared for "the death blow." He said that if the gentry was determined to rush to its own destruction they would have their way. "We have endeavored to save them, and they regard us as enemies for so doing."[33]

Greville, in his *Memoirs*, reported that the Government had lost the confidence of its own party members and that a change of ministries could occur at any time. "Peel and his colleagues are so well aware of this, that they think

[32] Extract, Foreign Office, Add. MSS 43278, B.M.
[33] Graham Papers.

something must, before long, occur to break up the Government . . . everybody is now beginning to see that this beginning of endowment must lead to still larger measures, and eventually the complete establishment of the R. C. Church."[34]

But Peel and Graham had the Queen's support. She was convinced of the good sense behind Peel's Irish policy and was disturbed about the bigotry it provoked.[35] And Peel, convinced that British interests demanded the destruction of Irish nationalism and that the needs of the nation were more important than the Conservative party and his own political power and career, carried on with his Irish policy, ignoring the risks involved.

Except for the Protestant minority, Ireland accepted the Maynooth bill as an installment on justice. O'Connell, although he was an opponent of State aid to religion, considered this measure a partial restoration of Catholic goods stolen by the Establishment. He praised Peel and Graham for their generosity in not placing embarrassing obstacles in the way of the Catholic hierarchy's acceptance of the increased grant. O'Connell told the Repeal Association that the intensity of Repeal enthusiasm in Ireland and pro-Irish sympathy in the United States forced the Government to reevaluate its Irish policy. He said that he realized that Peel was in competition with him for the support of Irish opinion and he welcomed the contest because it would benefit the Irish people, but he warned the Government that reform was not a satisfactory alternative to Repeal.[36]

The *Nation* also congratulated Peel for an "act of bold and generous justice to Ireland" and acknowledged his

34 *The Greville Memoirs, 1814-1860,* ed. by Lytton Strachey and Roger Fulford (London, 1938), 213.

35 Queen Victoria to the King of the Belgians, April 15, 1845, *Letters of Queen Victoria, 1837-1861,* ed. by Arthur C. Benson and Viscount Esher (New York, 1907), 2:42.

36 *Nation,* April 12, 1845.

courage in risking a distinguished political career to promote the Maynooth bill in the face of British no-Popery
opinion. Charles Gavan Duffy, the editor, assured his
readers that although the Maynooth bill was designed to
separate the Catholic clergy from the nationalist movement, the Catholic priests were "too poor" and Ireland
"too strong" to be swayed by bribes. Irishmen, he said,
welcomed concessions to national needs, but their right
to political independence was separate from their claims
to social, religious, and economic justice.[37]

In May 1845, when he was sure that the Maynooth bill
would be accepted by Parliament, Peel decided to introduce his Irish colleges bill. This piece of legislation was
designed to further the objective of destroying the nationalist coalition in Ireland by removing the Catholic
middle class from clerical influences and the pressure of
mass opinion by giving them educational and cultural
interests similar to those of Protestants of the same class.

Sir James Graham presented the colleges bill to the
House of Commons. He proposed establishing provincial
colleges in Cork, Galway or Limerick, and Belfast. Each
college would receive an annual appropriation of thirty
thousand pounds. Faculty members of the new Queen's
colleges would receive their appointments from the Crown,
which would retain sole visiting power. Faculty and students would imitate the living arrangements used in the
Scottish universities and reside outside the colleges. The
Government left the decision of whether each college or a
central university would confer degrees to future settlement. According to Graham the main principle of the
colleges bill was "the avoidance of all interference, positive or negative, with conscientious scruples in religion."
Therefore, courses in theology would not be financed by
the Government grant, but if individual Catholics or Prot-

[37] *Ibid.*

estants wished to endow chairs of theology the Government would be pleased to provide the classrooms.[38]

Unlike the Maynooth bill, the colleges proposal met with general approval in the House of Commons. A few M.P.'s like Sir Robert Inglis, the Conservative representative from Oxford, and Richard Lalor Sheil objected to the Government endowing "Godless education,"[39] but the only serious controversy over the merits of the scheme took place in Ireland, where the Government again succeeded in driving a wedge into the nationalist coalition.

On May 12, 1845, during a Loyal National Repeal Association meeting in Conciliation Hall, John O'Connell denounced the colleges bill and all the M.P.'s who supported it. He said that mixed or nondenominational education was unacceptable to Catholic Ireland. He also objected to the appointment of faculty members by the Crown, the residence of students outside the walls of the colleges and away from proper moral guidance, and the continuation of Trinity College as a Protestant monopoly. The Liberator's son demanded that the Queen's colleges in the South and West of Ireland be established as Catholic institutions with the deans of the colleges receiving their appointments from the Catholic hierarchy.[40]

John O'Connell's speech caught nationalist Ireland by surprise. His father had always been a champion of the principle of separation of church and state and friendly to mixed education—at least he had never complained about the national system of primary education founded on a nondenominational basis. However, the old man endorsed his son's attack on the colleges bill and in doing so precipitated a quarrel with the Young Irelanders in the Repeal Association, the first in a series of disagreements that finally led to their secession from Conciliation Hall.

38 *Hansard* 80:345ff.
39 *Ibid.*, 80:377ff., 380ff.
40 *Nation*, May 17, 1845.

Members of the Young Ireland group insisted that Ireland's future depended on cooperation between Catholic and Protestant in an effort to raise the cultural, economic, and political status of their common country. They believed that this cooperation could exist only when the two religious groups had an opportunity to mix on an intellectual and social level. That is why they were enthusiastic about the colleges bill. The new colleges would create an environment where Catholics and Protestants could meet, discuss common problems, and develop a truly national program, excluding sectarian interests, for the future of Ireland.

Thomas Davis, a brilliant graduate of Trinity College and a founder of the *Nation* along with John Blake Dillon and Charles Gavan Duffy, led the Young Ireland opposition to O'Connell in the Repeal Association. He agreed with two criticisms made by John O'Connell of the colleges bill: the proposal did not make adequate provision for the moral guidance of students and Royal appointments of faculty members did not promise good and objective teaching. But Davis did defend the principle of mixed education and pleaded with Repealers not to condemn a bill that facilitated badly needed intellectual intercourse between Catholics and Protestants.[41]

The members of the Catholic hierarchy were caught in a dilemma on the Government's program for nondenominational higher education. They wanted Peel to know that they were grateful for his generous concessions on Maynooth, but O'Connell insisted that they take a stand on the merits of the colleges bill. On May 23, 1845, the bishops met, discussed the provisions of the colleges bill, and then drew up a memorial rejecting the bill as it stood as dangerous to the faith and morals of Catholic students.

41 *Ibid.*, Charles Gavan Duffy, *Young Ireland,* 2:165ff.; Denis Gwynn, *Young Ireland and 1848* (Cork, 1949), 40-48; Michael Tierney (ed.), *Daniel O'Connell,* 201-204.

They indicated that they would endorse the Government's
plan if the bill was amended to give them some control
over faculty and administrative appointments in the colleges where Catholic students would be in the majority.[42]

This memorial was sent to the Lord Lieutenant who
forwarded it to Whitehall. In a courteous reply to the
bishops Graham announced the Government's intention
to proceed with the colleges bill as first presented to the
House of Commons. He said that it would be impossible
to devise a program of higher education for Ireland that
would meet the approval of both Catholics and Protestants, and therefore the Government decided that any
attempt to conciliate one group without offending the
other would be futile.[43]

Each faction in the Repeal Association interpreted the
bishops' memorial as an endorsement of its position. Young
Ireland, with some justice, claimed that the hierarchy
had no objection to a system of mixed education pro-
tecting the faith and morals of Catholic students.[44] O'Connell was equally convinced that the bishops had rejected,
without qualification, the entire principle of nondenominational education.[45] Peel's educational plan succeeded in
dividing Repealers but failed in its ultimate aim, the
unity of the Catholic and Protestant middle classes. The
colleges bill was passed, but the hostility of the bishops
forced Catholics to boycott the Queen's Colleges in Cork,
Galway, and Belfast and waste the excellent opportunity
to raise the intellectual level of nineteenth-century Irish
Catholicism.

When it finally passed through Parliament the colleges
bill contained a number of concessions to Catholic ob-

42 The resolutions of the Catholic bishops concerning their objections to
the colleges bill and their memorial to Lord Heytesbury were printed in
the *Nation*, May 24, 1845.
43 *Hansard* 80:1144ff.
44 *Nation*, May 24, 1845.
45 *Ibid.*, May 31, 1845.

jections. The bill permitted students to live in denomi-national residence halls under the supervision of clergy-men, providing the halls were built with voluntary sub-scriptions. In addition the Government permitted the different denominations to select deans of residence. Cath-olic bishops received invitations to take seats in the senate and on the visitorial board of the colleges. The authorities of the colleges could dismiss professors who interfered with the religious convictions of students. The Govern-ment asked Archbishop Murray to join the board which was to recommend faculty members to the Queen, a Catholic priest was appointed to head the college at Gal-way, and a Catholic layman was put in charge of the one at Cork. Everything was done to encourage divine services at the colleges.

Archbishops Crolly and Murray were prepared to ac-cept the colleges, but MacHale and a majority of the bishops refused to bless mixed higher education. They described the colleges bill as "a penal and revolting measure" and as an attempt "to bribe Catholic youths into an abandonment of their religion." Dr. Derry, bishop of Clonfert, refused the sacraments to parents who sent their sons to the Queen's colleges. MacHale went to Rome to argue the case against the colleges, and his efforts were rewarded with rescripts from the Vatican in 1847 and 1848 condemning the colleges as "a grave danger to the faith of Catholics." Rome went on to advise Irish Catholics to establish their own university, similar to the one at Louvain. This was attempted in the 1850's. John Henry Newman was invited to direct a Catholic university in Dublin. He accepted the offer but found it impossible to work with the anti-intellectual Irish hierarchy.

In 1850, with Archbishop Cullen presiding, the Synod of Thurles condemned the Queen's colleges, and the next year Rome again denounced them and forbade Catholic priests to accept administrative posts in the colleges. Only a small percentage of Irish Catholics ignored the wishes of their bishops and attended the Queen's colleges. Cardinal Cullen and the other bishops continued to agitate for a charter and an endowment for the Catholic university in Dublin. They argued that the British Government endowed denominational universities like Oxford and Cambridge, and justice demanded the extension of this same principle to Ireland.[46]

The college at Belfast was effectively used by Presbyterians and developed into Queen's University, one of the finest institutions of higher education in Great Britain. The Galway and Cork campuses are now part of the successful National University of Ireland.

With the passage of the colleges bill Peel's attempt to undermine Irish nationalism by destroying the Catholic coalition of priest, peasant, and middle class came to an end. Lord Stanley introduced a bill into the House of Lords in June, 1845, based on the report and recommendations of the Devon commission and designed to promote tenant farmer security by compensating them for improvements they made to their holdings. But the united opposition of Liberal and Conservative peers to any limitations on property rights forced the Government to withdraw the measure.

Peel's conciliation policy was terminated because of an unexpected disaster. During the heat of the controversy surrounding the merits and objectives of his Irish legislation, a fungus attacked the Irish potato crop and famine became the major figure on the Irish stage. Before it took its final bow a million and a half Irishmen had died of hunger and diseases associated with undernourish-

---

[46] William Edward Hartpole Lecky, *Leaders of Public Opinion in Ireland* (London, 1903), 2:271ff., contains an interesting discussion of the Catholic reaction to the Queen's colleges. E. R. Norman, *The Catholic Church and Ireland in the Age of Rebellion, 1859-1873* (Ithaca, 1965) presents a detailed and brilliant analysis of Cardinal Cullen's and the Irish hierarchy's views concerning mixed and denominational education.

ment: cholera, fever, and scurvy; many millions more approached death; and another million tried to escape death and poverty by fleeing to Britain, the United States, and Canada.[47] The frightful realities of death, disease, and emigration, and the bitter hatred for the system that produced these results, made issues such as tenant right, suffrage extension, denominational education, and even Repeal, seem insignificant. And of course they sabotaged any hope Peel had that his Irish policy would succeed in destroying Irish nationalism and creating a "respectable" pro-Union Irish Catholic opinion.

The Famine did present Peel with a strong case against the corn laws as an obstacle to the importation of food into starving Ireland. This argument proved effective and influenced the repeal of the corn laws in 1846. Although Peel demonstrated an active interest in the plight of the desperate Irish masses and was more concerned with providing them with food than the succeeding Whig administration, the Famine crisis and the resulting chaos in Ireland forced him to substitute a policy of coercion for one of conciliation.[48] In June 1846 he introduced an Irish coercion bill into the House of Commons to give the Government extra-legal powers to curb agrarian crime and unrest. British Liberals and Irish Repealers opposed the bill, and Disraeli's Tory faction, seizing an opportune moment to obtain revenge for Catholic emancipation, the Maynooth bill, and the repeal of the corn laws, joined the opposition and brought to a close the last Peel administration. He was defeated in the House of Commons on the

[47] Cecil Woodham-Smith, *The Great Hunger* (London, 1962), 411-13; Oliver MacDonagh, "Irish Emigration to the United States," and "The British Colonies during the Famine," *The Great Famine*, ed. by R. Dudley Edwards and T. Desmond Williams (New York, 1957), 317-88.

[48] For excellent discussions of the response of the British Government to the Famine crisis see Thomas P. O'Neill, "The Organization and Administration of Relief, 1845-52," *The Great Famine*, 207-59; and Woodham-Smith, *The Great Hunger*.

evening of June 25. That afternoon the House of Lords had voted its approval of corn law repeal.

In his brilliant though unsuccessful effort to pacify Ireland, Peel created the Tory hatred and lust for vengeance which destroyed the Conservative Government, his own career, and, for a generation, the party he did so much to create. After Peel's abortive attempt to exterminate the roots of Irish nationalism contributed to the instability of British party politics in the 1850's and 60's, no British Prime Minister had the courage to confront the Irish Question in all of its complexity until Gladstone took office in 1868. But by that time Irish nationalism had time to assume an identity independent of the economic, political, and religious grievances which created and nourished it, and Britain had already lost the opportunity "to kill Home Rule with kindness."

Bibliographical Note

Most of the secondary published papers, parliamentary, periodical, and newspaper sources used in writing this book are cited in the footnotes. I have consulted the following manuscript material:

ENGLAND

BRITISH MUSEUM
Sir Robert Peel Papers

PUBLIC RECORD OFFICE
Lord John Russell Papers

IRELAND

NATIONAL LIBRARY
William J. O'Neill Daunt Journal
William J. O'Neill Daunt Papers
Sir Charles Gavan Duffy Papers
Sir James Graham Papers, microfilm (the originals are in the possession of Sir Fergus Graham, Bart., Netherby Hall, Cumberland).
Kilmainham Papers (correspondence of the military secretary in Ireland).
Monteagle Papers
William Smith O'Brien Papers
Daniel O'Connell Papers
Richard Lalor Sheil Papers

STATE PAPER OFFICE
Correspondence of the Chief Secretary's Office

UNIVERSITY COLLEGE LIBRARY, DUBLIN
Daniel O'Connell Papers

Index